Social History of Africa

"CITY OF STEEL AND FIRE"

Recent Titles in
Social History of Africa Series
Series Editors: Allen Isaacman and Jean Allman

Making the Town: Ga State and Society in Early Colonial Accra
John Parker

Chiefs Know Their Boundaries: Essays on Property, Power, and the Past in Asante, 1896–1996
Sara S. Berry

"Wicked" Women and the Reconfiguration of Gender in Africa
Dorothy L. Hodgson and Sheryl A. McCurdy, editors

Black Death, White Medicine: Bubonic Plague and the Politics of Public Health in Colonial Senegal, 1914–1945
Myron Echenberg

Vilimani: Labor Migration and Rural Change in Early Colonial Tanzania
Thaddeus Sunseri

"God Alone Is King": Islam and Emancipation in Senegal: The Wolof Kingdoms of Kajoor and Bawol, 1859–1914
James F. Searing

Negotiating Development: African Farmers and Colonial Experts at the Office du Niger, 1920–1960
Monica M. van Beusekom

The Bluest Hands: A Social and Economic History of Women Dyers in Abeokuta (Nigeria), 1890–1940
Judith A. Byfield

Colonial Lessons: Africans' Education in Southern Rhodesia, 1918–1940
Carol Summers

Poison and Medicine: Ethnicity, Power, and Violence in a Nigerian City, 1966 to 1986
Douglas A. Anthony

To Dwell Secure: Generation, Christianity, and Colonialism in Ovamboland
Meredith McKittrick

Genders and Generations Apart: Labor Tenants and Customary Law in Segregation-Era South Africa, 1920s to 1940s
Thomas V. McClendon

"CITY OF STEEL AND FIRE"

A SOCIAL HISTORY OF ATBARA, SUDAN'S RAILWAY TOWN, 1906–1984

Ahmad Alawad Sikainga

HEINEMANN
Portsmouth, NH

JAMES CURREY
Oxford

DAVID PHILIP
Cape Town

Heinemann
A division of Reed Elsevier Inc.
361 Hanover Street
Portsmouth, NH 03801-3912

James Currey Ltd.
73 Botley Road
Oxford OX2 0BS
United Kingdom

David Philip Publishers
An imprint of New Africa
Books (Pty) Ltd.
P.O. Box 46962
Glosderry 7702
Cape Town, South Africa

www.heinemann.com

Offices and agents throughout the world

ISBN 0-325-07106-3 (Heinemann cloth)
ISBN 0-325-07107-1 (Heinemann paper)
ISBN 0-85255-967-4 (James Currey cloth)
ISBN 0-85255-962-3 (James Currey paper)

British Library Cataloguing in Publication Data available on request

Library of Congress Cataloging-in-Publication Data

Sikainga, Ahmad Alawad
  "City of steel and fire" : A social history of Atbara, Sudan's railway town, 1906–1984 / Ahmad Alawad Sikainga.
    p. cm.—(Social history of Africa, ISSN 1099–8098)
  Includes bibliographical references and index.
    ISBN 0-325-07106-3 (alk. paper)—ISBN 0-325-07107-1 (pbk. : alk. paper)
    1. Working class—Sudan—òbarah—History. 2. Railroads—Sudan—òbarah—Employees—History. 3. òbarah (Sudan)—Economic conditions. 4. òbarah (Sudan)—Social conditions. I. Title. II. Series.
HD8787.Z82 A8675   2002
962.5—dc21   2002068711

Paperback cover photo: Punching holes in boiler plate. Courtesy of the Sudan Archives at the University of Durham.

Printed in the United States of America on acid-free paper

06 05 04 03 02 SB 1 2 3 4 5 6 7 8 9

In memory of:
Muhammad Muhammad Salih (Wad al-Gubba), who served the
Sudan Railways for more than forty years, and Fatima Ahmad
Salah.

CONTENTS

	Illustrations	ix
	Preface	xi
	Abbreviations	xiii
	A Note on Transliteration	xv
	Introduction	1
	Photo Essay	17
1.	The Foundation of a Colonial Town: Atbara, 1906–1924	25
2.	The Evolution of a Company Town: Atbara, 1925–1939	43
3.	Railway Workers in an Urban Milieu	65
4.	Labor Protests, Trade Unions, and Nationalist Politics, 1940–1955	97
5.	The Making of a Militant Town: Atbara, 1956–1969	123
6.	Atbara under the May Regime, 1969–1984	149
	Conclusion	177
	Appendices	181
	Glossary	203
	Bibliography	205
	Index	215

ILLUSTRATIONS

MAPS

I.1   Railway System in the Sudan   xvi
1.1   Plan of Atbara, 1910   34
3.1   Map of Atbara   67

TABLES

1.1   Egyptian Army Railway Battalion   30
2.1   Sudan Railways Grade System   46
2.2   Sudan Railways Wage Structure, 1935   60
4.1   Wakefield Commission Wage Structure   113
6.1   Sudan Railways Job Evaluation Scheme, 1978   157
6.2   Sudan Railways Revised Job Evaluation Scheme, 1980   158
6.3   Sudan Railways Corporation Deficits, 1974–1984   166

PREFACE

My interest in the history of Atbara was motivated by personal and intellectual reasons. Although I am not a native of Atbara, I spent a great deal of time in the city visiting family members and relatives, many of whom were railway workers. Moreover, for someone who is interested in labor and urban history, Atbara is an ideal site. As the headquarters of the Sudan Railways, Atbara had the largest concentration of industrial workers in the Sudan. The overwhelming majority of the city's residents were railway employees and their families. Most important, Atbara was birthplace of the Sudanese labor movement. Since the 1940s, this working-class town has become known as a center of labor activism, solidarity, and radical politics.

The research and writing of this book would not have been possible without the help of numerous institutions and individuals. My research in the Sudan and England was generously funded by grants from the U.S. Department of Education Fulbright-Hays Faculty Research Abroad Program and the Ohio State University. I am particularly grateful to the College of Humanities, the Department of History, and the Department of African American and African Studies at the Ohio State University for providing me with release time to concentrate on writing this book. I wish to express my deep gratitude to the Sir William Luce Fellowship Committee and the Trevelyan College at the University of Durham, England, for giving me a fellowship that allowed me to spend the period from January to March 2000 in Durham to conduct research for this project. During this period I also benefited from my affiliation with the Center for Near Eastern and Islamic Studies, for which I am grateful. Very special thanks are due to Mrs. Jane Hogan and the staff of the Sudan Archives at the Palace Green Library of the University of Durham for their help and hospitality.

I could not have accomplished my research in the Sudan without the generous help of the staff of the National Records Office in Khartoum, who, despite the adverse conditions in the Sudan, have continued to give enthusiastic support and encouragement to researchers. I owe my greatest debt to the numerous Atbarawis for their generous willingness to share with me their memories and their experiences; the names of these individuals are listed in the bibliography. Sadly, two of the most prominent figures I had the privilege to interview have recently passed away: al-Hajj `Abd al-Rahman, a railway worker and an eminent trade unionist for more than four decades, and Ahmad Shami, leader of the Atbara branch of the Sudanese Communist Party from the early 1950s to 1964. I am especially thankful to al-Hajj's family for sharing with me some of his poetry and writings. I could not have accomplished my research in Atbara without the help and enthusiasm of my relatives and friends: Haydar al-`Atta, Abu Bakr Hussain Babikir, and Ali Mahjoub Fatah al-Rahman.

I am grateful to Dr. Martin Daly for reading an early draft of the manuscript and offering valuable suggestions, and to Dr. Mohammed Ahmed Mahmoud for translating some of the poems and being enthusiastic about this project since its inception. The criticism and suggestions of the anonymous readers for Heinemann have helped me sharpen my argument and refine my analysis.

Special thanks goes to Payne Hicks Beach Solicitors of London, England, for giving me permission to use one of the photographs of the late Mr. G. K. Wood on the book cover.

I am grateful to Lynn Zelem, Jim Lance, and the production staff of Heinemann/Greenwood Publishing Group and to Jeri Lambert of Impressions Book and Journal Services, Inc., for the meticulous care with which they edited and prepared the manuscript.

ABBREVIATIONS

CAIRINT	National Record Office (Khartoum) classification
CIVSEC	National Record Office classification
Dakhlia	National Record Office classification
DUP	Democratic Unionist Party
FO	Foreign Office (and Public Record Office classification)
ICFTU	International Confederation of Free Trade Unions
INTEL	National Record Office classification
NP	National Record Office classification
NRO	National Record Office, Khartoum
NUP	National Unionist Party
PALACE	National Record Office classification
PRO	Public Record Office
RCC	Revolutionary Command Council
Reports	National Record Office classification
SAD	Sudan Archives, University of Durham Library
SCP	Sudanese Communist Party
SECURITY	National Record Office classification
SMNL	Sudanese Movement for National Liberation
SR	Sudan Railways
SRWU	Sudan Railways Workers' Union
SSU	Sudanese Socialist Union
SWTUF	Sudan Workers' Trade Union Federation
WAA	Workers' Affairs Association
WFTU	World Federation of Trade Unions

A NOTE ON TRANSLITERATION

In transliterating Arabic words, I have adopted a flexible approach and stressed consistency rather than adhering to a particular system. For Arabic proper names, I have utilized the system used by the *International Journal of Middle East Studies*, without the diacritical marks except for ` to indicate the letter `ayn. For the place-names of provinces and larger towns, I have used conventional forms, e.g., *Khartoum* and *Omdurman* instead of *al-Khartoum* and *Umdurman*. Titles such as *shaykh* and *qadi* are transliterated. For Arabic plurals, I have added *s* to the transliterated word. Finally, in direct quotes and in documentary citations in the endnotes, I have retained the original spelling.

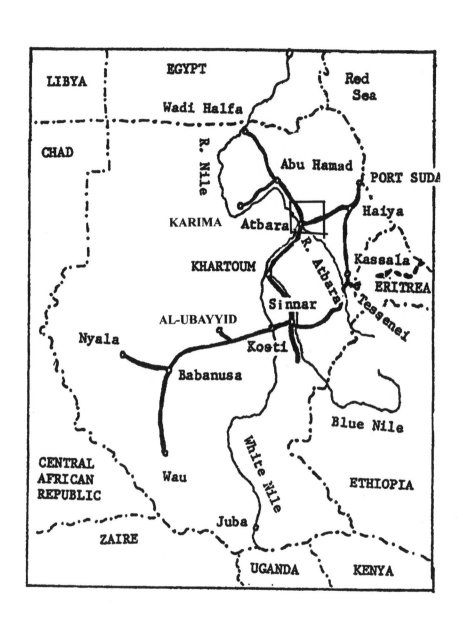

INTRODUCTION

I am Atbara
by al-Hajj `Abd al-Rahman[1]

You ask who I am!
I am Atbara
I am the garden of the future
I am a fortress sending light from above
I am Atbara
The mother of working youth
I am Atbara
Pregnant, waiting for the moment of labor
It is in the melodious clinking of iron and the drops of sweat
It is in the muttering lips creeping [back home] at dusk
It is the wrinkles of the faces returning in the evening
It lies in the midst of the tiny leaves of food
I will give birth to a giant
Not created out of a blood clot
I am Atbara
My mark is in the smoke with chests puffing out
In the blue uniforms overcrowding the roads at dawn
In the muscular forearms pressing iron against rocks
In the mighty leader penetrating veils like lightning
Though resting quiet
Volcanoes seethe inside me
I am Atbara
Truly, a capital city of iron
When my plants are blown away by the wind, flowers grow anew
Never will the soil watered by the drops of working people turn arid
Look! History embraces me as a symbol of eternal life
Never mind the judgement of the blind who denies my existence

"I am Atbara" is a celebration of the spirit of a working-class town and a glori-fication of labor resistance and militancy. Atbara, headquarters of the Sudan Rail-ways, is a small but politically significant Sudanese town that has attained great notoriety as a distinctive site of labor activism and radical politics. For over half a century, the railway workers of Atbara formed the core of the Sudanese working class and established the most dynamic and militant labor movement in Sudanese history. Atbara is also known for its extensive social networks and communal sol-idarity. It is not surprising that this working-class town was nicknamed City of Steel and Fire.[2]

By examining the experience of the railway workers of Atbara, this study will shed light on the development of urban working-class culture and politics and the role of organized labor in contemporary Sudan. In view of Sudan's current politi-cal and economic crises, it is difficult to imagine that this country once had one of the best organized and most radical trade-union movements in Africa and the Mid-dle East. On two occasions, Sudanese trade unions, professional associations, and other civic organizations led popular uprisings that brought down military regimes—those of Ibrahim `Abboud in 1964 and Ja`far Nimeiri in 1985.

In a sense, this book deals with a past but still remembered era in Sudanese his-tory. It is not, however, intended to be a sentimental reminder of a period of tri-umph and glory, nor does it aim at romanticizing workers' experiences. Its primary goal is to unravel the world the railway workers of Atbara created, and to explain how this group of workers developed both a militant, radical working-class cul-ture and a distinctive identity that have become the hallmark of Atbara. The prin-ciple argument here is that in order to understand the development of these traits, it is important to situate the railway workers in their historical and cultural con-texts and to stress the structural and ideological factors that shaped their con-sciousness and behavior. The tradition of labor militancy that characterized Atbara was a product of daily struggles inside and outside the workplace. Atbara railway workers, most of whom were rural immigrants, became part of a modern, indus-trial establishment with a highly regimented system of authority and a work cul-ture that fostered a strong sense of community and camaraderie. Association with the railway industry, which played a crucial role in Sudan's economic and social life, had a profound impact on workers' perspective and self-image. Atbara rail-way workers exhibited an acute awareness of their pivotal role in Sudan's econ-omy and their status as industrial workers in a country where the vast majority of the population engaged in farming and pastoral activities. However, one of the most critical factors that contributed to the radicalization of the railway workers' movement was its close link with leftist organizations such as the Sudanese Com-munist Party (SCP). This link had a profound impact on the ideological orienta-tion and the trajectory of the movement and became one of the defining charac-teristics of Atbara.

This study is grounded in the growing literature on labor and urban history in Africa, the Middle East, and elsewhere. The past three decades have witnessed the development of a substantial body of research, which transformed African labor history from a neglected field into a vibrant academic enterprise. The works of Richard Sandbrook, Robin Cohen, Richard Jeffries, Paul Lubeck, and others opened up the subject and put it at the center of research on African social history.[3] This early literature naturally reflected the theoretical paradigms of the 1970s and 1980s, which were preoccupied with the process of class formation, proletarianization, trade unions, and labor activism. Influenced by orthodox Marxism, these studies have portrayed the working class as a homogeneous entity whose members shared the same perceptions and aspirations by virtue of their position within the capitalist structure.[4]

In recent years, however, the study of African labor history has been dramatically reshaped by new questions and issues deemed crucial for understanding working-class culture, consciousness, and politics. The range of topics has vastly expanded to include working-class family life, leisure, popular culture, gender, and so forth. Beyond the initial focus on the predominantly male workers in the formal sector, the study of African labor history has moved to encompass female and casual labor, peasants, petty traders, slaves, and other marginal groups. In short, the new literature stresses the importance of examining workers in their broader social and political contexts, and in relation to other social groups—such as peasants, nomads, urban dwellers, and the middle class.

Beyond concern with wage laborers in government departments and private firms, there has been growing interest in the history of nonwage workers in the so-called informal sector of the economy. For instance, the works of Charles Van Onselen, Luise White, Claire Robertson, and several others have focused on prostitutes, taxi drivers, market women, and domestic servants, and underscored their role in the reproduction of labor.[5] Among the most important themes these studies have highlighted is the gender division of labor, which relegated women to nonwage economic activities.

The new literature has also bridged the gap between labor history and urban history by stressing the interdependence between the urban space and work, and by conceptualizing the city as the locus for reproduction of the working class. Indeed, the questions of how and where workers lived and the manner in which they developed neighborhoods and communities are crucial elements for understanding their culture and experience.[6]

While the early literature focused mainly on the role of industrial control, time, and discipline in shaping and molding African workers, considerable attention has now been given to the question of what African workers themselves brought to the workplace.[7] The most pioneering works in this regard have dealt with Southern Africa. For instance, in her study of Zulu mine workers in Natal, Keletso Atkins has shown how Zulu work habits and concepts of time, authority, and discipline permeated the workplace and forced employers to make major adjustments in working conditions.[8] Working-class culture has also figured prominently in Patrick Harries's study on Mozambican migrant workers in South Africa. Harries criticized the dominant paradigm in African labor history for its focus on workers' resistance, militancy, and activism. He rejected the notion that working-class culture

is shaped solely by the struggle against employers and the capitalist strategy of social control. By focusing on the culture of drunkenness, desertion, and social deviance among Mozambican migrant workers, Harries tried to underscore the wide
range of experiences and cultural resources that shaped the worldview of these
workers. In short, the emphasis on the cultural matrix represents a major departure
from the old paradigms that conceived of working-class politics and consciousness as a mere derivation of socioeconomic structure.

Historians of African labor have begun to move beyond the confines of the workplace and union halls, to examine workers in their families, neighborhoods, and
communities. Indeed, among the most important aspects of African workers' experience are leisure and social activities.[9] This was the subject of Phyllis Martin's
recent book, in which she explored recreational activities such as football, music,
dance, and fashion among urban residents in colonial Brazzaville. Martin's study
illustrated the manner in which these activities fostered development of strong social networks and emergence of particular identities among the African population
of this colonial town. According to Martin, leisure activities were "arenas of con-
test and mediation within European and African sub-communities as well as between them."[10]

The questions of gender and the impact of wage labor on household structure
and family life have attracted considerable attention in recent years. Lisa Lindsay
has dealt with the impact of wage labor and post–World War II colonial labor policies on household structure and family life among Yoruba railway workers in Nigeria.[11] As several scholars have pointed out, the postwar labor reforms aimed at the
creation of a more stable and differentiated working class, through the provision
of family wages, decent housing, and social services. According to Lindsay, these
policies were premised on the European conception of the male worker as head of
the household and primary breadwinner. Application of these concepts in the
African context had serious implications for gender relations and domestic life.
Lindsay argued that the notion of the male worker as breadwinner conflicted with
a Yoruba social structure in which women engaged in various commercial activities and enjoyed a considerable degree of economic independence. The promotion
of the model of the male-headed nuclear family and the emphasis on female domesticity formed the central theme of Thomas Klubock's recent book on the El
Teniente copper miners in Chile. Klubock's study showed how the North American mining companies relentlessly sought to organize gender relations to conform
to this model.[12] In short, the new literature has not only shown the need for a more
expansive working-class history but also underscored the importance of examining the history of African workers in different regional and cultural contexts. Such
an approach would illuminate not only the myriad factors that shaped workers'
consciousness and behavior, but also the different ways in which they constructed
their identity and expressed their consciousness.

Of particular relevance to this book is the literature on transportation workers,
especially dock and railway workers. The studies of Ralph Grillo, Richard Jeffries,
Timothy Oberst, Frederick Cooper, and others[13] have attributed the high level of

militancy of transport workers to a number of factors. Railroads and harbors had been a major source of revenue for both colonial and postcolonial governments and played pivotal economic and social roles. The sheer size of railway workers and their strategic position in the colonial economy allowed them to exert considerable influence. In his study of the post–World War II railway strikes in different parts of Africa, Timothy Oberst pointed out that railway corporations employed a significant number of skilled workers, which gave the workforce a degree of bargaining power and a remarkable ability to organize effective strikes. Oberst also stressed the fact that railway workers represented the most stable, homogeneous group of African workers, who embraced the ethos of railway employment and developed a strong sense of community and corporate identity. This point has also been emphasized in the studies of Ralph Grillo on Ugandan railway workers and Richard Jeffries on the railway workers of Sekondi in Ghana.

It is important at this point to ask about the significance of the experience of the railway workers of Atbara within and beyond the context of African labor history. To what extent did the experience of these workers resemble or differ from other Sudanese, African, and Middle Eastern workers? And what was unique about the world the railway workers of Atbara made?

The study contends that the experience of each group of workers—their culture, their identity, and the way in which they conceptualized their struggle and organized themselves were shaped by specific historical and cultural contexts. Like their counterparts elsewhere, the railway workers of Atbara exhibited a keen awareness of their strategic position in their country's economy. On the basis of their common work experience, these workers developed a strong sense of community, and built a militant tradition of labor activism and combative political culture. However, the railway workers of Atbara also exhibited several distinctive traits.

Within the Sudanese context, the railway workers were distinguished by their sheer size, stability, skills, and pioneering role in the development of the Sudanese labor movement. Unlike casual laborers who moved between wage and nonwage employment, the majority of the railway workers were permanent employees who spent the greater part of their lives in the city. They created a multifaceted world that reflected their rural background and their railway experience. To face the challenges of urban life, Atbara workers established extensive social networks, exemplified by regional associations, mutual aid institutions, and cooperative societies. Through their persistent struggles and confrontations with the colonial and postcolonial Sudanese governments, the railway workers of Atbara created a "culture of protest" that was drawn upon by successive generations of workers. This culture of protest became the defining characteristic of Atbara.

Atbara workers perceived themselves and were perceived by other Sudanese people as a special group of workers with a unique identity. Atbara's residents referred to themselves and were referred to by others as Atbarawis (sing. *Atbarawi*). The term *Atbarawi* was not limited to the geographic entity itself, but subsumes a number of traits. It conjures up images of militancy, strong social bonds, and working-class solidarity. Atbara has become known as *madina `ummaliyya* (working-class town), inhabited by low-income, struggling people. This occupational solidarity is at the core of the Atbarawi identity. The railway workers themselves developed a discourse that portrayed their struggle as an act of bravery and heroism. The nickname City of Steel and Fire, which refers to Atbara's industrial nature, was also a euphemism for its militant and radical character.

Atbara was a highly cosmopolitan Sudanese town. Its residents included Britons, Eastern Europeans, Greeks, Italians, Ethiopians, Indians, and Egyptians, just to name a few. The largest and the most influential immigrant community in Atbara were the Egyptian Coptic Christians. They dominated key railway divisions and built several churches and schools in the city. This religious and ethnic diversity contributed to the development of a vibrant, tolerant urban culture.

Beyond the Sudanese context, the experience of the railway workers of Atbara illuminates a number of themes that have much wider implications for African and Middle Eastern labor history. In many parts of Africa and the Middle East, the labor movement established close links with either politically moderate nationalist movements or leftist organizations that espoused some populist ideologies. In the Sudanese case, however, since its inception in the late 1940s, the railway workers' movement had been closely associated with a Marxist-Leninist party, namely the SCP. Until the party's destruction in 1971 in the aftermath of an abortive coup, the SCP was considered the largest and most influential communist party in Africa and the Middle East, second only to the South African Communist Party. Through its mobilization of workers, peasants, students, professionals, and other groups, the SCP built a powerful popular movement that played a pivotal role in Sudanese politics.

The link between the labor movement and the SCP raises important points. In the first place, it defies the essentialist notions that Muslim societies can only be understood through the prism of religion. With the exception of a few studies, the experiences of the left in Muslim societies as well as the struggle between Islam and secularism and its link with working-class history and politics has not been sufficiently addressed. For instance, Paul Lubeck's study of the labor movement in the city of Kano in northern Nigeria showed both the success and the limitations of Islamic social populism that was embraced by this group of Muslim workers. According to Lubeck, Kano workers developed an oppositional ideology within an Islamic framework to express their nationalist sentiments against European colonial rule and to resist their social and economic subordination in the postcolonial period.[14] Similarly, in his study of Iranian workers, Assef Bayat argued that following the Iranian Revolution in 1979, Islam had become "a key element in workers' subjectivity." Iranian industrial workers used Islamic ideology to express their occupational grievances and class interest. However, Bayat also stressed the complex and contradictory role of Islam in articulating class consciousness. Bayat contends that while Islam served as an ideology and a discourse to express common needs, it also contributed to exclusivism and a blurring of class lines.[15]

The success of the SCP in establishing a strong base among Sudanese workers and peasants—the overwhelming majority of whom are Muslims—is often attributed to a number of factors. Prominent among those was the "flexible" attitude of the party toward ideology and Islam. In its pronouncements, the SCP did not oppose Islam and emphasized that there is no contradiction between individual religious beliefs and communism. However, the SCP rejected the political role of the two dominant Islamic sects in the Sudan: the Khatmiyya and the Ansar.[16] From the SCP's perspective, the political parties that were affiliated with these sects represented the interest of a privileged elite who exploited the loyalties of their followers. The SCP focused its attention on workers, peasants, students, and the small educated class. A major factor behind the success of the SCP in mobilizing these groups was its ability to organize at the grassroots level and to develop dynamic and dedicated union leaders who enjoyed considerable respect and loyalty among the rank and file. What has not been discussed, however, is the complex nature of this alliance as well as workers' strategies and motivation. While the SCP succeeded in establishing a strong constituency among the railway workers, it had great difficulty in mobilizing them for its broad political agenda. Railway workers continued to express their sectarian loyalties in national politics. Their behavior mirrors the complex way in which culture shapes and transforms working-class politics and underscores the limitations of the proletarianization paradigm.

The experience of Atbara's railway workers also illustrates the critical role of institutions such as labor unions, political parties, and the state in shaping working-class history. Although the new literature on labor history has drawn our attention to the importance of such elements as culture, community, family life, and gender in understanding the workers' experience, the role of institutions should not be ignored. The case of Atbara workers will demonstrate the manner in which state policies seriously impacted every facet of workers' lives and will show how the alliance with the SCP shaped the trajectory of the labor movement. Most important, however, was the way in which the railway workers of Atbara transformed their union from an organization of collective bargaining into a dynamic institution that played a central role in the social, cultural, and political life of Atbara and the whole country. As Bill Freund noted, in many parts of Africa, trade unions were turned into undemocratic institutions and became mere "power brokers" between workers and the state.[17] Union leaders were often co-opted by governments and used their positions to gain material and political benefits. As will be shown in this study, since its formation in the late 1940s, the Sudan Railways Workers' Union (SRWU) created an organizational structure and a system of elections that fostered the emergence of leadership from the grassroots level and allowed unskilled workers to rise to the highest positions. Moreover, beyond the issues of working conditions and wage demands, the SRWU organized literacy programs among workers, built schools and clinics, and engaged in various forms of charitable activities. Over the years, the SRWU became an integral part of the social fabric of Atbara.

Another important characteristic of Atbara railway workers was the high level of militancy and radicalism of the artisans. This counteracts the labor aristocracy thesis, which portrayed artisans as a privileged group of workers whose primary concern was to preserve their entitlements and advantageous positions. According to this thesis, skilled workers tend to be unreceptive to appeals for solidarity with the lower strata of the working class.[18] However, as the recent literature has shown, artisans in Africa and the Middle East can hardly be considered an elite group. Skilled and unskilled workers lived in the same neighborhoods, engaged in similar activities, and were viewed as the same by their societies.[19] The railway artisans of Atbara represented the most militant and radical group of railway workers. They were best exemplified by al-Hajj `Abd al-Rahman, Qasim Amin, Hashim al-Sa`id, `Ali Muhammad Bashir, and al-Shafi` Ahmad al-Shaykh, who was executed in July 1971 following the failed Communist coup.

The story of the railway workers of Atbara also reveals the innovative ways in which workers organized protests against the authoritarian regimes that ruled the Sudan in the postindependence period. As will be shown in the following chapters, these methods ranged from the distribution of leaflets from the roofs of buildings, to the tapping of telephone lines to monitor contacts between the central government and the railway management during strikes, to the organization of rolling strikes by particular groups of workers in strategic railway divisions.

Atbara was not just a working-class town but a major center of literary activity and a prominent site of modernity. The city took the lead in the establishment of soccer clubs in the Sudan and had the oldest soccer stadium in the country. Atbara residents engaged in various forms of literary activities, ranging from poetry and drama to cinema. Many of the railway workers such as al-Hajj `Abd al-Rahman, al-Tayyib Hasan al-Tayyib, and Hashim al-Sa`id were accomplished poets, whose poetry not only celebrated workers' struggle and the militant character of Atbara, but also expressed romantic themes. It is worth mentioning that it was in Atbara that the first Sudanese movie was produced, in which al-Tayyib Hasan, the prominent labor activist, was the main character. These creative writings not only reveal the various ways in which workers perceived their struggle and expressed their identity, but also allow us to transcend the elitist definition of intellectuals and see these workers as intellectuals in their own right.

HISTORICAL AND CULTURAL CONTEXT

The Sudan, Africa's largest country, straddles the worlds of the Middle East and sub-Saharan Africa and exhibits a remarkable geographical, ethnic, and cultural diversity. In view of its intermediate position between these regions, the Sudan has been marginalized in the scholarly literature on the Middle East and Africa. According to conventional classification, the northern part of the Sudan is "Arabic" and Islamic, while the southern part is "African" and Christian. However, historical and social realities in the country defy this rigid classification. It is evident that the North itself is not a monolithic entity, but includes many non-Arab groups such as the Nubians, the Beja, the Nuba, the Fur, the Funj, and many people of West African descent. The adoption of an Arab identity by some northern Sudanese groups has something to do with politics and identity, and was a product of old and complex historical and structural processes that are still unfolding.

In the pre-Islamic era, the territories of the present-day northern Sudan were part of the ancient Nubian kingdom of Meroe. After the collapse of Meroe in A.D. 350 Coptic Christianity became the dominant religion for several centuries. However, the Muslim conquest of Egypt in the seventh century A.D. had a great impact on Nubia. Although Nubian Christian kingdoms resisted the Muslim dynasties of Egypt for several centuries, the continuous migration of Arabs and their intermarriage with local population led to the gradual decline of Christianity. A steady stream of traders, nomads, and holy men from Arabia and Egypt settled in Nubia. Using the matrilineal system of descent, these immigrants eventually dominated the political institutions of Nubia. Following the collapse of the last Christian kingdom, a new Muslim entity known as the Funj Sultanate emerged in 1504. During the next few centuries, other Muslim sultanates arose in Kordofan and Darfur.

The rise of these Muslim kingdoms accelerated the pace of Islamization. Their rulers encouraged the migration and settlement of individual Muslim holy men and Sufi teachers who played a major role in the spread of Islam among the Sudanese population. The most prominent Sufi orders in the Sudan were the Sammaniyya, the Khatmiyya, the Tijaniyya, the Majdhubiyya, and the Ahmadiyya. Sufi leaders attracted followers who regarded them as possessors of *baraka* (grace), which was believed to be inheritable. The most popular Sufi order in the northern region, particularly among the Shaiqiyya, the Manasir, and the Rubatab, was the Khatmiyya.

In addition to their religious functions, leaders of religious sects enjoyed considerable political and social influence under the successive regimes that ruled the Sudan. During British colonial rule, Sayyid `Abd al-Rahman al-Mahdi—leader of the Mahdiyya—and Sayyid `Ali al-Mirghani—leader of the Khatmiyya—enjoyed unparalleled influence. As we shall see later, these two sectarian leaders patronized the main parties that led the nationalist movement and dominated postindependence Sudanese politics.

As elsewhere in Africa, Sufism incorporated local beliefs, and quite often deviated from the orthodox teachings of Islam. Moreover, pre-Islamic Nubian traditions were not completely uprooted and have continued to influence popular culture in the northern region. These traditions can been seen in birth, naming, and marriage ceremonies. This aspect of Sudanese Islam is particularly important in understanding workers' attitude toward politics and ideology, a subject that will be elaborated upon in the next chapters.

Like other African and Middle Eastern countries, Sudan's modern history was shaped by its colonial experience. But Sudan had a distinctive colonial history. First, between the nineteenth and the twentieth centuries, the country experienced two colonial regimes: the Turco-Egyptian (1820–1884) and the Anglo-Egyptian Condominium (1898–1956). The former was overthrown by the Mahdist movement in 1884, which established an independent state in the Sudan until it was defeated by the Anglo-Egyptian forces in 1898. Second, the colonial state in the Sudan in the twentieth century was an oddity in view of the unique arrangement by which the country was ruled. The Anglo-Egyptian Condominium regime was theoretically a joint British and Egyptian administration. This unique arrangement was a result of geo-historical considerations that will be examined below.

Britain's conquest of the Sudan in 1898 was driven by strategic considerations, mainly to prevent other European powers from seizing the sources of the Nile and establishing a foothold on the Red Sea. The conquest was undertaken under the pretext of restoring Egyptian "sovereignty" over the Sudan. Hence, the Condominium Agreement, which was signed in 1899, intended to honor Egyptian claims and protect British interests. However, as mentioned earlier, Britain was in full control while Egyptians were relegated to the lower rungs of the administration.[20] Moreover, the agreement provided a rationale for subsidizing the costs of the reconquest and of the financial deficits in the Sudan until 1913, out of the Egyptian rather than the British treasury. The Condominium Agreement vested all civil and military authority in a British governor-general. Nominally subject to Khedival approval, the governor-general was in practice selected by the British Foreign Office and held all legislative and administrative authority. Since the Sudan was not a typical colony, its affairs were dealt with by the Foreign Office rather than the Colonial Office. The system of administration incorporated elements of the Turco-Egyptian and Mahdist regimes as well as the British practices in Egypt, India, and other colonies.

For a number of reasons, British administrators remained apprehensive about Egyptian presence in the Sudan. In their view, it was the Egyptian mismanagement of the Sudan in the nineteenth century that paved the way for the rise of the Mahdist Revolution. Most important, however, was British fear of the influences of Egyptian nationalism on the small class of educated Sudanese. This fear was confirmed by the emergence in the early 1920s of pro-Egyptian organizations such as the White Flag League, which was inspired by the Egyptian Revolution of 1919. Although the league's members were few in number, they included elements of the new urban lower-middle class as well as a few workers and artisans. The league called for the political unity of Egypt and the Sudan and organized anti-British demonstrations in various Sudanese towns in 1924. These protests created a golden opportunity for the British to get rid of Egyptian civilian and military personnel from the Sudan. After suppressing a series of mutinies by Egyptian and Sudanese army units in 1924, the British evacuated the Egyptian army from the Sudan.

Following the suppression of the 1924 uprising, British officials adopted a hostile policy toward the Sudanese educated class and sought the collaboration of tribal heads and leaders of the main religious sects, particularly Sayyid `Abd al-Rahman al-Mahdi of the Ansar. Through land grants, contracts, and agricultural schemes, the Mahdi's family accumulated considerable wealth and enjoyed strong economic and political influence, particularly in central and western Sudan. Similarly, the Khatmiyya sect received British patronage and grew in wealth and influence, particularly in the urban areas of northern and eastern Sudan. However, as a result of the Khatmiyya's close ties with Egypt, the British increasingly favored the Mahdists, whose animosity toward Egypt had deep historical roots.

The importance of these religious sects lay in the fact that they became the main patrons of the political parties that led the nationalist movement and ruled the country in the postindependence period. The nationalist parties emerged from the Graduates' General Congress, established by the small class of Sudanese intelligentsia in the late 1930s. The congress was an umbrella organization, which included several competing factions. Leaders of the congress believed that the only way to gain mass support was to ally themselves with the two religious sects, who had a large number of followers, particularly in rural areas.

By the mid-1940s, several nationalist parties had emerged. Prominent among those were the Umma Party (nation), which was patronized by Sayyid `Abd al-Rahman al-Mahdi; the Ashiqqa Party (blood brothers), patronized by Sayyid `Ali al-Mirghani of the Khatmiyya; the Sudanese Movement for National Liberation, which became the Sudanese Communist Party; the Muslim Brothers; and several regional and ethnic organizations. The Ashiqqa called for Sudan's unity with Egypt while the Umma opposed it. The regional base of support for the Umma Party was the western part of the country and the White Nile area, while the Ashiqqa's influence was mainly in the northern riverine region and the eastern part of the Sudan. Besides their slogans and regional bases of support, there was hardly any ideological difference between the two sectarian parties. Both came to express the interest of the dominant socioeconomic classes in the country and had little to offer to the mass of workers, peasants, and marginalized groups.

During and after the colonial period, cash-crop production, particularly cotton, remained the backbone of the Sudanese economy. The largest cotton scheme was the Gezira Scheme between the Blue Nile and the White Nile. The scheme was officially launched in 1925 as a partnership involving the Sudan government, the Sudan Plantation Syndicate, and thousands of tenants. By 1956 the scheme covered about one million *feddans*.[21] Other cotton schemes were established in the eastern, western, and central Sudan. In addition to cotton, Sudan's export included gum arabic, cattle, and grain.

Cash-crop production and the expansion of trade brought about major transformation in the structure of the Sudanese society. It led to the emergence of a bourgeois class that included religious leaders, tribal heads, and merchants. In the urban centers, a small group of entrepreneurs, most of whom were foreigners, dominated the import/export sector of the economy. Below those groups was a small class of civil servants, technocrats, and other white-collar workers. The lower rung of the social hierarchy was occupied by a large number of workers, peasants, nomads, and agricultural laborers.

In view of Sudan's dependence on cash crops, its vast territory, and its poor communication, the railways played a crucial role in the transportation of these crops. Although the establishment of the railroad system was initially linked with the Anglo-Egyptian military campaign against the Mahdist state in the 1890s, it gradually became the main means of transportation in the country. By World War II, the Sudan Railways was the largest employer of industrial labor in the Sudan, with about 20,000 employees, most of whom were stationed in Atbara.

Atbara was a colonial town, which owed its growth entirely to the establishment of the railway system in the Sudan at the end of the nineteenth century. In 1898 it was nothing more than a military camp near the site of a major battle between the Anglo-Egyptian army and Mahdist forces.[22] Following the conquest of the Mahdist state and extension of the railway line to different parts of the Sudan, the headquarters of the Sudan Railways were transferred in 1906 from Wadi Halfa to Atbara. Within a few years "Fort Atbara" had been transformed into a bustling and cosmopolitan railway center, with a population that included Britons, Greeks, Italians, Eastern Europeans, Egyptians, Middle Easterners, and Ethiopians, among others. These foreigners occupied the higher echelons of the railway administration, while the Egyptian Army Railway Battalion did most of the work on the main line and in the workshops in Atbara. However, for economic and political reasons that will be discussed later, the railway battalion was evacuated from the Sudan in 1924, a move that paved the way for the development of a Sudanese railway workforce. Atbara's location and the availability of railway employment attracted a large number of immigrants from the neighboring northern region. Within two decades, Atbara metamorphosed into a major company town, with distinctive characteristics.

Using their numerical strength and their strategic position in the colonial economy, the railway workers of Atbara led Sudanese workers in the struggle for recognition and for better working conditions. From the late 1940s they engaged in fierce battles against the colonial government, which resulted in legalization of trade unions, wage increases, and other benefits. In addition to their vigorous resistance to postcolonial regimes, Sudanese labor unions became the backbone of a powerful popular movement that included a wide array of professional, regional, and civic associations. These groups saw themselves as the vanguard of progressive sociopolitical change, and continued to challenge the dominant political forces in the country.

The hostility of the postindependence Sudanese governments toward the labor movement was due to the movement's close association with the Sudanese left and the radical orientation of its leadership. Although trade unions have faced systematic repression by successive Sudanese governments, the most serious setback occurred under the regime of Ja`far Nimeiri (1969–1985). Following an abortive communist coup in July 1971, Nimeiri launched a repressive campaign against the labor movement in general and the railway workers in particular. In addition to dismissing and detaining many trade-union leaders, Nimeiri tried to undermine the railway department by decentralizing it and by building an extensive network of paved roads. Nimeiri's campaign not only crippled the Sudanese labor movement but also dealt a serious blow to the railway workers of Atbara. But the final assault on Atbara occurred in the early 1990s when the current government of the National Islamic Front persecuted many trade-union leaders and dismissed thousands of railway workers.

The organization of this study is determined by its conceptual framework, which stresses the cultural matrix, workplace experience, and urban life in shaping the consciousness and identity of the railway workers. The first three chapters examine the transformation of Atbara from a small railway center into a major company town, and the development of the railway labor force. The first chapter follows the evolution of Atbara from 1906, when it became the railway headquarters, to the evacuation of the Egyptian Army Railway Battalion in 1924. It outlines the development of the railway system in the Sudan and provides a social profile of Atbara. The chapter stresses two important aspects of Atbara's history during this period: the military character of the railways and the cosmopolitan nature of the city, both of which had a lasting legacy. The chapter argues that the military and cosmopolitan nature of Atbara laid the foundation for the development of a distinct tradition of work habits, social life, leisure, and political activism. The last part of the chapter deals with the political unrest that preceded the evacuation of the Egyptian Army Railway Battalion in 1924, and its consequences. The evacuation of the railway battalion paved the way for the development of a Sudanese railway workforce; this is the main theme of chapter two. The inquiry focuses on the transformation of a largely migrant population into a stable railway community, their socialization into the norms of the railway industry, and the structure of the workplace and working conditions. The discussion highlights the role of the regional and cultural backgrounds of these workers and the workplace experience in shaping their consciousness and attitude. Chapter three follows workers into their neighborhoods and communities, and shows how these migrant workers established families and communities and developed extensive social networks and leisure activities that reflected their rural background and urban experience. Chapter four focuses on the period from World War II to Sudan's independence in 1956, arguably the most pivotal period in Atbara's history. It was during this period that the city emerged as a center of labor activism and radical politics. The inquiry revolves around the impact of the war on the city and its workers, the development of working-class organizations, the protests of the 1940s, trade unions, and the relationship between the labor movement and anticolonial struggle. The significance of these protests is that they laid the foundation for the militant, radical tradition of the city and shaped the trajectory of the railway workers' movement. The final two chapters focus on the evolution of Atbara during the postcolonial period, the struggle of the railway workers against successive Sudanese governments, and the conditions that led to the destruction of the railway workers' movement and the decline of Atbara as a center of labor activism. Chapter five covers the period from Sudan's independence in 1956 to the end of the second parliamentary democracy in 1969. During this tumultuous period, which was punctuated by military coups, political repression, and popular uprisings, the Sudanese labor movement became a powerful political force that occupied a prominent position in Sudanese society. Building on their earlier tradition of militancy and radicalism, the railway workers of Atbara engaged in fierce struggles for better working conditions and developed innovative ways to fight repressive and authoritarian regimes. In addition to these struggles, the chapter examines the main characteristics of the railway trade union and its role in Atbara's social and political life. The final chapter deals with the destruction of the railway workers' movement and the decline of Atbara. The chapter contends that these tragic developments were a direct result of the major social and political changes that took place in the Sudan under the military regime of Nimeiri.

Nimeiri's repression of trade unions and his systematic purge of labor activists seriously crippled the labor movement in general and the railway workers in particular. Realizing the potential threat of the railway workers, Nimeiri introduced a number of measures to undermine the railway corporation. Moreover, his regime encouraged foreign investment, particularly in agriculture; deliberately neglected the railways; and built a network of paved roads. The final blow occurred in 1981, when in response to a lengthy railway strike, Nimeiri launched a massive campaign against the workers and dismantled the railway corporation.

In view of the critical role of many individuals in both the development of the railway workers' movement and the shaping of Atbara's history, a brief biographical section is provided in appendix 5.

SOURCES

This study is based on a range of written and oral sources in the Sudan and Britain. In the Sudan, the National Records Office in Khartoum (NRO) is a rich source of information on all aspects of precolonial, colonial, and postindependence Sudanese history. The most important materials for this study are the records of Berber and Northern provinces, which include a large number of files on Atbara; the civil secretary files; the annual reports of various government departments, including the Sudan Railways; newspapers and magazines; and other official publications. At Atbara, the records of the Research and Development Unit of the Sudan Railways contain vital information on the organizational and operational aspects of the railway department as well as on the working conditions of employees. Another useful source of information in Atbara is the office of the Sudan Railways Workers' Union, which holds important materials such as union publications, magazines, photographs, and videotapes.

Archival sources in Britain include the Public Record Office in London and the Sudan Archives of the University of Durham. At the Public Record Office, the Foreign Office files cover many aspects of the Anglo-Egyptian administration in the Sudan. The richest source of information on Sudanese history in Britain is the Sudan Archives at the University of Durham, which includes papers of officials, soldiers, missionaries, and private individuals who served or lived in the Sudan during the Anglo-Egyptian period.

It would have been virtually impossible to write a social history of Atbara without oral accounts, which were difficult to collect in view of the current political climate. Political repression, government hostility toward trade unions, and difficult living conditions have silenced trade-union leaders and prompted many others to leave the country and join the growing number of Sudanese exiles in Egypt, Europe, and North America. Moreover, since the 1980s the railway workers in general and Atbara in particular have suffered disproportionately from political repression and economic hardship. As a result, many Atbarawis have either moved to other Sudanese towns or left the country altogether. Despite these difficulties, I was able to interview a wide range of people who were associated with Atbara.

They include active and retired railway workers, officials, teachers, political ac-tivists, trade-union leaders, religious figures, merchants, political activists, and members of the Coptic community. Moreover, I interviewed a number of widows, wives of railway workers, and other women in Atbara who wanted to remain anonymous. Outside Atbara and Khartoum, I interviewed former railway em-ployees in their home villages in the Northern Province as well as union leaders living in England, North America, and Egypt. Finally, my own experience in At-bara has given me important insights into the city's history and social landscape.

NOTES

1. Al-Hajj `Abd al-Rahman was a railway worker, a prominent trade union leader, and a gifted poet. I am grateful to his family for sharing with me some of his poetry.

2. Although the nickname City of Steel and Fire refers to the industrial nature of Atbara, it is also a metaphor for its radical character.

3. Richard Sandbrook and Robin Cohen, eds., *The Development of an African Working Class* (London: Longman, 1975); Jeff Crisp, *The Story of an African Working Class: Ghana-ian Miners' Struggles, 1870–1980* (London: Zed Books, 1984); Paul Lubeck, *Islam and Urban Labor in Northern Nigeria: The Making of a Muslim Working Class* (Cambridge: Cambridge University Press, 1986). Richard Jeffries, *Class, Power and Ideology in Ghana: The Railwaymen of Sekondi* (Cambridge: Cambridge University Press, 1978). For an overview of the main works and issues in the field of African labor history, see Bill Freund, *The African Worker* (Cambridge: Cambridge University Press, 1988).

4. For a critique of this literature, see Frederick Cooper, "Work, Class and Empire: An African Historian's Retrospective on E.P. Thompson," *Social History* 20 (May 1995): 235–41, and his most recent book, *Decolonization and African Society: The Labor Ques-tion in French and British Africa* (Cambridge: Cambridge University Press), 1996.

5. Charles Van Onselen, *New Babylon: Studies in the Social and Economic History of the Witwatersrand, 1886–1914* (London; Longman, 1982); Claire Robertson, *Sharing the Same Bowl? A Socioeconomic History of Women and Class in Accra, Ghana* (Bloomington: Uni-versity of Indiana Press, 1984); Luise White, *The Comforts of Home: Prostitution in Colo-nial Nairobi* (Chicago: University of Chicago Press, 1990).

6. Frederick Cooper, ed., *Struggle for the City: Migrant Labor, Capital, and the State in Urban Africa* (Beverly Hills: Sage, 1983).

7. Cooper, "Work, Class and Empire," 236.

8. Keletso Atkins, *The Moon Is Dead! Give Us Our Money! Cultural Origins of an African Work Ethic, Natal, South Africa, 1843–1900* (Portsmouth, NH: Heinemann, 1993). See also Elias Mandala, *Work and Control in a Peasant Economy: A History of the Lower Tchiri Val-ley in Malawi, 1859–1960* (Madison: University of Wisconsin Press, 1990), and Patrick Harries, *Work, Culture, and Identity: Migrant Laborers in Mozambique and South Africa. 1860-1910* (Portsmouth, NH: Heinemann, 1994).

9. Phyllis M. Martin, *Leisure and Society in Colonial Brazzaville* (Cambridge: Cambridge University Press, 1995); Anthony Kirk-Greene, "Imperial Administration and the Athletic Imperative: The Case of the District Officer in Africa" in William Baker and James A. Man-gan, eds., *Sports in Africa: Essay in Social History* (New York and London: Africana Pub-lishing Company, 1987); Remi Clignet and Maureen Stark, "Modernization and Football in Cameroon," *Journal of Modern African Studies* 3 (1974): 409–421.

10. Martin, *Leisure and Society*, 3.

11. Lisa A. Lindsay, "Putting the Family on Track: Gender and Domestic Life on the Colonial Nigerian Railway" (Ph.D. diss., University of Michigan, 1996).

12. Thomas Miller Klubock, *Contested Communities: Class, Gender, and Politics in Chile's El Teniente Copper Mine, 1904–1951* (Durham: Duke University Press, 1998).

13. R.D. Grillo, *African Railwaymen: Solidarity and Opposition in an East African Labour Force* (Cambridge: Cambridge University Press, 1973); Richard Jeffries, *Class, Power and Ideology in Ghana: The Railwaymen of Sekondi* (Cambridge: Cambridge University Press, 1978). Frederick Cooper, *On the African Waterfront: Urban Disorder and the Transformation of Work in Colonial Mombassa* (New Haven: Yale University Press, 1987); Timothy Oberst, "Transport Workers, Strikes and the 'Imperial Response': Africa and the Post World War II Conjuncture," *African Studies Review* 31, no. 1 (1988): 117–134.

14. Lubeck, *Islam and Urban Labor in Northern Nigeria*, 262–300.

15. Assef Bayat, "Historiography, Class, and Iranian Workers," in *Workers and Working Classes in the Middle East: Struggles, Histories, Historiographies*, ed. Zachary Lockman (Albany: State University of New York, 1994), 202.

16. Gabriel Warburg, *Islam, Nationalism, and Communism in a Traditional Society: The Case of Sudan* (London: Frank Cass, 1978), 148–149.

17. Bill Freund, *The African Worker* (Cambridge: Cambridge University Press, 1988), 94.

18. Giovanni Arrighi, "International Corporations, Labor Aristocracies and Economic Development in Tropical Africa," in *Imperialism and Underdevelopment*, ed. R.I. Rhodes, (New York: Monthly Review Press, 1970); Giovanni Arrighi and John Saul, eds., *Essays on the Political Economy of Africa* (New York: Monthly Review Press, 1973).

19. Richard Jeffries, "The Labor Aristocracy? A Ghana Case Study," *Review of African Political Economy* 3 (1975): 59–70. See also Zachary Lockman, ed., *Workers and Working Classes*, 202.

20. P.M. Holt and M.W. Daly, *A History of the Sudan: From the Coming of Islam to the Present Day* (London and New York: Longman, 1988), 117–128.

21. One feddan = 1.038 acres, or 0.420 hectares.

22. This battle, which came to be known as the Battle of the Atbara, paved the way for the Anglo-Egyptian advance to Omdurman, the capital of the Mahdist state.

Staff of the Traffic Division of the Sudan Railways, 1940.

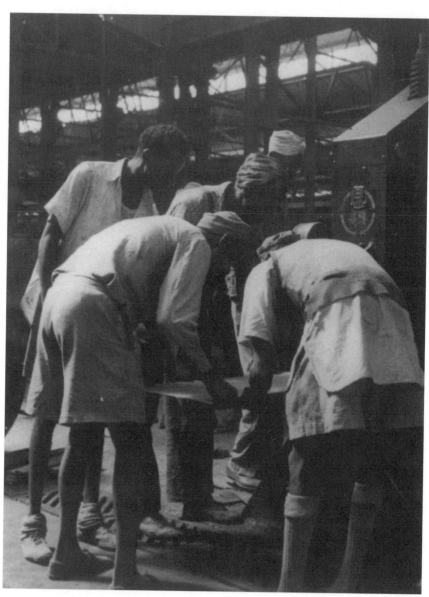

Group of workers punching holes in boiler plate.

Sudanese workers in the Workshop Division.

Sudan Railways and Steamers Police.

Atbara Engineering Workshops.

Atbara Club, 1907.

Egyptian Club, 1909.

Atbara Football Team, 1914–1915.

Members of the Northern Province's Committee of the Sudanese Communist Party. Standing from left to right: Hashim Sorkti, Khidir Mabrouk, Taj al-Sir Hasan Adam, Al-Amin Hajj Abbo, Yusuf Jadalla; sitting from left to right: Hashim al-Sa`id, Ahmad Shami, `Abdalla `Ibaid, Al-Hajj `Abd al-Rahman.

Women attending an adult education class.

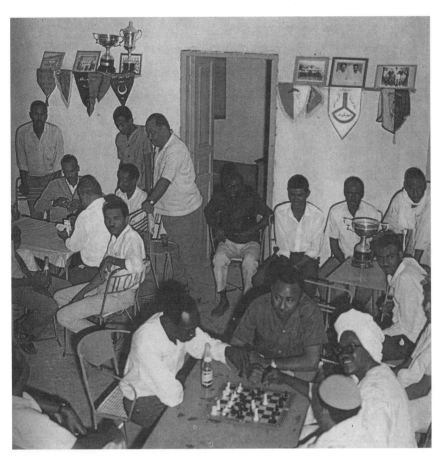

Typical scene of a social club in Atbara.

1

THE FOUNDATION OF A COLONIAL TOWN: ATBARA, 1906–1924

This chapter examines the transformation of Atbara from a small military depot into a major railway center. After outlining the establishment of the railway system in the Sudan, the discussion will focus on the development of the railway labor force, the spatial and demographic growth of Atbara, and the 1924 uprising and its consequences. The most conspicuous features of Atbara during this phase of its history were its military character and its cosmopolitan nature. Until 1924, the bulk of the railway labor force was military personnel, namely the Egyptian Army Railway Battalion and the British Royal Engineers. Moreover, Atbara was largely a town of foreigners who came from diverse backgrounds. Its inhabitants included Britons, Egyptians, Greeks, Italians, Eastern Europeans, and Middle Easterners. This chapter argues that this setting played a crucial role in the development of working-class culture and affected the social structure of Atbara in many ways. The military nature of the railways created work habits and notions of time and discipline that became the hallmark of the Sudan Railways. Moreover, the presence of many foreigners in Atbara had important sociological and political implications. It led to the emergence of a cosmopolitan, urban culture, and distinct forms of social and leisure activities. Foreign workers and artisans, particularly Egyptians, brought with them political ideas that appealed to the small class of Sudanese civil servants and artisans. This was manifested in the protests of 1924, which led to the evacuation of the Egyptian military and civilian personnel from the Sudan. The impact of foreign artisans can also be seen in the development of a technical vocabulary that stemmed from various European and Middle Eastern languages. This hybrid vocabulary was modified and adopted by the Sudanese railway employees and became an integral part of the workplace language.

THE DEVELOPMENT OF THE RAILWAY SYSTEM
IN THE SUDAN

The establishment of the railway system in the Sudan at the end of the nineteenth century was primarily a military affair. Extension of the railway line from Wadi Halfa near the Egyptian border was an integral part of the strategy of the Anglo-Egyptian forces against the Mahdist state. In a vast, desert country, the railway facilitated the movement of troops and supplies and gave the Anglo-Egyptian army a tremendous advantage over the Mahdist forces.

Development of the railway system in the Sudan can be traced to the last three decades of Turco-Egyptian rule. In 1870 a track was laid from Wadi Halfa to Sarras, 33 miles south, with the grand intention of extending it to al-Fashir in Darfur. After reaching Sarras, however, the project was abandoned due to lack of funds. Work on this line recommenced in 1884 in connection with the relief expedition sent to rescue General Gordon, besieged by Mahdist forces in Khartoum. The line was extended to the village of `Akasha, but was once again abandoned after the fall of Khartoum and retreat of the relief force.[1]

With the commencement of the Anglo-Egyptian campaign in 1896, the old line was extended along the Nile about 150 miles to Kerma. In view of the decision to build a new railway across the Nubian Desert, from Wadi Halfa to Abu Hamad, the Kerma line was abandoned. In August 1897 the Wadi Halfa–Abu Hamad line was completed, and in July 1898 it reached the mouth of the Atbara River, where a fortified camp was built and remained the terminus of the railway for several months. Atbara camp became the base for the families of thousands of Sudanese soldiers in the Egyptian Army.

After the defeat of the Mahdist army at Omdurman in 1898, the railway was quickly extended to the Blue Nile opposite Khartoum. A temporary wooden bridge was built across the Atbara River for carrying track-laying material, locomotives, and rolling stock. The floods of 1899 destroyed the bridge, which was then replaced by a steel bridge.[2]

Following the establishment of the Anglo-Egyptian regime, railway expansion was determined by both economic and political considerations. In their effort to limit Egyptian influences in the Sudan, the British decided to link Khartoum and the Nile region with the Red Sea coast. This line was built to make the Sudan less dependent on Egypt for transport, and to reduce the cost of transshipments by cutting the distance from Khartoum to the Mediterranean.[3] Work on this line began in 1904, and by 1906 Atbara was linked with the newly built Port Sudan harbor. During the same year, the Kareima–Abu Hamad line was completed.[4] One of the main goals behind building this line was to reorient Sudanese Nubia with the country's hinterland, away from Egypt.[5]

Completion of the Nile–Red Sea railway put Atbara at the heart of the whole network. It had become the major junction of three lines: Atbara–Wadi Halfa, Atbara–Khartoum, and Nile–Red Sea. It was for this reason that Atbara was chosen as the headquarters of the Sudan Government Railways.[6]

In 1909 the railroad was extended from Khartoum North across the new Blue Nile Bridge to Khartoum itself, from where it was pushed forward, reaching Wad Medani and Sinnar on the Blue Nile in 1910. From Sinnar, the line was extended westward to Kosti on the White Nile and to al-Ubayyid in Kordofan in 1912.

The next phase of railway extension began in the mid-1920s with the expansion of cash-crop production, particularly cotton in the Gezira and Kassala regions. In 1924 Kassala, in the fertile Gash River region, was linked with Haya on the Red Sea line. One of the most important new extensions, however, was the Kassala–Gedarif–Makwar line, which was completed between 1926 and 1929. This line linked the cotton-growing areas of central Sudan with Port Sudan and provided relief to the Sinnar–Khartoum line, which was already overburdened. This marked the end of the most important phase in railway development. By 1930 the total length of the railway open for traffic was 1,990 miles, which made Sudan's system the largest in Africa.[7]

The Organization of the Sudan Railways

The organization of the Sudan railways began to take shape during the early years of the Anglo-Egyptian campaign. Continuous expansion and the growing responsibilities of the railway entailed major changes in its administrative structure.

It is worth noting that during the period from 1896 to 1924, the Sudan Railways was essentially military, a fact reflected in its early official name, the Sudan Government Military Railways. Although the name was changed in 1902 to Sudan Government Railways, the military character of the railways did not change.[8] Until 1925 all the directors, their assistants, and the senior officials were British military and naval officers. British civilians began to arrive after 1900. In 1908 the title "director" was changed to "general manager," who made all the major decisions.[9] In 1908 a more elaborate hierarchy involving heads of divisions and assistants was set up, and it was decided that all proceedings should be formal and strictly confidential. The Sudan Government Railways (SGR) began to take its shape as a corporate entity.[10] The major divisions were headquarters, traffic, locomotive, stores, and harbor. Heads of these divisions were responsible directly to the general manager.[11]

During the first two decades of its existence, the SGR encountered serious challenges that severely impacted its performance. These problems arose from the nature of the track as well as the climatic conditions in the Sudan. The original line was laid with 50-pound flat-footed rails, except for the section from Summit Station in the Red Sea Hills to Port Sudan, which was laid with 75-pound track.[12] The gauge was 3 feet 6 inches throughout the system.[13] The nature of the track severely affected the speed and volume of traffic. In the early years, the train journey from Wadi Halfa to Khartoum took about 55 hours, but was reduced to about 34 hours by World War I.[14]

In a country as vast as the Sudan, with diverse climatic and topographic conditions, the maintenance and repair of the railway remained a serious and continuing problem. From Wadi Halfa the line runs through the Nubian Desert and joins the Nile again at Abu Hamad, where a branch line runs downriver to Kareima. The country between Wadi Halfa and Abu Hamad is bare desert, rising from 410 feet above sea level in the north to 2,000 feet at No. 5 Station, 105 miles from Wadi Halfa. From Abu Hamad to Atbara, the inland country is desert with little cultivation along the riverbank, and the line follows the river fairly closely. In the desert region between Wadi Halfa and Abu Hamad, the track was often covered with sand, which resulted from heavy dust storms.

From Port Sudan, the line runs through the Red Sea Hills, reaching a height of 3,008 feet at Summit Station. It then crosses the desert to join the Wadi Halfa line at Atbara, 296 miles from Port Sudan. The Red Sea region is a bare, rocky country, intersected by dry watercourses; during the last 75 miles to Atbara, the line traverses a flat desert. The Red Sea line presented the greatest problems for repair and maintenance: the track was often washed out by torrential rains and floods, and the high altitudes and steep inclines in this hilly region were a source of numerous accidents.

From Atbara the main line runs southward, more or less following the Nile to Khartoum. Here the country is less desertlike but with little vegetation. From Khartoum the line follows the Blue Nile to Sinnar and strikes westward to the White Nile, which it crosses at Kosti. Between the Blue Nile and the White Nile, the line runs through the flat and fertile Gezira region. From Kosti the line continues westward for 190 miles to al-Ubayyid, the capital of Kordofan. This savanna region's frequent rainfall caused numerous washouts.

The period after World War I witnessed a major reorganization of the SGR. In 1918 the railway and steamer departments were combined.[15] The headquarters of the steamers section and workshops were in Khartoum North.[16] In 1918 a catering section was established in the railway department to provide catering on all principal trains. The railways also managed hotels in Khartoum and Port Sudan.

By the mid-1920s, the Sudan Government Railways and Steamers had 108 trains and 19 shunting locomotives, giving a total of 127 engines.[17] In view of the length of journeys and the unpredictable weather conditions, which could hold trains for a whole night or longer, trains were provided with restaurants and sleeping cars. There were also mail and hospital cars. All first-, second-, and third-class passenger cars were electrically lit. There were also 1,015 goods vehicles, with a total capacity of 24,236 tons. The steamers section had 37 passenger steamers, 114 barges, and dozens of small boats.[18]

The post–World War I reorganization led to some improvements in the performance of the SGR. Tonnage increased from 46,000 in 1903 to 232,000 in 1919.[19] In 1922 the total number of passengers carried was 392,562.[20] With regard to freight traffic, the total tonnage carried in 1922 was 572,974 tons.[21] In 1912, gross revenue from the railways exceeded LE 500,000 and reached LE 1 million in 1919.[22]

THE DEVELOPMENT OF THE RAILWAY WORKFORCE

Like other government departments, the SGR had great difficulty attracting local Sudanese to wage employment. Typically, rural people were not willing to abandon their farming and pastoral activities for low-paying and arduous railway work.[23] In other parts of Africa, colonial governments resorted to such methods as forced labor and the recruitment of socially dislocated groups, runaway and liberated slaves, refugees, and war captives. In the Sudanese case, the railway authorities depended on foreign labor—particularly Egyptian Sa`idis, Mahdist prisoners from the Anglo-Egyptian military campaign, and ex-slaves—who were employed as daily laborers during the extension of the railway line to different parts of the country.[24] In the dry and hot climate of the Sudanese desert, the work of Mahdist prisoners proved indispensable. According to Sir Edward Midwinter of the Royal Engineers, these people were the only ones who could carry the rails that had often become extremely hot from the heat in the Nubian Desert.[25] Many Mahdist prisoners were enlisted by the Egyptian Army Railway Battalion to perform plate-laying and other unskilled jobs.

The composition of the labor force changed over time. During the Turco-Egyptian phase, from 1870 to 1884, British personnel dominated the technical posts while Egyptians occupied most of the administrative positions. Egyptians, Greeks, and Maltese were the artisans, while Sudanese Nubians formed the unskilled labor force.

During the last two decades of the nineteenth century, officers of the Corps of Royal Engineers of the British Army and the Egyptian Army Railway Battalion dominated the railway labor force. In 1898 the personnel of the railways included 9 officers and 34 noncommissioned officers and men of the Royal Engineers, assisted by 444 British civilians, who did accounting and clerical work, and the Egyptian Army Railway Battalion. The latter comprised 33 staff officers, 2 quartermasters, and 2,882 noncommissioned officers and men.[26] The unskilled labor force consisted of Mahdist prisoners as well as Sa`idis from upper Egypt.[27]

The Royal Engineers who served in the SGR included men with vast experience in railway work.[28] Prominent among those was Lieutenant E. Percey Girouard, the director of the SGR from 1896 to 1897. Girouard was a French Canadian who had trained in the Canadian Pacific Railway. He was hired for service in the Sudan in 1896 while he was passing through England on his way to Mauritius to raise a company of engineers. Girouard played a central role in building the railway from Wadi Halfa to Abu Hamad. He returned to England and subsequently served in South Africa, Nigeria, and East Africa.[29] Other Royal Engineers who headed the SGR were G.B. Macauley, the director between 1897 and 1906, and E.C. Midwinter, who held the post from 1906 to 1925. There were many others such as W.E. Longfield and P.C. Lord, who spent twenty-five years in the Sudan Government Railways.[30]

From 1896 to 1924 the Egyptian Army Railway Battalion was the backbone of the railway workforce. This unit had been raised at Aswan in southern Egypt and was deployed to Wadi Halfa in 1896. Its men were recruited from different parts of rural Egypt.[31] With its headquarters at Atbara, the battalion became responsible for the construction, operation, and maintenance of the line. In 1913 it numbered about 27 officers, 19 clerks, and about 2,429 men. However, for financial reasons, the battalion was gradually reduced. Its strength in 1923 appears in Table 1.1.[32]

Table 1.1   Egyptian Army Railway Battalion

	Officers	Men
Headquarters Company	10	261
Traffic	3	461
Engineering	11	996
Workshops	3	285
Civilians (clerks, watchmen)		123
	27	2,126

The soldiers of the railway battalion wore a different uniform but were subjected to the same military rules and discipline as the rest of the Egyptian Army. Upon joining the unit, the men would go through a short training course after which they were posted directly to their jobs; they were expected to learn their trade on the job. Some noncommissioned officers were employed as clerks, firemen, plate-layers, builders, fitters, shunters, guards, point men, and so forth.[33] The vast majority of men were organized into large units for new line construction, maintenance, and handling of cargo. After their discharge from the army, many of these Egyptians found employment in the SGR.[34]

Although the battalion formed the backbone of the permanent labor force, daily labor continued to play a major part of the railway work, particularly the maintenance and construction of new lines. The Sudan government continued to bring Egyptian Sa`idis to do the heavy tasks such as digging earth and carrying tracks. Employment of Sa`idis had to do with British stereotypes about their physical abilities. A British official described the Sa`idi as a "bigger, stronger man than the average native of the Sudan, ... having been accustomed to hard agricultural and manual labor all his life."[35] For instance, about 1,700 Sa`idis were employed on the construction of the Kassala line. They were divided into fifty gangs, each supervised by a *shaykh*. They were paid on a piecework basis, so the rates of pay varied according to the nature of the work.[36]

During the first two decades of the twentieth century, a small number of Sudanese railway employees rose through the ranks to hold technical and clerical posts. They included Muhammad Khair Ahmad, who was born in Wadi Halfa in 1890 and joined the SGR in 1912 as a telegraph clerk. He became stationmaster in 1925 and remained in the service until his retirement in 1945. Another was

Muhammad al-Haj `Abd al-Latif. He was born in Berber and began his railway career in 1909 as a telegraph clerk. After passing through the grades, he was promoted to stationmaster in 1935.[37] Other Sudanese who became stationmasters early on were `Abd Abdalla Muhammad Ali, who was born in Dongola and joined the railways in 1909; Ahmad Ali Satti, also of Dongolawi origin, who started his career in 1912; and Ibrahim Awad, who began his career in 1910 as a telegraph clerk. This first generation of Sudanese workers remained in the service of the Sudan Railways for more than thirty-five years. Despite their small number, they formed the nucleus of the Sudanese railway workforce.

Among the most important tasks that required intensive labor during the early years were the construction, maintenance, and re-laying of the line. This was highly regimented and monotonous work. After a preliminary survey had been made, a railhead party was sent from the base to extend the line. The railhead party would then build a camp at which food and medical supplies were provided. A complete train of material was dispatched daily from the base. A second party followed, eight miles behind the railhead, consisting of one permanent-way inspector and about 130 laborers. A third party followed thirty to forty miles behind. After the tracks were laid, bridge and station builders would follow. The progress of the railhead was between one and one-and-a-half miles a day, depending on the climate and the nature of the terrain.[38]

A constant problem for the SGR was the washouts that often destroyed several miles of the high bank and cut the line for as long as two months. For maintenance purposes, the whole railway system was divided into eight districts of an average length of 270 miles. Each district had a motor trolley and was staffed by British engineers, permanent-way inspectors, and Egyptian and Sudanese platelayers. Maintenance of the line was performed by section gangs, or working parties supervised by headmen.[39]

THE RISE OF ATBARA AS A RAILWAY CENTER

In her study of the literature on urbanization in Africa, Catherine Coquery-Vidrovitch has criticized the notion that European colonizers actually created cities in Africa. For the most part, colonizers either used preexisting towns and villages, or established settlements near trading areas with easy access to natural resources and food supplies.[40] In some cases, however, European colonizers did establish new garrisons, ports, and railway stations where nothing existed before. Although Atbara belongs to this category, which includes Conakry, Nairobi, and Port Sudan, it actually grew around an old settlement, namely the village of al-Dakhla.

The region in which al-Dakhla was located had witnessed the development of one of the oldest civilizations in the Nile Valley. It was in this region that the kingdom of Nubia had prospered from 750 B.C. until its destruction by the army of Axum in A.D. 350. According to oral tradition, the name Atbara was derived from the Nubian combined word *at-bara*, which referred to the riverbank and the land adjacent to it.[41]

After the destruction of Meroe, the northern part of the Sudan was dominated by a series of Christian kingdoms. However, the gradual infiltration of Muslims eventually led to the collapse of these Christian kingdoms and the emergence of the Muslim Funj Kingdom in A.D. 1504. From its capital in Sinnar on the Blue Nile, the Funj Kingdom dominated the Nilotic parts of northern Sudan until the Turco-Egyptian conquest in 1820.

Oral accounts also suggest that during the Funj period, the junction of the Atbara River and the Nile was uninhabited until the beginning of the eighteenth century, when it was occupied by subsections of the Arabic-speaking Ja`aliyyin. As a result of an internal conflict, some Ja`aliyyin clans moved from their home in Jelessi, south of the present-day town of Damer, and occupied the southern bank of the Atbara River. They then crossed the Atbara River and settled in the more fertile land north of the river until the Turkish conquest in 1820.[42]

When the Turks arrived in this area, they established a fort at al-Qayqar, at the junction of the Nile and Atbara rivers. Like the rest of the Sudanese communities, the local inhabitants of this area suffered from the atrocities of the Turks and consequently split into three separate settlements at the confluence of the Nile and the Atbara River. These were al-Dakhla, al-Mugran, and al-Tilayh.[43]

The origin of the name al-Dakhla is unclear, but it is believed that it stemmed from the Arabic verb *dakhal* (enter) because pilgrims and traders regarded it as an entrance to the desert route to the Red Sea.[44] During the eighteenth and nineteenth centuries, al-Dakhla functioned as a resting station for pilgrims and commercial caravans to the Red Sea.

This area attained great notoriety during the Anglo-Egyptian military campaign against the Mahdist state in the late 1890s. In 1897 the Anglo-Egyptian forces established a reconnaissance station near al-Dakhla to gather intelligence on the Mahdist forces that were encamped near al-Nikhaila. The old Turkish fortification was restored, and a small dockyard to repair steamers was established. Finally, on April 8, 1898, a major battle was fought between the Anglo-Egyptian forces and the Mahdist army of Mahmud wad Ahmad. Mahmud's defeat paved the way for the Anglo-Egyptian advance to Omdurman, the capital of the Mahdist state. Although this battle has become known as the Battle of the Atbara, the actual site was al-Nikhaila, a few miles east of al-Dakhla.

From 1898 to 1905, Atbara was just a railway station. However, following the extension of the railway line to Khartoum and the completion of the Red Sea line in 1905, Atbara became a major junction and was thus chosen as the railway headquarters. Until that time, Wadi Halfa had been the headquarters since the inception of the railways.

The first railway division to arrive at Atbara in the winter of 1905 was the engineering department, headed by Lieutenant R.E. Russell of the Royal Engineers.[45] When Russell and his crew arrived there was nothing except "a small station shed formed by a few sleepers planted vertically in the sand with others laid across them as a roof."[46] There were no houses or markets, and the residents had to depend on trains coming from Wadi Halfa and Port Sudan for their supplies. Railway employees lived in tents until houses were built. The engineering division was charged with the task of designing and building the headquarters and drawing a town plan. Lieutenant Russell prepared a sketch for a new railway station, workshops, offices, residential quarters, a club, and a hospital. The remaining divisions—traffic, mechanical, headquarters, and administrative staff—arrived when the principal buildings had been completed. By 1914 Atbara had begun to take its shape as a railway center and colonial town.

As previously mentioned, Atbara at this phase of development was already a highly cosmopolitan town. The artisans of the railway were drawn from different nationalities: Greeks, Maltese, Poles, Albanians, Syrians, Ethiopians, Indians, and Sudanese. The Greek community, for instance, comprised about one hundred families.[47] According to the 1914 Sudan Government Railways annual report, the inhabitants of the railway cantonment numbered about 1,975. Of those, there were 85 British civilian personnel, 36 British troops, 132 Europeans, 731 Egyptian civilians, 653 soldiers of the Egyptian Army Railway Battalion, 36 Syrians, 5 Indians, and 230 Sudanese, of whom 80 were former Mahdist soldiers.[48] Unfortunately, there were no population figures for the rest of the city, but it is clear that Atbara had a small but extremely diverse population.

The largest foreign community by far was the Egyptian, which included the officers and men of the railway battalion, civilian staff, and Sa`idi laborers.[49] Most of the Sa`idis were employed during construction of the railway line. They were subsequently employed permanently and settled in Atbara. The Sudanese community consisted mainly of former Mahdist war prisoners who were captured during the Anglo-Egyptian campaign, runaway and liberated slaves from the neighboring areas, and a few West Africans.[50]

At the beginning, the inhabitants of al-Dakhla evinced little interest in railway employment and continued their farming activities. However, after a great deal of persuasion and inducements in the form of food rations and consumer goods, the railway department was able to attract a few villagers to work as *tulbas* (unskilled laborers). They worked on a part-time basis for two or three hours per day, then returned to their farms.[51] Railway employment in Atbara attracted some Sudanese, particularly from the riverine areas north of Atbara. They included Ja`aliyyin, Rubatab from the Abu Hamad area, Shaiqiyya from the Kareima and Meroe districts, and Nubians from the Dongola and Wadi Halfa regions.

Organization of the Urban Space

As in other colonial towns, the occupation and the organization of urban space in Atbara was regulated by a set of laws introduced by the Anglo-Egyptian colonial administration from the early years of the twentieth century. These laws covered everything from land ownership to the type of building material required for houses. One year after the conquest of the Sudan, the Town Lands Ordinance had been introduced to provide for settling land-ownership cases in towns. It authorized the government to obtain any land required, either by purchase or by exchange, thus enabling the government to plan towns without interference from property owners.[52] Landowners were ordered to erect buildings conforming to certain standards. A decade later, the Town Building Regulations were introduced. They included detailed instructions as to the type of buildings allowed for each class of land, and laid down sanitary regulations. Landholders had to apply to the municipal authorities or to the provincial government to obtain building permits. Three classes of residential areas were recognized according to the size of the plot and the type of building material.[53]

The majority of property owners, who lived in the "official" part of the city, were foreigners. The early generation of Sudanese residents established informal settlements in different parts of the town. One year after the foundation of Atbara, a number of native quarters emerged to the east of the railway line and near the railway cantonment.[54] One of the oldest native quarters in Atbara was Hay al-Darawish (the dervish quarter), which was established by former Mahdist soldiers, many of whom were Baqqara from Kordofan and Darfur or West Africans. Another old settlement was `Ishash, in the southeastern part of town. It was called `ishash (straw) because it consisted mainly of straw huts and hovels that provided accommodation for the poorest segments of the town's population. The majority of those were ex-slaves and West African immigrants who were known locally as *Fellata*. Some immigrants, particularly the Ja`aliyyin and Rubatab, preferred to settle among their kinsmen at al-Dakhla. Not far from al-Dakhla, hospital workers and dressers established a quarter called Hay al-Tamargiyya (hospital workers' quarter). The informal urban settlements where the majority of low-income people lived fell outside the official

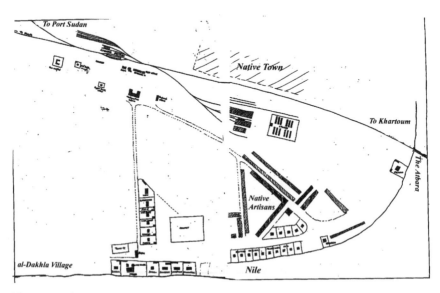

Map 1.1   Plan of Atbara, 1910.

classification and were dubbed "native lodging areas." Since they were considered illegal, the municipal authorities could evict tenants and remove these settlements at any moment. Indeed, this occurred in various Sudanese towns and was often justified by lack of sanitation and the need for further planned expansion.

From the beginning, the physical layout of Atbara reflected its colonial character. The railway line divided the town roughly into western and eastern zones. The native quarters were located east of the railway line, while the area west of the line was decidedly foreign. To avoid the hot climate of Atbara, senior British officials built their bungalows on the bank of the Nile about half a mile west of the line. The western zone also included the railway station, offices, workshops, and houses of British and Egyptian employees. In the town center next to the workshops was the central market, where many merchants and Egyptian officials settled.[55]

It is important to point out that most of the railway buildings, particularly the residential quarters, were built on land appropriated from the inhabitants of al-Dakhla.[56] The acquisition of the farmland of al-Dakhla reached a peak in the late 1920s and sparked a strong reaction by the inhabitants, a subject that will be examined in chapter 3.

Social Life in a Colonial Town

Among the most important factors that shaped the pattern of social life and leisure activities in Atbara was the fact that it was largely a town of foreigners who introduced new forms of entertainment and lifestyle. Moreover, the military character of the railways and its highly regimented work had a great impact on social activities outside the workplace.

European staff, particularly the British, found life in Atbara extremely boring and monotonous. They particularly detested its hot climate and constant dust storms. In describing the daily routine there, G.R. Storrar, a British railway engineer, wrote in 1907:

> Staying in Atbara does not give one very much to write about, as there is not much variety of life here. The day begins with a look around the work between 7–8 am, breakfast 8–9, office 9–12, lunch 12–2:30, office 2:30–4, and tennis in the evening.[57]

While the men went to work, the few wives who lived there entertained each other through visits, tea parties, and other activities.[58]

To overcome the boredom of Atbara, European officials tried to develop a more familiar environment and create their own world in this remote land. They gave their streets European names such as Broadway Avenue, which ran along the bank of the Nile.[59] In the evenings, they held parties, dances, musicals, and theatrical activities.

To a large extent, social life and leisure activities in Atbara were centered in clubs. One of the oldest was the Atbara Club, established in 1907 and affiliated with the Red Sea and Port Sudan Clubs. Atbara Club remained an elite club, limited to senior

British railway employees and administrative staff.[60] Another British club was the Atbara Sports Club, founded in 1910 for sport and social activities. The club had tennis, hockey, and cricket teams. Tennis was very popular in the early days, followed by golf and hockey. Atbara Golf Club was founded in 1914 and it affiliated with the English Golf Union in 1933. At that time, it had about ninety members. Golf tournaments were held regularly among various railway clubs in Khartoum North and Port Sudan.[61] However, these tournaments were limited to Europeans. The establishment of social and sport clubs at this early stage set the pattern for leisure activities in Atbara. Clubs proliferated in the 1930s and 1940s and became one of the most distinctive features of this railway town.

As mentioned earlier, the largest expatriate community in Atbara was the Egyptians. In 1910 the Egyptian Club was founded for recreational purposes. Club membership included both Muslims and Copts, with the latter predominating. Although there are no accurate figures on the number of Copts in Atbara, it is clear that they were the most active and dynamic segment of the Egyptian community. As a minority in a predominantly Muslim society, the Copts remained a close-knit community and tried to preserve their distinctive identity by establishing a variety of communal organizations. In 1912 they established the Coptic Orthodox Benevolent Society, which ran a Bible society, a Sunday school, a Christian girls' school, and an Egyptian Coptic school.[62] Another Christian community in Atbara was the Greeks. Most Greeks were artisans in the railway department while a few owned liquor stores, restaurants, and small hotels. In 1907 they established a local branch of the Hellenic Society, which had its headquarters in Khartoum.[63]

1924 UPRISING AND ITS AFTERMATH

It is a commonplace that the period of the early 1920s was a watershed in Sudanese colonial history. It was a period of political unrest, popular protests, and mutinies that involved Sudanese and Egyptian army units in the Sudan. These events culminated in the evacuation of the Egyptian Army, including its railway battalion, from the Sudan. The background causes and the course of these events have been examined in numerous studies in a manner that warrants no further elaboration. Here, it is necessary to stress the fact that the removal of the railway battalion was prompted by both economic and political considerations.

For several years before the 1924 incidents, the efficacy of keeping the Egyptian Army Railway Battalion in the Sudan was a subject of serious debate. From the perspective of the British colonial administration, the revenue generated by the railways and steamers represented more than half of the Sudan's income. It was essential then that the railway department cut down costs and eliminate unnecessary expenses. In this regard, the use of foreign military personnel to operate the railway was considered too expensive. According to official estimates, an Egyptian soldier cost about twice as much to maintain as a Sudanese civilian laborer. The total cost of the railway battalion in 1923 was LE 67,767, or LE 16,000 more than the cost of comparable civilian labor.[64]

Another economic consideration had to do with the anticipated completion of the Gezira Scheme and the production of cotton. From the mid-1920s, cotton was the main cash crop and the backbone of the Sudanese colonial economy. It was deemed necessary that the railway be prepared in every way to deal with the expected growth in cotton exports.

In 1923 the Sudan Government invited Felix Pole, general manager of the Great Western Railway, to visit the Sudan to inspect and report on the SGR.[65] Although Pole's report did not specifically recommend evacuation of the railway battalion, British officials were determined to get rid of it. In 1923 about 100 Egyptian troops were eliminated from the engineering division.

These economic considerations were given further impetus by the political climate that prevailed in Egypt and the Sudan in the early 1920s. The development of Egyptian nationalism after World War I and the Egyptian revolution of 1919 appealed to some segments of the small class of educated Sudanese, who established a number of political organizations in various urban centers. The most prominent of these was the White Flag League, which was founded by `Ali `Abd al-Latif, an ex-army officer of slave parentage. The league adopted the slogan Unity of the Nile Valley and called for Sudan's independence and unity with Egypt. It established branches in several towns and attracted a significant number of educated Sudanese. In 1923–1924, the league held demonstrations in various Sudanese towns.

Throughout the first two decades of Anglo-Egyptian rule, the British viewed Egyptian civilian and military personnel in the Sudan as the main vehicles of disseminating anti-British sentiments among Sudanese. The opportunity to get rid of the Egyptian Army occurred when Sir Lee Stack, the governor-general of the Sudan and sirdar of the Egyptian Army, was assassinated in Cairo on November 19, 1924.[66]

Given the large concentration of Egyptian military and civilian personnel in Atbara, the town became one of the major centers of unrest during the summer of 1924. In addition to the large Egyptian presence in the town, many Sudanese civil servants were either members or sympathizers of the White Flag League. Since the appearance in Egyptian newspapers of reports that the battalion was going to be disbanded and sent to Egypt, discontent and insubordination among the soldiers had risen. The first protest occurred on August 9, 1924, when a train carrying Salih `Abd al-Qadir, a postal employee at Port Sudan and a member of the White Flag League, arrived at the Atbara station. `Abd al-Qadir had been arrested in Port Sudan and was on his way to Khartoum. When the train arrived in Atbara, he was cheered by a crowd of Sudanese and Egyptian railway employees, who carried banners and shouted anti-British slogans.[67] After the train's departure, they marched toward the central market and continued their demonstration until midnight.

On the morning of August 10, many of the soldiers of the railway battalion, armed with sticks and iron bars, marched to the railway headquarters. They smashed windows, pulled down the British flag, and proceeded to the workshops where they caused serious damage to the machines and rolling stock. Fearing attacks on civilian personnel and their families, British officials then ordered a detachment of the 9th Sudanese Battalion to guard the workshops, stores, power station, and headquarters, and assembled all British and European families at the Atbara Sports Club and armed them with rifles. Reinforcement of British troops was also requested from Khartoum. When the men of the railway battalion heard the news that a train carrying enforcements was coming from Khartoum, they proceeded to meet it at the station. In order to avoid a bloody confrontation, British officials decided to disembark the troops on the outskirts of Atbara. The plan worked and the British troops, which included a company of mounted rifles, were stationed at the railway rest house and the Atbara Sports Club.

On the morning of August 11, the railway soldiers staged another demonstration and marched through the central market. With much difficulty they were rounded up and confined to their barracks by two British platoons of mounted rifles. At the barracks a confrontation erupted between the Egyptian soldiers and their British guards. The latter opened fire and wounded twenty-one men, of whom four later died. With the assistance of a detachment of the 9th Sudanese, the British troops were able to subdue the mutineers, and sixteen of the alleged ringleaders were arrested.[68] Using the Public Order Ordinance, the governor of Berber Province issued an order prohibiting all public gatherings and demonstrations. However, this order did not deter the civilian population of the city from organizing a demonstration during the funeral services.

In solidarity with their comrades in Atbara, the men of the railway battalion at Abu Dis went on strike and threatened to hold up mail trains. However, on the following day, they were brought to Atbara where they were confined to barracks. By August 14 the rest of the men of the railway battalion had been placed with their comrades in the barracks. On August 16 a special court of inquiry was held to investigate the circumstances that had led to the uprising in Atbara and to assess the damage.[69] The next day, arrangements for the evacuation of the railway battalion had begun. The first detachment left for Egypt on August 19, and by August 28, the last party of the railway battalion had left Atbara under escort.

It is important at this point to raise questions about the significance of the 1924 uprising in Atbara's history and the extent to which it contributed to the city's militant and radical tradition. Although the uprising involved mainly Egyptian military and civilian personnel, it was evident that certain segments of the Sudanese civilian population, particularly in the railway department, had been actively involved. Some Sudanese railway employees were either members or sympathizers of the White Flag League. As early as 1920, British officials feared that railway workers were going to strike to obtain wage increases, and began to take measures to prevent it.[70] The White Flag League had established a number of cells among the railway employees. It was reported that several members of the White Flag League were Communists.[71] For instance, Ali Ahmad Salih, a former railway artisan and member of the league, tried to recruit workers in Khartoum, Port Sudan, and Atbara. As a result of his efforts, artisans from the departments of Power and Water, Railways, Tramways, and some private companies had formed a Workmen's Society and affiliated to the White Flag League.[72] Moreover, several Eastern and Central European artisans with socialist leanings were actively trying to indoctrinate Sudanese workers.[73] Another organization called Jami`yat al-shabiba al-wataniyya bi Atbara (The patriotic youth of Atbara) organized demonstrations and distributed pro-Egyptian and anti-British leaflets in the summer of 1924.[74]

In the broader context of Sudanese history, the 1924 movement was limited in terms of scale, duration, and influence. This was an urban-based movement that was confined to the small class of Sudanese junior civil servants, and had little impact on the rural population. Apart from the Unity of the Nile Valley slogan, the movement had no clear ideological vision or program. In the aftermath of the rebellion, the government began to cultivate the allegiance of tribal heads through the application of indirect rule, and to marginalize the educated class. As a result of the defeat of the movement and the hostility of the colonial government, the Sudanese intelligentsia became more introspective, focusing their activities mainly on the formation of literary groups that stressed education. A number of literary magazines and newspapers were established in the early 1930s. The most influential of these was *al-Fajr* (The dawn). Nonetheless, the 1924 uprising marked the beginning of secular opposition to the colonial regime. In the context of Atbara's history, the uprising and the evacuation of the Egyptian Army Railway Battalion paved the way for the development of a Sudanese labor force and sowed the seeds for the tradition of political activism that emerged in the 1940s.

CONCLUSION

Between 1906 and 1924 Atbara was transformed from an ordinary station into a vibrant railway center and a unique colonial town, with a predominantly foreign population and a segregated urban space. During this phase of its history, Atbara resembled a military garrison, for the great majority of its residents were military personnel. Yet it was also a cosmopolitan town, inhabited by diverse nationalities and ethnic groups. These factors shaped Atbara's history and became its defining characteristics.

NOTES

1. SAD 294/9: *Brief Historical Outline of the Sudan Government Railways and Steamers*, 5 January 1930.

2. Ibid.

3. M.W. Daly, *Empire on the Nile: The Anglo-Egyptian Sudan, 1898–1934* (Cambridge: Cambridge University Press, 1986), 203–204.

4. Ibid.

5. Ibid.

6. E.W.C. Sandes, *The Royal Engineers in Egypt and the Sudan* (Chatham: Institution of Royal Engineers, 1937), 401.

7. SAD 294/9: *Brief Historical Outline of the Sudan Government Railways and Steamers*, 5 January 1930.

8. Richard Hill, *Sudan Transport* (London: Oxford University Press, 1965), 55.

9. Ibid., 145.

10. Hill, 77.

11. SAD 114/3: *Handbook of the Egyptian Army*, 1911, 115.

12. SAD 294/9: *Brief Historical Outline of the Sudan Government Railways and Steamers*, 5 January 1930.

13. Ibid., 7.

14. Hill, *Sudan Transport*, 50–51.

15. Ibid.

16. Frederick George Augustus Pinckney, *Sudan Government Railways and Steamers* (London: Institution of Royal Engineers, 1926), 15.

17. Ibid.

18. Ibid.

19. Ibid.

20. Ibid., 17.

21. Ibid., 18.

22. M.W. Daly, *Empire on the Nile*, 206.

23. On colonial labor policies, see Ahmad Alawad Sikainga, *Slaves into Workers: Emancipation and Labor in Colonial Sudan* (Austin: University of Texas Press, 1996).

24. SAD 554/1/160: G. Storrar Diaries.

25. Sir Edward Midwinter, "Sudan Government Railways," *The Atbarabian* 2 (November 1928): 5.

26. Sandes, *The Royal Engineers*, 240–41.

27. SAD 554/1/160: G. Storrar Diaries.

28. During the first two decades of the Sudan Railways, there were thirty-five British officers, many of whom were drawn from the Royal Engineers, (Sandes, 173–174).

29. Ibid.

30. Ibid., 401.

31. SAD 114/3: *Handbook of the Egyptian Army*, 113–117.

32. Hill, *Sudan Transport*, 96.

33. Ibid.

34. Ibid.

35. SAD 424/11, H.D. Bindley, "Sudan Railways, 1925–1935," *Journal of Institution of Civil Engineers* 1 (November 1935): 58.

36. Pinckney, *Sudan Government Railways and Steamers*, 7.

37. *Sudan Railways Bulletin*, February 1945.

38. Ibid., 9.

39. Ibid., 10.

40. Catherine Coquery-Vidrovitch, "The Process of Urbanization in Africa (from the Origins to the Beginning of Independence)," *African Studies Review* 34 (April 1991): 35–36.

41. Al-Tayyib Muhammad al-Tayyib, interview by author, Khartoum, 23 October 1999.

42. Ibid.

43. Ibid.

44. Muhammad Idris Ahmad, "Madinat Atbara: dirasa fi gughrafiyat al-Mudun" (master's thesis, Cairo University, 1978), 4–5. According to one account, the whole area in which al-Dakhla grew was also known as al-Dadariyya; interview with Muhammad ʿAli Mustafa, Atbara, 13 October 1999.

45. Ibid.

46. Sandes, *The Royal Engineers*, 401.

47. Hill, *Sudan Transport*, 77.

48. *Sudan Government Railways Annual Report*, 31 December 1914.

49. SAD 114/3: *Handbook of the Egyptian Army*, 113.

50. Al-Tayyib, interview.

51. Ibid.

52. Gabriel Warburg, *Sudan under Wingate: Administration in the Anglo-Egyptian Sudan, 1899–1916* (London: Frank Cass, 1971), 162.

53. El-Sayed El-Bushra Mohammed, "The Evolution of the Three Towns," *African Urban Notes* 6, no. 2 (1971): 18.

54. SAD 50/1/6: Storrar Diary, 12 November 1907.

55. Ibid.

56. This area extended from Atbara Bridge in the south to the middle of al-Dakhla. NRO, NP 2/29/312, Petition by Twenty-five Residents of al-Dakhla to the Governor, Berber Province, 20 January 1928.

57. SAD 50/1/6, G.R. Storrar Diaries.

58. SAD 294/18/1–66: "A Young Bride's First Impressions of the Sudan."

59. SAD 730/9: Hugh Quinland Memoires, 7 April 1982.

60. NRO, NP 2/33/386, DC Atbara to Governor, Northern Province, 8 December 1945.

61. SAD 294/7/1–56.

62. NRO, NP 2/33/386, enclosed in DC Atbara to Governor, Northern Province, 8 December 1945.

63. NRO, NP 2/34/384, Clubs and Societies Functioning in Atbara, enclosed in DC Atbara to Governor, Northern Province, 8 December 1945.

64. Hill, *Sudan Transport*, 96–97.

65. NRO, Departmental Reports, 30/6/81, Report on the Sudan Government Railways by Sir Flex Pole, 1923.

66. Hasan Abdin, *Early Sudanese Nationalism, 1919–1924* (Khartoum: Khartoum University Press, 1986), 86; Mohammed Omer Beshir, *Revolution and Nationalism in the Sudan* (London: Rex Collings, 1974), 73–80.

67. SAD 294/6/2: Memorandum on Events at Atbara from 9 August 1924 onward.

68. Ibid.

69. Ibid.

70. NRO, NP 1/1/3: Civil Secretary to Governor, Northern Province, 13 October 1920.

71. Jaafar Muhammad Ali Bakheit, *Communist Activities in the Middle East, 1919–1927, with Special Reference to Egypt and the Sudan* (Khartoum: University of Khartoum, 1968); Gabriel Warburg, *Islam, Nationalism, and Communism in a Traditional Society: The Case of Sudan* (London: Frank Cass, 1978), 93–96; Mohammed Nuri El-Amin, *The Emergence and Development of the Leftist Movement in the Sudan during the 1930s and 1940s* (Khartoum: Khartoum University Press, 1984).

72. Abdin, *Early Sudanese Nationalism*, 86.

73. Ibid., 188.

74. NRO, NP 1/20/191: Leaflet by the Patriotic Youth of Atbara, 4 September 1924.

2

THE EVOLUTION
OF A COMPANY TOWN:
ATBARA, 1925–1939

The central theme of this chapter is the transformation of Atbara from a small railway center into a major company town, with a large and heterogeneous population. The chapter will focus on the structure of the workplace, the regional and social origins of the railway workers, and their transformation into stable wage earners. The primary goal is to show how the workplace experience shaped the perspective and attitude of these workers and led to the emergence of a strong sense of solidarity and a distinctive identity.

Atbara's transformation was brought about by a number of interrelated developments. The withdrawal of the Egyptian Army Railway Battalion and the retrenchment of foreign railway personnel during the depression years paved the way for the emergence of a Sudanese railway labor force. Moreover, the expansion of cash-crop production from the mid-1920s and the consequent sharp increase in railway traffic engendered substantial growth in the railway workforce. By the end of World War II, the Sudan Railways had over 20,000 employees, 90 percent of whom were Sudanese. The bulk of this labor force was stationed at Atbara, where the main workshops and division headquarters were located.

SUDAN RAILWAYS DURING THE INTERWAR PERIOD

As mentioned earlier, the growth of the railway labor force after the mid-1920s was closely associated with the expansion of cash-crop production and sharp increase in railway traffic. By 1945 the Sudan Railways (SR) had about 2,014 miles of track, and its steamer service operated over 2,000 miles of waterway.[1] In addition to cotton, the Sudan's exports included gum arabic, grain, and livestock. The transportation of these products to Port Sudan on the Red Sea became the primary responsibility of the SR. Export tonnage nearly doubled between 1933 and 1934, and surpassed 300,000 tons in 1937–1938.[2] By the mid-1940s the railways carried annually nearly 1¼ million tons of commodities. Gross revenue generated by the SR increased from LE 2.16 million in 1934 to LE 2.84 million in 1937, but declined slightly in 1938–1939. The ratio of expenditure to gross revenue ranged between 52.3 and 58.6 percent. Between 1934 and World War II, the railways provided about 15–20 percent of the government's normal revenue before the Egyptian subsidy and Gezira figures were factored in.[3]

In the early 1930s the SR carried out extensive reforms. In addition to changing its administrative regulations and operational rules, the SR introduced diesel locomotives in 1933. Although the number of diesel locomotives rose during the next two decades, the SR continued to rely on steam engines until the late 1950s.[4]

In addition to its routine work of carrying goods and passengers, the SR provided several other services. For example, its engineering division was responsible for the construction and maintenance of many government buildings and bridges in the country.[5] In 1925 a mechanical transport branch was established within the mechanical division to provide service to road vehicles, motor trolleys, lorries, and trucks. Moreover, the SR maintained power stations at Port Sudan and Atbara for its own use and for the use of municipalities.[6]

The Structure of Railway Employment

The nature of railway operations involved a particular type of organization, administrative structure, forms of supervision, and division of labor. Railway corporations were usually divided into functional departments with a number of subdivisions and districts. Each unit or division had its own functions, chain of authority, staff, and workers, at headquarters as well as at outlying stations.

The SR was organized into the following divisions: headquarters, engineering, mechanical, traffic, accounts, stores, and hotel and catering services. The engineering division was responsible for construction and maintenance of the track. Its activity increased considerably during rainy seasons, which often resulted in washouts. It has already been mentioned that the engineering division of the SR was responsible also for construction of many government buildings, bridges, and government houses throughout the country. The division's workforce included civil engineers, permanent-way inspectors, track supervisors, superintendents of ways and works, district surveyors, carpenters, and builders, as well as a large number of unskilled laborers. In 1941 the engineering division had about 6,379 employees.[7] The backbone of this workforce was *umal al-darisa*, permanent-way workers. The organization of the permanent-way workforce changed over time. Before 1934, for instance, the entire railway system was divided into sections, each with British civil engineers, inspectors, surveyors, headmen, and a contingent of permanent-way workers who were organized into *kalas*, or gangs, supervised by native headmen. A reorganization of the engineering division in 1934 divided the entire railway system into four districts, each with two British engineers and two native surveyors. The districts were subdivided into four or more sections, each with a track supervisor. In districts that included large towns, a British superinten-

dent of works and a native assistant surveyor were posted to supervise the maintenance of buildings in the town.[8] In emergencies such as washouts, the permanent-
way workforce was supplemented by daily laborers. On these occasions, work
continued around the clock, often in hazardous conditions.[9] Special classes and ex-
aminations in permanent-way rules and regulations were held annually for all Sudanese staff involved in track work.

The traffic division was in charge of the management, organization, and scheduling of trains. In 1941 it had a workforce of 4,545. They included train crews of
engine drivers, firemen, guards, conductors, ticket collectors, and brakemen. In addition, there were stationmasters who supervised traffic, ticketing, and other paper-
work; signalmen; switchmen; and so forth. Traffic employees were in charge of
the most sensitive aspect of railway activity, namely the operation and movement
of trains. To ensure safety, the bulk of the *General Rules Book* was devoted to traffic operations. Breaching these rules carried severe penalties.[10]

One of the most challenging tasks that faced the traffic division was making train
timetables. In making timetables, several factors had to be taken into account. These
included difference in type and speed of train service, unequal distance between
stations, and varying time required for stops at stations for traffic and locomotive
purposes. The traffic division organized four types of train services: mail and passenger, cattle, through goods, and pick-up goods. In terms of speed, there were six
categories of trains: express, express-mixed, mixed, cattle, goods, and pick-up
goods.[11] The fact that the SR operated on a single track rendered the scheduling of
train services extremely difficult and caused numerous delays.

The heart of the system was the mechanical division, which was responsible for
maintaining rolling stock and manufacturing tools and parts. Within the division
there were seventeen workshops, each specializing in a particular trade. Among the
most important of these were the running-shed, carpenter, boilermaker, and fitter
workshops. These workshops were grouped under three broad sections. One section manufactured passenger and freight wagons. Another was responsible for the
maintenance and repair of rolling stock as well as manufacturing spare parts. The
third was the electric section, which was in charge of making and repairing electric
equipment. It is worth noting that the Atbara workshops had the largest foundry in
the Sudan, in which a wide range of railway parts and equipment were made.

The mechanical division had the largest concentration of skilled workers. In
1941 it had a labor force of 5,535, with a diverse and complex hierarchy of skills.
They included mechanical engineers, fitters, turners, pattern makers, charge men,
checkers, carpenters, and apprentices. Unlike the mobile workers in the traffic and
engineering divisions, the artisans of the mechanical division worked in a factory-
like setting. They were assigned to specific locations, where they remained under
direct supervision. The division's employees began their working day at 6 A.M. and
finished at 2 P.M. In view of its critical role in preparing the rolling stock, work at
the running-shed workshop continued around the clock.

These various divisions were functionally integrated. For instance, the traffic division relied heavily on the mechanical division in making train timetables. The

running-shed workshop provided such vital information as the number of minutes required by a locomotive to haul a particular class of train between two stations.[12]

Among the most conspicuous features of railway employment was the sharp division of labor and the complex job hierarchy, made evident by the elaborate grade system employed by the railway. Until the late 1940s, the SR had over 300 grades distributed among the various divisions. This distribution is shown in Table 2.1.

From the perspective of railway management, these grades reflected variations of skills required in each division. In other words, skill level was the main criterion for determining the rank and salary of railway employees.

The development of a highly stratified job hierarchy based on skill level had many implications. It not only created major social distinctions among railway employees but also shaped their behavior and self-image. Job rank became a status symbol. For instance, locomotive engineers and train drivers enjoyed considerable prestige both inside and outside railway circles. Similarly, the artisans, particularly the graduates of Atbara Technical School, saw themselves as a cut above the rest of the workers. At the bottom of the hierarchy were permanent-way workers and the mass of *tulbas* (unskilled laborers) who were viewed by skilled workers as illiterate and backward. These distinctions extended beyond the workplace. One of the most vivid illustrations of social distinctions among the workers was establishment in the 1930s of two separate clubs, one for skilled artisans who had graduated from the technical school and the other for unskilled workers.[13]

The expansion of the railway network had many sociological and political implications. In addition to integrating remote regions into the colonial economy, the railroad played a key role in the process of urbanization. Many railway stations such as Sinnar, Kosti, and Babanusa became major commercial centers. Most important, however, was the role of the railroad in facilitating the movement of people and ideas across vast regions. It gave young people in the countryside the

Table 2.1   Sudan Railways Grade System

Division	Number of grades
Mechanical	200
Traffic	46
Engineering	31
Stores	16
Catering	40

opportunity to move away from their homes, earn income, establish households, and gain economic and social independence. Equally important is the fact that railroads became a vehicle for the dissemination of new ideas, modes of behavior, and political and cultural influences in the rural areas. Babo Nimir, a prominent tribal head in southern Kordofan, aptly expressed the impact of railway influence. When Nimeiri's regime (1969–1985) tried to reform the system of native administration, Babo Nimir commented that as far as he was concerned, the system of native administration had ended with the arrival of the railway line at Babanusa. Implicit in Babo's statement was the vital role of the railways in bringing new ideas that impacted the social fabric of rural communities. The multifaceted role of the railways in Sudanese society shaped the attitude of its employees and their self-image. Railway employees took great pride in their work and viewed themselves as harbingers of modernity.

THE DEVELOPMENT OF THE RAILWAY LABOR FORCE

As mentioned earlier, the abrupt evacuation of the Egyptian Army Railway Battalion created a huge vacuum that had to be filled immediately. The most critical areas for railway operations were the traffic and mechanical divisions. The few Sudanese workers who had sufficient training in traffic operation carried out their task without any delay to train services.[14] The most serious challenge, however, was replacement of five hundred Egyptian soldiers in the engineering division. In this regard, the SR had to rely on foreign artisans.

Immediately after the withdrawal of the battalion, the SR management requested Thomas Cook & Sons in Cairo to dispatch a contingent of European artisans. About forty artisans, mostly Eastern and Central Europeans, were dispatched to Atbara.[15] Together with British engineers, these artisans formed the backbone of the skilled labor force, particularly in the workshops. At the same time, railway management retained many Egyptian civilian personnel in clerical and accounting posts. In other words, expatriates dominated technical posts and the upper echelon of the railway administration for many years.

The presence of foreign artisans had great significance in the context of Atbara's radical history, for many of them were Communists. One of those artisans was a Pole named Pobonski, often referred to by his British colleagues as "our tame Bolshevik."[16] It was reported that Pobonski was allowed into the Sudan despite the fact that he had been officially blacklisted. Moreover, an organization known as the Hammer and Sickle Society existed in Atbara in the 1930s. According to official reports, this society was formed by a group of discontented railway officials who wanted to form trade unions. The extent of the activities of these artisans and their influence on their Sudanese colleagues is not clear.

The development of a skilled Sudanese labor force was a gradual process closely linked to the provision of technical education. Until the mid-1920s, technical training for Sudanese was provided at Gordon Memorial College and the Omdurman School for Stone Masons. In 1924 the technical school was transferred from Omdurman to Atbara. Atbara Technical School became the main center for training future Sudanese artisans. The school admitted boys between the ages of twelve and fifteen. Before entering the school, boys must have completed their elementary education, though intermediate-school students were also admitted. Admission was by examination and interview, and the course of study was three years. Two-thirds of the curriculum was devoted to technical subjects and one-third to general subjects such as English, Arabic, and Islamic studies.[17] After completing their course of study, the students would enter the railway service as apprentices, where they would remain for five years until they were appointed skilled artisans.

The railways also maintained an enginemen's school and an electrical engineering school, with a branch at Port Sudan. The role of these schools was to produce competent enginemen, electricians, and charge men. The traffic division established a training school, which taught the principles of railway traffic.[18]

Learning railway skills required many years of practical training. The example of engine drivers illustrates this pattern. Candidates for the job went through a lengthy program of training, beginning as engine cleaners. This was a period of probation during which candidates were given grounding in safety regulations and were introduced to the various parts and workings of the locomotive. They were kept in the workshops, where they received frequent instruction—individually and in classes. At the end of this period, they would be tested before they were promoted to firemen. They spent several years at this level, during which they received practical rather than theoretical training. However, before the fireman was ready for promotion to engine driver, he was required to master the *General Rule Book of Engine Drivers*, which consisted of 313 rules occupying 171 pages. The engine driver was required to know these rules thoroughly. After passing a test, the fireman would first be promoted to shunting driver, and finally, to main-line driver.[19]

Over the years, a small cadre of Sudanese main-line and engine drivers had emerged. Although British railway engineers were initially apprehensive, they were impressed by the performance of Sudanese train drivers. In 1946, for instance, three Sudanese engine drivers and two main-line firemen were awarded special watches for their "high standard of work throughout the year." The drivers were Sir al-Khatim al-Makki, `Abd al-Majid Gindeil, and `Awad `Uthman. The firemen were `Uthman Hasan Abu al-`Ila and Muhammad Hussain Ibrahim.[20]

One of the main problems that faced the SR was its dependence on expensive foreign artisans and technical workers. Shortly before the withdrawal of the railway battalion, the chief mechanical engineer expressed the view that a European artisan might cost twice as much as a Sudanese, but two Sudanese would do more work than one European.[21] In the early 1920s the SR began to reduce the number of foreign artisans. In 1923, for instance, sixty-two European artisans in the mechanical division were retrenched.[22]

Retrenchment of foreign artisans gained momentum during the depression years. By 1932 about 31 percent of the British, 33 percent of the Egyptians, and the overwhelming majority of the Greeks had been retrenched.[23] In 1941 the SR had 18,551 employees.[24] Of those, 16,750, or 90 percent, were Sudanese.[25] Foreigners included 213 British officials and 56 Greeks, of whom nine were classified staff. The overwhelming majority of foreigners were Egyptians; they numbered 654, of whom 248 were classified officials. The number of Syrians, Eastern and Central Europeans, and Ethiopians was negligible. According to official employment policy, the first priority was to be given to qualified Sudanese, followed by non-Sudanese domiciled in the Sudan. Nonetheless, Egyptians continued to form an important segment of the railway workforce.[26] The railway management retained many Egyptian employees at the end of their service on the condition that they accept the salary and terms of service of local Sudanese.[27]

In 1939 about twenty Egyptians whose contracts had expired signed new ones, in which they agreed to be treated as local employees. Some of these Egyptians had invested the greater part of their lives in the SR and established strong ties with the Sudan. Moreover, most of those classified as Egyptians had actually been born and raised in the Sudan.

One of the most important categories of the Egyptians who chose to remain in the service of the SR were the *muwaladin*, or offspring of Sudanese and Egyptian parents. The following examples illustrate this pattern. Al-`Ubaid Sidahmad was one of those who signed a new contract in 1939. Al-`Ubaid had an Egyptian father and a Sudanese mother, both of whom lived in the Sudan. Al-`Ubaid joined the SR in 1904 and became a steamer engineer in 1927. Another Eqyptian who decided to remain in the Sudan was Muhammad `Abdalla. His father was Egyptian and his mother Ethiopian. Muhammad joined the SR as a fitter in 1918 and became a steamer engineer in 1938.[28] Many Egyptians who continued to work in the SR were Coptic Christians. One of them was Nassif Armanios, who joined the railways in 1928 as a telegraph technician. Another Copt was Kamal Girgis who moved to the Sudan with his parents. After receiving his education, Kamal joined the railways as an accountant in 1929.[29]

By the 1940s a cadre of Sudanese artisans and technical staff had emerged, some of whom served for many years and occupied senior positions in the SR. The most prominent Sudanese employee who had a remarkable career in the SR was Hasan Ahmad Khalifa. Hasan joined the traffic division in 1907. In 1910 he became traffic inspector as well as the superintendent of Sudanese staff. In 1931 Hasan was promoted to traffic superintendent, and four years later, he was promoted to headquarters traffic inspector, a post he held until his retirement in 1939.[30]

Hasan Ahmad Khalifa was known for his efficiency and dedication. Throughout his career, he was heavily involved in promoting the welfare of railway employees, particularly education for workers' children, and the proper running of social and sports clubs. In 1929 he was made an honorary member of the Most Excellent Order of the British Empire (MBE). He also received both the Silver Jubilee and the Coronation Medals of King George V. Hasan was invited by the Sudan government to join an official delegation of prominent Sudanese to attend the coronation of King Farouk of Egypt.[31] After his retirement from the SR in 1939, Hasan was immediately appointed third-class magistrate in Omdurman's Municipal Council. In 1940 he was awarded the Egyptian Order of the Nile for his service as a warden during the war. Hasan returned to the SR in 1942 as headquarters staff inspector, a post he held until his final retirement in 1946.

Other Sudanese who rose to prominent positions included Muhammad Shurbaji, the first Sudanese traffic inspector; Muhammad al-Amin al-Khalifa `Abdullahi,[32] the first Sudanese locomotive foreman; and his brother `Abd al-Salam, who came from Gordon Memorial College for training in the traffic division.[33] Among the early Sudanese artisans who were trained at Atbara Technical School were Sulayman Musa, al-Shafi' Ahmad al-Shaykh, Qasim Amin, al-Tayyib Hasan al-Tayyib, and al-Hajj `Abd al-Rahman, all of whom became prominent trade-union leaders in the late 1940s.

By the end of World War II, over 90 percent of the railway employees were Sudanese. For instance, of the 7,300 employees in the mechanical division, 6,680 were Sudanese. Over 90 percent of the 4,600 staff in the traffic division were Sudanese. Similarly, 98 percent of the staff of the engineering division were Sudanese.[34] In short, within two decades, Sudanese workers had formed the overwhelming majority of railway labor force and become the most dynamic group of workers in the country.

The Sudan Railways Police Force

An important segment of the railway workers was the police force, which was responsible for maintaining security on trains, on steamers, at harbors, and in the railway cantonment in Atbara. In its early years, the railway police force was part of the Egyptian Army Railway Battalion. It consisted of twenty-five constables, many of whom were former Mahdist war prisoners. Following the withdrawal of the battalion, the old force was disbanded and a new one—called the Sudan Railways Police Force (SRPF)—was formed. The SRPF was established in Atbara in 1925 and was commanded by British officers.[35] The force began with 150 noncommissioned officers and men and soon reached 500 men. Many of those men had served in the Sudanese units of the Egyptian Army. At the top was the commandant of police, assisted by a superintendent, a chief inspector, and two other officers, all stationed at Atbara. The commandant reported directly to the railway manager. The first commandant was Harry Dibble, a retired British officer who served in the Egyptian Army. Dibble played a leading role in the development of the force. His assistant was Hugh Quinlan, a World War I veteran who joined the SR in 1922.[36] In 1928 the railway police was integrated into the Sudan Police Force, but its duties remained limited to the railways and steamers. Members of the SRPF had their own badge, which displayed the front of an engine set between the letters "S" and "R" (for Sudan Railways).

In addition to its role in maintaining security, the railway police force played a major role in Atbara's social life. The railway police had one of the best musical bands in the country. The first bandmaster, who trained most of the band members, was Daoud Adam, whose remarkable career deserves special attention.

Of all the Sudanese railway employees, Daoud had the longest years of service in the SR. He was born around the middle of the nineteenth century at al-Fashir in Darfur. At the age of twenty-five, Daoud was recruited into the Turco-Egyptian Army and sent to Egypt, where he learned music. In the 1880s Daoud was part of the Turco-Egyptian force that was stationed in the Red Sea region. After the defeat of the Egyptian forces, Daoud returned with the rest of his unit to Egypt. In 1896 he enlisted in the musical band that was attached to Herbert Kitchener, the sirdar of the Egyptian Army. During the Anglo-Egyptian campaign against the Mahdist state, Daoud fought in the Battle of the Atbara and was awarded the medals of Queen Victoria and Abbas, the khedive of Egypt. After the conquest of the Sudan, Daoud remained a member of the sirdar's band, which was stationed at the palace in Khartoum. The palace band played on such important occasions as King George's visit to Port Sudan and the official opening of al-Ubayyid railway line in 1912.[37]

Daoud retired in 1912 and settled in Khartoum as a pensioner. During a visit to Khartoum sometime in the mid-1920s, Edward Midwinter, general manager of the SR, met Daoud in the civil secretary's office and induced him to join the railway police band. After the withdrawal of the Egyptian Army Railway Battalion, Daoud became the *soul* (Turkish for "sergeant major") of the Sudan Railways Police Band. In 1939 Daoud received the Silver Jubilee Medal, presented to him by Stewart Symes, governor-general of the Sudan. In 1946 Daoud was still in the service of the Sudan Railway Police Force, and an article in the August issue of the *Sudan Railways Bulletin* described him as "perhaps the oldest serving railway man in the world."[38]

The railway police band performed at official ceremonies, festivals, and social occasions such as weddings. It attained great notoriety throughout the country in the 1960s and 1970s. One of the best-known members of the railway police band was the late `Abdalla Deng, a man of Dinka origin who was an excellent saxophone player.

THE DEVELOPMENT OF THE RAILWAY COMMUNITY IN ATBARA

As mentioned previously, the railway workforce in Atbara expanded in tandem with the sharp increase in railway traffic during the interwar period. Atbara became a major center of employment and received a steady stream of immigrants from neighboring and distant regions. In the span of two decades, Atbara's population jumped from an estimated 2,750 people in 1926 to over 30,000 in 1945.[39] At the time of the first census in 1955, Atbara had about 36,298 people.[40]

The overwhelming majority of Atbara's residents had come from the northern riverine region. By joining the railway workforce, these immigrants, most of whom were farmers and pastoralists, had become part of a complex and highly regimented industrial system that involved particular work habits and notions of authority, time, and discipline.

The transformation of rural immigrants into industrial workers is a subject that has attracted academic attention for many years. However, the bulk of the early literature on African labor history was preoccupied with the process of proletarianization, which was premised on the notion that the transition from farmer to worker represented successive stages in an evolutionary process. According to this thesis, just as in nineteenth-century Europe, the industrial environment in which African immigrants worked would inevitably force them to abandon their rural work ethic, adopt the industrial discipline and work culture, develop class consciousness, and engage in collective action against employers.[41] However, the trajectory of African workers of rural origin was much more complex than the linear process implied in the proletarianization thesis. As recent studies have shown, African workers brought to the workplace a great deal of their rural culture, attitudes, and work habits. The new literature has shifted the focus from the impact of the industrial environment on African workers to the role of African workers themselves in shaping the workplace.[42] Like Russian peasants who joined the industrial workforce in Moscow during the 1930s, African workers neither remained the archetypal farmers nor did they become the ideal workers employers had endeavored to create.[43] They developed a vision and created a new identity that reflected both their work experience and their rural background.[44]

In order to clarify the interaction between the cultural background of Sudanese workers and employment in the railway system, the following section will highlight some of the most important characteristics of the communities from which these workers were drawn.

Social Profile of Atbara's Railway Workers

It was mentioned in chapter 1 that the early generation of railway workers were recruited from among Mahdist prisoners, ex-slaves, and other displaced people. Freed and runaway slaves from the neighboring areas of Berber, al-Bawga, Darmali, and Kannur continued to flock into Atbara, particularly in the 1920s. One of the most important factors that led to the influx of runaway and liberated slaves from Berber district was the antislavery campaign of P.G. Diggle, an agricultural inspector at al-Bawga, and T.P. Creed, assistant district commissioner in Berber Province.[45] Both officials defied the prevailing government policy that discouraged slaves from leaving their masters, and issued certificates of manumission to slaves who came to district headquarters to complain about their owners. Most of these ex-slaves were attracted to Atbara, where they found employment either in the SR or in the informal sector of the urban economy.[46]

Railway employment attracted thousands of freeborn farmers and pastoralists from the Northern Province. According to the 1955 census, eighty percent of Atbara's residents had been born in the northern riverine region.[47] The predominance of immigrants from the northern region was also evident in the names of residential neighborhoods and regional associations that emerged in Atbara in the 1930s, a topic that will be discussed in the following chapter.

The preponderance of people from the far north in Atbara can be attributed to a number of factors. Prominent among those was the region's poor economic conditions. The principal economic activity was agriculture. Land was privately owned but cultivable land was confined to a narrow strip along the banks of the Nile. Private ownership of land had become prevalent since the late eighteenth century as a result of the policies of the Funj rulers and Turco-Egyptian regime (1820–1884). Coupled with this was the application of Islamic rules of inheritance, which resulted in great fragmentation of land. As a result, land could no longer support the growing population. For many years, these conditions had driven people from this region to other parts of the Sudan, a pattern that continued under colonial rule.[48] Moreover, the proximity of Atbara and the availability of train and steamer services in the region made it easier for many young people to migrate to Atbara. While the Rubatab, Manasir, and Shaiqiyya areas were connected to Atbara by the Kareima railway line, the Dongola region was linked by the steamer service.

The population of the northern region consisted of several ethnic and linguistic groups. The area near the Sudanese-Egyptian border was inhabited by the Nubians (Halfawiyyin, Mahas, and Danagala), who spoke the Nubian language in addition to Arabic. The population of the area between Debba—near the bend of the Nile—and Abu Hamad consisted of the Arabic-speaking Bedairiyya, Shaiqiyya, Manasir, and Rubatab. The region around Atbara was inhabited mainly by the Ja'aliyyin.

The overwhelming majority of the inhabitants of the northern region were Muslims. However, as in other parts of Africa, the practice of Islam in this area was shaped by the pre-Islamic tradition and by the spread of Sufi orders. As elsewhere in Africa, Sufism incorporated local beliefs, and quite often deviated from the orthodox teachings of Islam. Moreover, pre-Islamic Nubian traditions were not completely uprooted and have continued to influence popular culture in the northern region. These traditions can be seen in birth, naming, and marriage ceremonies. This aspect of Sudanese Islam is particularly important in understanding workers' attitude toward politics and ideology, a subject that will be elaborated on in the next chapters.

The principal economic activity in the northern region was agriculture. Farming was based on the *saqiya*, a term that refers both to the waterwheel and the land irrigated by it. A saqiya holding was the common property of those who held a share in the fruits of its cultivation. Agricultural production required the participation of several individuals: the *samad*, or the overseer of production; the *arwati*, who drove the animals that propelled the saqiya; the *tarbal*, or laborer who tended the crop; and the *basir*, or craftsman who repaired the waterwheel. Work on the saqiya was extremely arduous; it involved cleaning the *kodaiq* (a ditch in the riverbank beneath the waterwheel from which the water is drawn), cleaning the *jadwal* (water conduit), and bird scaring. The saqiya had to be worked day and night. The work was divided into two shifts: the *fijrawi* (morning shift) and *`ishawhi* (evening shift). Some agricultural tasks were beyond the capacity of the shareholders of a single saqiya and demanded other forms of organization. These included construction of the primary distribution canal and preparation of a new site for saqiya cultivation. Village work parties called *nafir*, whose service would be reciprocated on other occasions, performed these tasks. The nafir was usually supplied with food and drink. It is worth mentioning that during the nineteenth and early twentieth centuries, slave labor was used extensively throughout the region, in both the domestic and the agrarian sectors.[49] In brief, the vast majority of immigrants who joined the railway workforce were accustomed to particular work habits and communal forms of labor organization. Most of them had some skills in metallurgy, carpentry, and blacksmithing.

In addition to the railway department, the growing urban economy created many employment opportunities. As Atbara expanded, its economic base grew considerably. The growing need for goods and services stimulated a wide range of activities in both formal and informal sectors of the economy. For instance, farmers in the neighboring villages of Kannur, Umm al-Tiyour, and al-`Akad became the primary suppliers of vegetables, milk, and other daily needs. Retail and wholesale trade was dominated by Ja`aliyyin, Rubatab, and Shaiqiyya merchants. Among the most prominent merchants in Atbara were al-Rayyah al-Faki, Muhktar `Abd al-Hadi, Ibrahim al-Shush, Ahmad Hasan Bayram, Ibrahim al-`Arabi, Muhammad Hasan Abu Sham, and Ibrahim `Uthman. Greek traders such as Marketto and Socotelis were prominent in the liquor and catering business. However, in view of the liquor regulations and low incomes, the vast majority of Atbara's residents could not afford to buy imported liquor. Instead, they attended *anadi*, where they could buy inexpensive, locally made drinks. As in other Sudanese towns, the anadi were at the heart of the "informal" urban economy. They were run by ex-slaves and other displaced women who could not find alternative means of living.

One of the most vibrant sectors of the urban economy in Atbara was in bicycle trade and repair. Although public transport was available, the overwhelming majority of railway workers preferred to use bicycles. Atbara was dubbed the bicycle capital of the Sudan. As noted in Nancy Hunt's recent work on nurses in the Belgian Congo, bicycles became a symbol of modernity. In the 1930s, Congolese nurses used bicycles as their main means of transportation to provide services in the rural areas. The expansion of bicycles corresponded to a period of growing commercial cultivation, forced labor, and colonial hygiene. In this way, Hunt argues, bicycles played a major role in the "systematic remaking of the Congolese rural and social space in the name of 'Modernization.'"[50]

In addition to its railway function, Atbara was a major administrative unit in Berber Province. As a district headquarters, Atbara had a sizable administrative bureaucracy, including clerical staff, teachers, health workers, accountants, and so forth. Another important industrial establishment in Atbara that created jobs for the city's residents in the late 1940s was the cement factory, the first in the Sudan. It began as a private enterprise, but was nationalized by the Sudan government in 1970.

Nonetheless, these establishments could not rival the position of the railway department as the main employer in Atbara. Railway workers remained the main consumers for retail traders, café and restaurant owners, and other business establishments.

Social Networks and Corporate Identity

Several studies have stressed the unique nature of railway employment and its role in shaping workers' attitudes and fostering a strong sense of solidarity among them.[51] In many respects, railway employment resembled military service. Both institutions have complex hierarchies, chains of command, strict rules, and a high level of discipline. As in the case of military service, railway corporations made considerable effort to mold their employees and inculcate in them an ethos of obedience, loyalty, and solidarity. The conduct of railway employees was governed by a set of rules laid down in considerable detail as to how jobs should be performed and how workers should behave. Breaking these rules carried severe penalties.

The rules and regulations governing the conduct of the employees of the SR were laid down in the *General Rules Book* (Arabic: *la`iha*). The first edition appeared in 1909, but as railway operations expanded and became complex, the *General Rules Book* was revised several times: in 1925, 1931, 1939, 1950, and 1958. Railway employees were required to know the 313 rules that covered in considerable detail topics ranging from train movement and signaling to the conduct of railway employees to types of goods allowed on trains.[52] The first rule states:

> All persons employed by the Sudan Railways must devote themselves exclusively to the Railway service; they must reside at whatever place may be appointed, attend at such hours as may be required, pay prompt obedience to all persons placed in authority over them and conform to all the Railway Rules and Regulations.[53]

Railway employees were required to acquaint themselves with this manual and carry it when they were on duty. They were also required to wear railway uniforms while on duty and respect the chain of command at all times. The safety of passengers was to be their first priority. Article 20 stipulated that the railway department had the right to punish any employee by immediate dismissal, fine, or suspension for insubordination, negligence, bribery, drunkenness, and any other professional misconduct.[54]

In addition to work manuals and direct supervision, the SR used several other methods to instill discipline, loyalty, and thrift among its Sudanese employees. The most important of these methods was official publications. In 1927, for instance, the railway management published a monthly magazine called the *Atbarabian*. The *Atbarabian* was published in English and directed mainly at British personnel. The first editorial committee included J.H. Dunbar, H.D. Crawley, and B. Cooper. The magazine was between twenty to twenty-five foolscap pages in length and circulated 250 copies per month.[55]

Although the *Atbarabian* was established as a forum mainly for literary and creative works, it also became a major vehicle for indoctrinating railway employees, particularly British supervisors. For example, the August 1927 issue contains an article on loyalty, with a quotation from Elbert Habbard, as follows:

> If you work for a man in Heaven's name, work for him. If he pays you wages that supply your bread and butter, work for him. Speak well of him. Stand by him and stand by the institution he represents ... as long as you are part of the institution, do not condemn it. If you do, you are loosening the tendrils that hold you to the institution, and the first high wind that comes along, you will be uprooted and blown away in the blizzard's track, and probably you will never know why.[56]

The *Atbarabian* ceased publication and was followed by the *Sudan Railways Bulletin (SRB)*, established in 1937. The SRB was much more comprehensive and open to Sudanese contributors. Items were published in both English and Arabic. However, before the bulletin was sent to print, it had to be approved by the general manager of the SR.[57] The *SRB* continued the *Atbarabian*'s mission in that it was used as a forum to mold railway employees and inculcate in them the ethos of the industry.

One of the most important and oft-repeated themes in the bulletin was the value of manual labor, which had something to do with British stereotypes about Sudanese. At the core of these stereotypes was the notion that Sudanese were lazy and averse to manual labor because they associated it with servile status.[58] Indeed, the perception of the native as lazy was a common theme in the discourse of colonial officials throughout Africa. Commenting on Sudanese workers, a British engineer wrote,

> One is confronted with a number of young natives who begin with a fundamental horror of hard or sustained effort of any kind, little idea of discipline, complete ignorance or indifference to the most obvious signals of mechanical distress, and a temperament unfitted to anticipate danger.[59]

In an article entitled the "Dignity of Labor," published in the September 1945 issue, a British official wrote: "the belief that manual labor is shameful is to be found only among backward peoples. A man who is ashamed of his hands is usually ashamed of working with his brain."[60] He went on to tell his Sudanese readers:

> The dignity of labor enters into the upkeep of a man's house and *hosh*. He who is too dignified to keep his place clean with his own hands, and too poor or too lazy to get somebody else to do it for him is in a helpless state. Be sure of it, such a man will foul any house you give him.[61]

The organization of the railway itself played a critical role in molding employees. Railway divisions and subsections can be considered as corporate entities. Workers in each unit or section shared a common work experience and developed what Grillo called a "corporate ethos." In describing corporate solidarity among the Ghanaian railway workers at Sekondi, Richard Jeffries wrote,

A situation such as that of the Location workshops, where three or four thousand workers are concentrated in approximately four square miles, most of them working at machines just a few yards from each other, makes for regular and easy communication between them, and a strong awareness of common interest.[62]

As in Ghana, Nigeria, Uganda, and elsewhere, the railway workers in Atbara developed a deep sense of corporate identity. They used workplace connections as a basis for social interaction in the community. Workers from the same division often attended the same club, café, and restaurant. Moreover, railway divisions became major sites for political mobilization, particularly during the labor uprisings in the 1940s.

It should not be assumed that Sudanese railway workers were passive agents, whose behavior was determined by the indoctrination and socialization process that railway employment entailed. As elsewhere in Africa, these workers brought to the workplace many aspects of their rural culture and social organization. The most conspicuous of those were village networks. Typically, the early generation of workers who had established themselves in the town played a major role in helping newcomers from their home areas. In addition to providing shelter and guidance, early workers helped their relatives and fellow villagers find employment.

The existence of village networks in Atbara became a major incentive for many people in the northern region to migrate to the town. According to oral accounts, there was a popular belief among the region's inhabitants that any newcomer in Atbara would easily find a relative or a fellow villager who would guide him and help him find a job.[63] The case of Musa Ahmad Mitay, who became one of the most prominent trade-union leaders, is a good example. Musa was born in the village of al-Dakar in Meroe District, Northern Province. He migrated to Atbara in 1941 where his brother and his cousin were living. Like many members of his generation, Musa's initial goal was to enlist in the army. However, in view of the potential risks of military service, particularly during World War II, Musa's brother discouraged him from joining the army. Through their cousin, who was a gardener in the residence of the general manager of the railways, Musa landed a job in the engineering division.[64] Several others of Musa's contemporaries replicated his story.

The use of village networks in the workplace had numerous implications. It not only affected the composition of the railway workforce but also created certain occupational patterns. Workers from the same village or ethnic group clustered in particular divisions. It is well known, for instance, that the majority of permanent-way workers were Rubatab from the Abu Hamad area. This is attributable to the fact that some of the senior personnel in the division were from Abu Hamad. They used their influence and brought many of their kinsmen and fellow villagers to this division.[65] Similarly, the Shaiqiyya were conspicuous in the workshops, the traffic department, and the railway police, while the majority of railway administrators and ticket collectors were from Berber, al-Bawga, and neighboring villages. The Nubians from the Wadi Halfa and Dongola regions dominated the catering and the steamer services, while Egyptian Copts were prominent in the accounting and stores sections.[66]

The clustering of people from the same village in certain divisions also influenced the organization of work. For instance, one of the most hazardous and arduous jobs that required a great deal of collective effort and care was that of permanent-way workers. In addition to earth digging, their task involved carrying and re-laying heavy track and sleepers. These workers organized themselves into gangs that resembled village work parties. They often tried to reenact the working environment in the village by chanting work songs that were popular in the rural areas.[67]

The impact of Sudanese railway workers on the workplace can also be seen in the unique railway vocabulary they developed. The vast majority of these workers spoke their native Sudanese languages. However, their job involved handling thousands of items and learning a wide variety of names and terminologies that came from European languages. Over the years, railway workers created a unique vocabulary that blended Sudanese colloquial Arabic with European terminologies.

The terms that were used daily in workshops, dockyards, and steamers had diverse origins that included ancient Nubian, Middle Eastern, European, and Turkish languages. For instance, the word *sandal* (barge) had a Byzantine-Greek origin, while *qarina* (keel) was borrowed from Latin. Similarly, the word *wardiya* (turn of duty) was from the Venetian Italian *guardia*.[68] While the marine vocabulary was ancient, railway terms came mainly from European vocabulary for the steam engine. Some terms were introduced first in Egypt by Maltese artisans who worked in the British naval dockyard in Malta. Maltese artisans taught them to their Egyptian counterparts while working on the Suez Canal. Many of these Egyptian artisans served in the SR. Italian origins can be seen in terms such as *kumsari* from *commissario* (ticket collector) and *farmala* from *fermola* (vehicle break). Similarly, the permanent-way head gang was *hikimdar*, a military title introduced by the Egyptians.[69] Other innovations were the titles *mahwalji* for switchman and `*atashqi* for charge man. Over the years, this language has become deeply rooted in Atbara to the extent that even city residents who were not associated with the railway department have become familiar with it.

WAGE STRUCTURE AND LIVING CONDITIONS

As elsewhere in Africa, the colonial government in the Sudan considered wages an expense that must be kept to a minimum. Colonial officials linked the issue of wages to labor market conditions, skill level, and productivity.

To reduce labor costs, colonial governments hired casual laborers who oscillated between wage employment and other activities, and paid them wages that could barely meet their subsistence need. The questions of housing, health, social services, and family needs were not taken into account. It was only after the wave of strikes and labor protests in the late 1940s that officials began to address these issues.

The administrative hierarchy and wage structure in the SR reflected both the internal structure of the railways and the system of civil service in the Sudan. The labor force of the Sudan Railways was highly stratified. At the top were the managerial and engineering staff, all of whom were British. Below them were clerical employees and middle-rank officials, the majority of whom were Egyptian. Below were the artisans and skilled workers. At the bottom were the mass of unskilled workers who were Sudanese.

Government employees in the Sudan were divided into two categories: classified and unclassified staff. Classified staff referred to civil servants. Unclassified staff referred to those who were employed permanently on monthly rates of pay, temporary employees on monthly salaries, and daily laborers. Classified scales and rates of pay were left to each government department to determine. In 1937 the colonial administration introduced a system known as the Block Grant to create uniform wages. Under this system, the head of a government department was given an appropriation to cover the cost of wages and other expenses, and was allowed to determine the rates of pay for various categories of employees within his department.[70]

The rates of pay in the railways were subjected to a series of revisions between 1924 and the 1940s. Wages and conditions of service were greatly affected by the depression. The sharp decline in world demand for cotton was accompanied by a fall in local production owing to a series of crop diseases and locust invasions. Government revenue fell from LE 6,981,590 in 1929 to LE 3,653,394 in 1932. The government resorted to retrenchment and salary reductions. In 1931 the starting salary of Sudanese civil servants was cut by 30 percent, a move that prompted a strike by Gordon Memorial College students. The strike was settled when the government compromised on the matter of starting salaries.[71]

But in 1935 the department adopted rates of pay for workers at the bottom of the pay scale, thus setting the basic wage for the lowest paid worker at barely more than LE 1 per month. The rates of pay are shown in Table 2.2.

One of the most important characteristics of the pay scale in the railway department was the huge difference between skilled and unskilled workers, and between them and clerical staff. An artisan was paid up to five times as much as an unskilled laborer; the clerk was earning a salary twice and even four times the wage of the artisan, and fifteen times the basic wage of the unskilled laborer.[72] Moreover, there was a great difference between the wages of Sudanese artisans and those of foreign artisans. The latter were given expatriate allowance as well as housing.

CONCLUSION

During the period covered by this chapter, Atbara was transformed from a small railway center into a major company town. Atbara witnessed dramatic changes both in the size and in the composition of the railway workforce. These changes were brought about by the withdrawal of the Egyptian Army Railway Battalion and by the surge in cash-crop production and railway traffic. The drastic reduction of foreign personnel accelerated the pace of Sudanization of the railway workforce.

Among the most important characteristics of the railway labor force that emerged in Atbara was its complex hierarchy and social stratification. Sudanese workers

Table 2.2   Sudan Railways Wage Structure, 1935

	Base salary	Cost of living allowance
General laborers	LE 1.350	LE. 1.800
Fitter mates	1.800	3.600
Laborers, Engineering	1.050	1.350
Platelayers	1.200	1.650
Tulbas	1.350	2.700
Shunters	1.800	3.000
Boilers	1.800	3.000
Point men	1.500	2.700
Line burners	1.200	1.650

occupied the lower rung of this hierarchy, below European and Egyptian personnel. Moreover, the fact that the overwhelming majority of Atbara's workers came from the same regional and cultural backgrounds played a critical role in promoting the development of networks and influencing the workplace environment. Finally, the railway labor force was predominantly male, which engendered the development of a particular ideology, defining social roles among the railway workers.

Despite the many forms of control and the relentless efforts of the railway to mold them, these workers had a great impact on the workplace. They used a common regional background and cultural heritage to create a more familiar work environment and to face the challenges of city life. In the process, they developed a distinct identity and created a world that reflected both their workplace experience and their social and cultural backgrounds.

NOTES

1. *Sudan Railways Bulletin*, February 1945, 1.
2. M.W. Daly, *Imperial Sudan: The Anglo-Egyptian Condominium, 1934–1956* (Cambridge: Cambridge University Press, 1991), 93.

3. Ibid.

4. Richard Hill, *Sudan Transport* (London: Oxford University Press, 1965), 132–33.

5. The most important bridges that were built and maintained by the SR were the Atbara Bridge over the River Atbara, the Blue Nile Bridge at Khartoum, and Kosti Bridge on the White Nile.

6. Ibid., 37.

7. SAD 294/12/53, *Sudan Railways Annual Report* (1941), appendix no. 34a.

8. SAD 424/11, H.D. Bindley, "Sudan Government Railways, 1925–1935," *Journal of the Institute of Civil Engineers* 1 (November 1935): 60.

9. Hashim Muhammad Ahmad, interview by author, Oxford, U.K., 17 July 1997.

10. *Sudan Railways Bulletin*, March–April 1947, 2.

11. *Sudan Railways Bulletin*, October 1945, 4.

12. Ibid.

13. Al-Hajj `Abd al-Rahman, interview by author, Khartoum, 23 August 1995.

14. SAD 556/1/13: G. Storrar's Diary.

15. C.R. Williams, *Wheels and Paddles in the Sudan, 1923–1946* (Edinburgh: Pentland Press, 1986), 35.

16. Ibid.

17. Hill, *Sudan Transport*, 136.

18. K.D.D. Henderson, *A Survey of the Anglo-Egyptian Sudan, 1898–1944* (London and New York: Abbey Press, 1943), 37.

19. Gerard K. Wood, "Training Native Engine Drivers on the Sudan Railways," *Crown Colonist* 5 (1935): 552–54.

20. *Sudan Railways Bulletin*, February 1946, 1.

21. Hill, *Sudan Transport*, 98.

22. Ibid.

23. SAD 294/12, *Sudan Government Railways Annual Report* (1941), appendix no. 34a.

24. Ibid.

25. Ibid.

26. NRO, CIVSEC 1/58/164, Employment of Non-Sudanese, 15 March 1939.

27. Ibid.

28. Ibid.

29. Ibid.

30. *Sudan Railways Bulletin*, May–June 1946, 5.

31. Ibid.

32. Grandson of the Khalifa `Abdullahi.

33. Hill, *Sudan Transport*, 154.

34. K.D.D., *Survey of the Anglo-Egyptian Sudan*, Henderson, 38.

35. Ibid.

36. SAD 730/9, Memoirs of Hugh Quinlan, 7 April 1982.

37. *Sudan Railways Bulletin*, July–August 1946.

38. Ibid.

39. Frederick George Augustus Pinckney, *Sudan Government Railways and Steamers* (London: Institution of Royal Engineers, 1926), 19; see also NRO Kh. 33/1/1. Note on the Growth of Towns, Civil Secretary's Office, 8 June 1948. These were just estimates and should, therefore, be taken cautiously.

40. Sudan Government, Department of Statistics, *First Population Census* (1955–56): 27.

41. For a critique of the proletarianization thesis, see Frederick Cooper, "Work, Class and Empire: An African Historian's Retrospective on E.P. Thompson," *Social History* 20 (May 1995):235–41, and *Decolonization and African Society: The Labor Question in French and British Africa* (Cambridge: Cambridge University Press, 1996), 1–20.

42. Among the most important examples of this new literature are the works of Keletso Atkins, *The Moon Is Dead! Give Us Our Money! Cultural Origins of an African Work Ethic, Natal, South Africa, 1843–1900* (Portsmouth, NH: Hienemann, 1993), and Patrick Harries, *Work, Culture, and Identity: Migrant Laborers in Mozambique and South Africa, c. 1860–1910* (Portsmouth, NH: Hienemann, 1994).

43. See David L. Hoffman, *Peasant Metropolis: Social Identity in Moscow, 1929–1941* (Ithaca and London: Cornell University Press, 1994), 1–11.

44. Russian workers of peasant origin had retained a great deal of their rural culture and village forms of labor organization despite the relentless efforts of Soviet authorities to transform them into disciplined and loyal workers; see Hoffman, 60–63.

45. Ahmad Alawad Sikainga, *Slaves into Workers: Emancipation and Labor in Colonial Sudan* (Austin: University of Texas Press, 1996), 100–2.

46. NRO CIVSEC, 60/2/7: A.C. Willis, Report on Slavery, 1926, 44.

47. Sudan Government, Department of Statistics, *First Population Census* (1955–56): 1, (Khartoum, April 1960).

48. SAD 519/5, Sudan Railways, Some Aspects of Development in Northern Province (7 May 1953).

49. Sikainga, *Slaves into Workers*, 2–4.

50. Nancy Rose Hunt, *A Colonial Lexicon: Of Birth Ritual, Medicalization, and Mobility in the Congo* (Durham and London: Duke University Press, 1999), 174.

51. Richard Jeffries, *Class, Power and Ideology in Ghana: The Railwaymen of Sekondi* (Cambridge: Cambridge University Press, 1978), and R.D. Grillo, *African Railwaymen: Solidarity and Opposition Man East African Labour Force* (Cambridge: Cambridge University Press, 1973), 65.

52. SAD, Sud. A., PK 1563, Sudan Railways Corporation, *General Rulebook* (1 July 1950).

53. Ibid., 4.

54. Ibid., 10.

55. C.R. Williams, *Wheels and Paddles in the Sudan*, 41.

56. SAD, PK 1500, *Atbarabian* 1 (August 1927): 6.

57. *Sudan Railways Bulletin*, December 1945, 4.

58. For further details, see Sikainga, *Slaves into Workers*, 36–72.

59. Gerard K. Wood, "Training Native Engine Drivers," 553.

60. *Sudan Railways Bulletin*, September 1945, 5.

61. Ibid.

62. Jeffries, *Class, Power and Ideology in Ghana*, 195.

63. `Awadalla Dabora and `Abdalla `Abd al-Wahid, interview by author, Atbara, 11 October 1999.

64. Musa Mitay, interview by author, Atbara, 12 October 1999.

65. Al-Tayyib Muhammad al-Tayyib, interview by author, Khartoum, 23 October 1999.

66. Ibid.

67. Muhammad Muhammad Salih, who was a permanent-way railway worker for over thirty years, related these stories to the author.

68. Hill, *Sudan Transport*, 157.

69. Ibid.

70. Sikainga, *Slaves into Workers*, 140–141.

71. M.W. Daly and P.M. Holt, *A History of the Sudan: From the Coming of Islam to the Present Day* (London and New York: Longman, 1988), 141.

72. PRO, FO 371/69236, Report of the Independent Committee of Inquiry, 14 April 1948.

3

RAILWAY WORKERS IN AN URBAN MILIEU

Atbara um dalat
Rabbayt al-yatama wa markaz al-`azabat[1]
(Atbara, the city of platforms,
Sustainer of orphans and hub of spinsters)

The above verse encapsulates the popular image of Atbara, as a place where or-phans could survive and unmarried women could find shelter. It subsumes the most important traits that Atbara was known for, namely strong social bonds, commu-nal support, and solidarity. The poem is also a powerful illumination of the world the railway workers of Atbara made. Through their activities and networks, these workers tamed the city and made it a hospitable place. In order to unravel the var-iegated world of the railway workers, it is essential that we examine their experi-ence outside the workplace and get a sense of where and how they lived by following them to their neighborhoods and communities. It was in these neigh-borhoods that workers lived with their families, interacted with one other, spent their leisure time, and developed extensive social networks. Neighborhoods were sites of myriad activities and daily struggles that fostered the development of a dy-namic working-class culture and a distinctive urban identity.

STRUGGLE OVER THE URBAN SPACE

Recent literature on African urban history has shown that both the occupation and the organization of the urban space were arenas of intense struggle between con-flicting notions of urban order and way of life. Colonial administrators in Africa sought to build well-organized and orderly cities by controlling the flow of Africans into urban centers and determining where and how immigrants lived. However, despite the relentless efforts of colonial officials, thousands of Africans flocked into cities and established informal settlements, where they engaged in activities that were deemed illegal by colonial authorities. Colonial urban regulations were particularly rigorous in railway, mining, and company towns. Until the 1940s, the

Sudan Railways enjoyed considerable authority in the administration of Atbara and ran the city in a quasi-military fashion.

The rapid growth of Atbara's population during the 1930s and 1940s led to a major expansion in the city's physical layout. The majority of rural immigrants who went to the city during the interwar period settled in the old quarters of al-`Ishash, al-Dakhla, and al-Faki Medani. As these quarters became overcrowded, new residential neighborhoods such as Umbakol, al-Qala', and al-Hasaya emerged.

The rapid growth of the railway labor force generated an urgent demand for houses and office buildings. In this regard, the railway department focused its attention on the western part of Atbara, particularly the land adjacent to the Nile. However, this farmland belonged to the people of al-Dakhla. Since the transfer of the railway headquarters to Atbara in 1906, the people of al-Dakhla lost huge tracts of land to the railway department. In 1920 alone, the SR appropriated about 200 feddans of al-Dakhla land on which it built most of its offices and houses.[2]

The appropriation of al-Dahkla land had become a contentious issue in the late 1920s. The railway department was determined to acquire 250 feddans, which would have resulted in displacement of the majority of al-Dakhla's residents. In 1927 the general manager of the SR engaged in lengthy discussions with the district commissioner of Atbara and the governor of Berber Province, on the question of how to obtain land on the riverbank. According to his plan, al-Dakhla residents would be given monetary compensation as well as agricultural land farther north. However, provincial authorities had serious reservations about these drastic measures. Instead, they suggested that the appropriation should exclude farmland.

When al-Dakhla residents learned about these plans, they were infuriated.[3] They would lose not only fertile land but also a substantial amount of rental income. Many residents were landlords who rented houses to railway workers. Al-Dakhla people expressed their opposition both verbally and in writing to district authorities. Despite their vehement opposition and protests, the railway management and provincial authorities went ahead with the appropriation plan. By 1928 al-Dakhla residents had lost twenty saqiyas and were left with only ten.[4] Their resistance had broken down as a result of official threats, persuasion, and inducements. The loss of land left bitter memories and divided the community. To this day, some members of al-Dakhla community regard those who gave up their land as traitors.[5] It was on this land that the British Quarter was built. It was the most opulent and exclusive part of Atbara, with beautiful bungalows, gardens, tennis courts, and clubs.[6]

In contrast to the British Quarter, the Sudanese section east of the railway line was crowded with rugged buildings and informal settlements. The new immigrants took advantage of lax regulations and established residential neighborhoods, most of which did not conform to official standards. Beer brewers, prostitutes, and non-wage workers settled in al-`Ishash, Zagalona neighborhoods, where they engaged in various economic activities. For many years, prostitutes had established themselves in an area known as the Abyssinian Quarter, which was located in the city center near the market.[7]

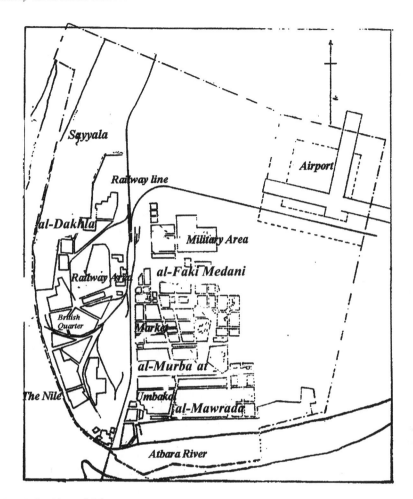

Map 3.1 Map of Atbara.

In 1937 the district authorities began to discuss plans for a reorganization of the old residential neighborhoods of al-`Ishash, al-Murba`at, and al-Dakhla. Two years later, a committee comprising the general manager of the SR, the governor of Berber Province, the survey officer, the health inspector, and the civil, legal, and financial secretaries made specific recommendations. Accordingly, residential quarters were classified as first-, second-, third-, and fourth-class areas. This classification was based on building materials and the size of plots. First-class houses were built with red brick and concrete, and the size of the plot was 400 square meters. Second-class houses were also built from red brick and concrete, but the size of the plot was 300 square meters. The third- and fourth-class houses were built from mud bricks known locally as jalous, and the size of the plots were 200 square meters.[8] The first-class area in Atbara included the British Quarter and the railway cantonment, while the second-class area included al-Faki Medani, which was re-planned in 1947 to fit the new classification. The majority of the Sudanese quarters were classified as third class areas. This included Umbakol, Gala`a, and al-Dakhla, while al-`Ishash was considered a "native lodging area."[9] In 1945 al-`Ishash was replanned, most of its old houses were destroyed, and the inhabitants were given new plots farther east. The new area was called al-Mawrada, which was classified as a fourth-class area.[10] The change from al-`Ishash to al-Mawrada subsumes several elements that had to do with ethnicity and social identity. In many Sudanese towns, the al-`*Ishash* (straw huts) were associated with former slaves, West African immigrants, and marginal groups, and were considered dens of so-cial deviance. The `Ishash of Atbara was inhabited by many Arabic speaking work-ers such as the Rubatab, the Shaiqiyya, and the Ja`aliyyin. The new residents and municipal authorities decided to adopt the more "respectable" name of al-Mawrada, although the term al-`*Ishash* continued to be used.

The reorganization of the urban space in Atbara also involved removal of broth-els and *anadi* (beer houses). In line with the new urban policy, the prostitutes were segregated in a separate quarter.[11] In the mid-1940s, beer brewers were also as-signed to a special quarter south of the market.[12]

In 1949 the municipal authorities considered the idea of extending the city south of the Atbara River. This idea was abandoned owing to objections by the residents of al-Mugran village as well as the difficulty of transportation.[13]

In the early 1950s al-Dakhla village was replanned and divided into old Dakhla and New Dakhla. While the former consisted of old houses and farms, the new Dakhla was classified as a third-class area. Similar steps were taken in 1953–1954 with regard to Faki Medani and Hasaya.

By the mid-1950s the physical layout of Atbara resembled a half circle, stretch-ing from the banks of the Nile in the west, to the river Atbara in the south, to the area east of the railway track (see map). Despite this expansion, residential space in Atbara remained segregated. Europeans lived in their exclusive quarter in the western part of town, the Egyptians and a few Sudanese lived in the central area near the market, while the overwhelming majority of the Sudanese settled in the eastern part of town. According to old residents of Atbara, with the exception of ser-vants and gardeners, Sudanese were not allowed to wander in the British Quarter.[14]

MANAGING THE TOWN

The reorganization of the urban space in Atbara led to the incorporation of many areas into the city's boundaries. In this way, thousands of people were brought under the direct control of municipal authorities. Atbara had become a major urban center and could no longer be run as a mere railway depot.

Until the late 1940s, the administration of Atbara was in the hands of a district commissioner (DC). The town itself was the headquarters of a district, which was part of Berber Province. Its authority extended beyond Atbara town to include several neighboring villages such as Kannur, al-Mugran, and al-`Kad. In addition to the district commissioner and his assistant, the administrative bureaucracy included the police commandant, the health inspector, clerical staff, and many other officials.

As in the rest of the Sudan, in the 1920s the colonial administration introduced the system of native administration, according to which it delegated limited authority to local leaders. In 1927 a bench of magistrates was established in Atbara. The bench's president was Sirour Muhammad al-Saflawi, shaykh of al-Dakhla. Sirour was a popular leader who enjoyed considerable influence among his people. The bench was supposed to represent the various communities in Atbara. In 1931 its members included:

Sirour al-Saflawi	Shaykh of al-Dakhla
Mukhtar `Abd al-Hadi	Egyptian merchant
`Abdalla Faham	Syrian
Mikha'il Girgis	Egyptian Copt
Al-Rayyah al-Faki	Merchant
Babikr Ahmad al-Rayyah	Merchant

In 1928 the DC proposed that the bench's jurisdiction be limited to Sudanese residents. He therefore recommended replacement of foreign members by Sudanese. According to his plan, Syrian and Egyptian members would be replaced by al-Zubair `Abd al-Karim—a Rubatabi from Abu Hamad—and Muhammad Hassan Abu Sham—a Shayqi from Meroe District.[15]

The fact that the town of Atbara included the villages of al-Dakhla and al-Sayyala created a dilemma for the district authorities. In 1933 the DC proposed to the province governor establishment of a village court under Sirour al-Saflawi. Its members would include al-Rayyah al-Faki, Mukhtar `Abd al-Hadi, Muhammad Hasan Bayram, Muhammad Mahjoub, Babikr Ahmad al-Shaykh, Muhammad Sulayman, and Jallal al-Hasan. With exception of Jallal al-Hasan, who was the shaykh of al-`Ishash, all of these figures were prominent merchants in Atbara.[16] However, when this proposal was presented to the civil secretary in Khartoum, it was rejected. Instead, the civil secretary's office recommended that a town bench was more appropriate for "an almost entirely detribalized town like Atbara, with a population well versed in the practical application of the codes and having little knowledge or respect for native custom."[17]

As in the rural areas, application of native administration bolstered the authority of local leaders. As mentioned earlier, the most prominent native administrator in Atbara was Sirour al-Saflawi, whose clout and profile grew considerably during the colonial period. Sirour used his position on the bench of magistrates to entrench his power. He exercised tremendous influence over the bench by nominating kinsmen as members.[18] Old residents of Atbara described the way in which Sirour displayed his power and authority: he used to tour the central market on his horse, carrying a whip with which he flogged any offender instantly.[19]

A major development in the administration of Atbara took place in 1947 when a municipal council was formed. The council was established under the 1937 Local Government Ordinance. In its early phase, it was charged with the responsibility of administering such services as roads, electricity, public health, and education.

According to council rules, members were elected, but the district commissioner retained the right to appoint a few. The council membership consisted of the chairman—usually the district commissioner—vice chairman, twelve members representing the various quarters of the city, two members representing the railway cantonment, and four members appointed by the district commissioner. Members came from various socioeconomic backgrounds. They included government officials, railway workers, merchants, and native administrators.

The council was established during the height of the nationalist movement and became, therefore, a site of competition among the various political parties. In the early 1950s, the council members included Sirour al-Saflawi, known for his loyalty to the Ashiqqa Party, and `Abdalla Muhammad al-Hasan, son of a prominent member of the Umma Party.[20] Another prominent member of the council who was also a member of the Ashiqqa Party was Muhammad Mutwali Badr, a railway engineer who represented the railway cantonment. Representatives of al-Mawrada and al-Murba`at included Bashir Abu Shoush, Muhammad Hasan Abu Sham, and Muhammad Hasan Bayram, all of whom were prominent merchants and followers of the Khatmiyya order. Another railway representative was `Abdalla `Abd al-Basit Bakumba, a Nuba from Kordofan and mechanic in the railway workshops. Appointed members included L.T. Virgo, an assistant to the general manager of the railways; Ahmad Zaki, a railway clerk and president of the Egyptian club; and al-Rayyah al-Faki. The latter was a prominent merchant from Shendi District.[21] The DC chose representatives of the Syrian, Greek, and Coptic communities. However, he often selected Syrians to represent these communities—a practice that prompted great resentment among the Copts and Greeks. In 1953 it was decided that representation of these communities would be rotational.[22]

With the approach of self-rule and Sudanization of the civil service in the early 1950s, the Sudanese controlled the leadership of the council, and in 1953 `Abdalla Mas`oud became its first Sudanese president. He was a senior railway official, who became deputy general manager of the SR. He was followed by Muhammad al-Fadl, a chief engineer and the first Sudanese general manager of the SR.[23]

From its establishment in the late 1940s, the power and territorial jurisdiction of the council generated a heated debate among authorities. The debate centered on whether or not the council should have jurisdiction over the railway cantonment. Since 1906 the railway cantonment had been a separate administrative entity within the town. Its residents in 1938 included 353 Britons, 38 Europeans, 1,100 Egyptians, 3 Syrians, 2 Indians, and 1,708 Sudanese.[24] The cantonment had its own laws, standing orders, and regulations.[25] Administration of the cantonment was in the hands of the railway management. With the exception of sanitation, the railway management retained exclusive authority within the cantonment.

Establishment of the municipal council created a dilemma for the district authorities. On the one hand, they considered the railway cantonment a "modern" enclave that should not be associated with the "native" part of town. According to the official view, the railway department had maintained a high standard of public order, sanitation, and other amenities in the cantonment. Hence, the railway department should not allow the cantonment to come under "an inexperienced and impecunious native committee."[26] On the other hand, there were many Sudanese officials living in the cantonment, and the DC argued that exclusion of these elements would deprive the council of the participation of the "most intelligent and public spirited native officials."[27] In the end, the DC resolved that with certain safeguards, the cantonment could come under the council's jurisdiction and still maintain its "high standards." One of the most important safeguards, in his view, was the fact that the province governor had the authority to change municipal regulations.

Another issue of potential conflict between the municipal council and the railway management was land allocation and building regulations. The DC argued that the railway management should retain its authority over land allocation within the cantonment, while the municipal council would be responsible for the rest of the town's land, subject to the requirements of the provincial board of public health and medical authorities. The railway management retained its authority to appropriate land for future expansion.[28] In short, the railway remained a powerful, independent administrative entity in Atbara.

Two years before independence, the Atbara municipal council was reorganized and its authority expanded. In 1954 the council took over virtually all the responsibilities of the district commissioner.[29] In addition to law and order, the council took charge of public health, road building and maintenance, housing, educational and social services, taxation, and welfare.[30]

The major source of revenue for the council was taxation and the annual dues paid by the railway department in exchange for health and other services. The council also owned property in the city, which it rented out to retail traders, butchers, and merchants. For instance, the council owned 102 shops, 90 fruit and vegetable shops, and 74 butcher houses. Rental income from these facilities amounted to SL 6,350 in the mid-1950s.[31] In 1958 the council's expenses totaled SL 107,106, of which SL 40,975 was spent on salaries, SL 38,840 on health services, SL 14,380 on water supply, and SL 4,266 on education.[32]

Although the municipal council became responsible for all aspects of urban policy and the provision of various services, the railway department continued to reign supreme in Atbara.

Infrastructure and Social Services

In order to understand the living conditions of the railway workers and the rest of Atbara's population, it is important that we examine social, educational, and health services in the city.

Until the late 1940s, Atbara had no running water. In the early days, water was pumped from a well near the railway workshops, put in small tanks, and then carried by donkeys to the homes of senior railway employees. With the city's expansion in the 1930s, a water supply station was established to provide clean water to the British Quarter and the cantonment. The rest of Atbara's residents received water from wells and rivers.[33] The first step toward provision of running water in the native quarters east of the railway line was taken in 1951, when a small supply center was established at al-Faki Medani. It was only in 1958 that the rest of the city's neighborhoods were supplied with running water.[34]

With regard to electricity, the railway department had one power station that supplied electricity to its workshops and the houses of its senior staff. Another plant was built in 1956 to provide power to the rest of the city. In 1960 the task of supplying electricity was transferred from the railway department to the local branch of the Ministry of Works. A year later the Light and Power Corporation became responsible for electric services in Atbara.

Until the mid-1960s, the distribution of electricity in Atbara was uneven. While all houses in the first-class areas were supplied with electricity, 66 percent of those in the third-class area and 4 percent of those in the native lodging area had power. By the mid-1970s, 90 percent of houses in Atbara had electricity.[35]

One of the most noticeable problems in Atbara was the lack of paved roads, which had a negative impact on transportation in the city. The most popular means of transport and the hallmark of Atbara were bicycles. About 60 percent of the city's residents depended on bicycles as their primary means of transportation.[36]

Until the early 1950s, Atbara had no modern sewage facilities. Like other Sudanese towns, Atbara had the bucket system, serviced by health workers during the night. In 1952 the municipal council introduced the sewage system, known locally as siphon. At the time, the cost of a single siphon was SL 35, which was far beyond the means of the vast majority of the city's population. With a subvention from the government and railway department, the municipal council provided loans with flexible terms to low-income residents to build siphons. By 1958 about 2,500 houses, mainly in the first- and second-class areas, had siphons.[37] The bucket system was gradually replaced by pit latrines in the third-class quarters.

Educational services in Atbara were affected by the fact that it was largely a town of foreigners, particularly in its early phase. Atbara had two missionary schools: the Church Missionary Society School and the American Mission School. An overwhelming majority of Egyptian residents sent their children to the American Mission School.[38] However, when the idea of closing the CMS School was contemplated in 1926, the Coptic community petitioned the provincial authorities to allow them to open a Coptic school. Despite their initial suspicions that such a school would be fertile ground for Egyptian propaganda, British authorities approved the request.[39]

Admission to the Coptic and American Mission schools was open to all town residents, regardless of religion. Both schools had many Sudanese Muslim students. In 1948 the American Mission School had 119 Muslim students. However, one of the thorny issues was whether or not Muslim students would attend religious classes. In February 1948, for instance, some Sudanese parents complained that the American Mission School did not exempt their children from religious classes and Christian prayer. The school administration defended its position on the ground that religious instructions and prayers were a major part of the school curriculum.[40]

Until the mid-1940s, Atbara had one government intermediate school. The students of Atbara Intermediate School fared well in the annual entrance examination for Gordon Memorial College. For instance, in 1944, seventeen boys were admitted to the college, five of whom were sons of railway artisans.[41]

The railway department maintained three sub-grade schools, two for boys and one for girls. Following its establishment, the municipal council took over responsibility for these schools, while the higher grades remained under the jurisdiction of the Ministry of Education. The ministry provided an annual subvention to the council, which covered 40 percent of the cost of sub-grade schools. The municipal council devoted considerable attention to adult education. In 1950 the council combined the two sub-grade schools into a primary school for boys. The girls' school continued to operate in a private house until 1956 when it was upgraded to a primary school.

In response to the growing demand for education, the council built two additional sub-grade schools in 1956, one for boys and one for girls. By 1958 the number of pupils in sub-grade schools in Atbara was 380 boys and 250 girls. There were seven primary schools, with 1,430 boys and 650 girls. These schools had 40 male and 12 female teachers.[42] In 1974, Atbara had thirty-five primary schools, thirteen intermediate schools, three secondary schools, and a polytechnic. There were 34,214 students in government schools and 2,746 in private schools.[43]

The municipal council also ran three *khlwas*, or Quranic schools, which provided instruction in Islamic studies. Occasionally the municipal council gave assistance to talented students whose financial conditions inhibited them from continuing their education beyond the primary level. The council also established youth clubs to provide training and guidance to school dropouts.

Given the high illiteracy rate among workers, the railway department devoted some attention to the question of adult education, which became one of the primary responsibilities of the welfare division. In addition to its role in career advancement, literacy was essential for learning technical skills. In 1935 the engineering division opened a school in Atbara to provide instruction in the Arabic language for its traffic staff. The course of study was three months. The school was closed during the war years, but was reopened in 1944.[44]

In 1954 the council opened twenty centers in which 600 adults were enrolled. By 1956 there were thirty-eight centers. During the same year, 258 men and 184 women completed the course. A year later, about 1,200 men and women enrolled in these centers. The municipal council created the special post of adult education officer to be in charge of these centers.[45]

In comparison to other Sudanese towns, Atbara enjoyed a relatively high literacy rate. According to the 1973 census, literacy among the population over ten years of age was 69 percent. Typically, there was a huge gap between men and women. The rate was about 81 percent among men and 54.6 percent among women.[46]

Beyond the question of literacy, the provision of these educational institutions in Atbara had many social implications. Education was the primary means of social mobility for the sons and daughters of railway workers. It gave them the opportunity to acquire valuable skills and find government jobs, particularly in the railway department. In other words, education led to the emergence of an educated middle class in Atbara and changed the social profile of the city.

HOUSEHOLD STRUCTURE
AND WORKING-CLASS FAMILY LIFE

The subject of working-class family life involves gender ideologies and notions of domesticity and patriarchy that embrace both urban and rural contexts. Contemporary literature on working-class history has stressed the notion that working-class formation and consciousness is structured by gender ideologies and involves the reorganization of relations between men and women. Colonial labor policies in Africa and elsewhere were based on the European notion of the male worker as the head of household and primary breadwinner. Women had limited opportunities in the wage labor market and were relegated to the informal sector or to the domestic sphere, where they bore and raised children.[47]

Household structure and family life among the railway workers of Atbara were shaped by a complex web of rural tradition, Islamic precepts and practices, and local gender ideologies. The notion of the male breadwinner was deeply rooted in the precolonial history of northern Sudan, from where the vast majority of the railway workers had come. Shari`a rules of inheritance, which allowed women to inherit a small percentage of property, seriously affected their economic status. Despite the fact that women's activities among the farming communities in the northern Sudan extended beyond the domestic sphere, they had little control over their produce. Most important, women were considered dependents of their husbands.

The cultural and social values of the inhabitants of the northern region stress the importance of marriage and family life. Marriage was considered a symbol of maturity, responsibility, and manhood, and a vehicle for gaining social respect within the community. People tended to marry early, between their early to mid-twenties. A man who reached thirty years of age without marriage was considered irresponsible, and his social status within the community would diminish. However, these concepts and practices were not fixed; for socioeconomic reasons, early marriage has declined sharply, particularly in the urban centers.

In many parts of the Sudan, kinship and lineage played a crucial role in marriage. The most preferred marriage for a man was with the daughter of his paternal uncle. The next preference was the daughter of his maternal cousin, aunt, followed by relatives and people from the same village.[48] According to the local tradition of northern Sudan, a man was supposed to marry within his extended family to safeguard the family's "honor" and reputation. However, these practices have declined rapidly—particularly in the urban centers, where marriages cut across ethnic and regional boundaries.

Unfortunately, reliable data on household structure and marital status of railway workers in Atbara is scant. The first population census was conducted in 1955–1956, followed by a social survey in 1964–1965 and another census in 1973. Although the results of these surveys must be taken with great caution, they do provide some clues about the social profile of Atbara's residents. According to the 1955 census, the total population of Atbara was 36,298, of whom 19,948 were male and 16,350 female. The number of people over the age of puberty was 11,875, of whom 7,110 were married and 4,765 single. In other words, 59 percent of the population over the age of puberty were married. The rate of marriage was much higher among females: of the 9,318 females over the age of puberty, 7,636 were married and 1,682 single. Ninety percent of the marriages were monogamous.[49]

At the beginning of their careers, the majority of people who went to Atbara were single men. After finding a job, the new immigrant would share a house with a group of people from his home village. After saving money for the dowry, the immigrant would either go to his village or ask his parents to choose a bride for him. While most workers brought their families to the city, those who could not afford the cost of housing left their families in the village and visited them during vacations.

One of the main problems that faced married workers was housing. With the notable exception of senior technical and administrative staff and workers in the outlying stations, the railway provided very limited housing to its employees. The majority of workers in Atbara had to find their own accommodation. While bachelors lived in small groups in rented houses, those with families faced great difficulties. According to the 1964–1965 population survey, about 58 percent of the city's residents lived in rented houses.[50]

Housing conditions had a great impact on working-class domestic life and gender relations. According to the 1964–1965 survey, the average number of persons per household in working-class neighborhoods was six, with more in some neighborhoods such as al-Mawrada and al-Dakhla. In view of the lack of cooling systems during the hot months of the summer, the entire family slept in the *hosh* (enclosure) and often shared it with other families. In addition to lack of privacy, overcrowding made it difficult for families to maintain traditional rural living arrangements, in which male and female members of the family slept in separate quarters. However, housing conditions in Atbara improved considerably following the establishment in the 1960s and 1970s of new residential areas, where residents were given relatively large plots of land.

One of the most important items of household expenditure was food. As in other Sudanese towns, the overwhelming majority of people in Atbara ate *foul* (fava beans), which was common throughout the urban centers in the Sudan. Foul was often eaten twice a day—for breakfast and dinner—while beef stew was cooked for lunch. The most common vegetable dishes were *bamiya* (okra) and *molokhiyya* (sauce). To obtain dairy products, many workers kept livestock such as sheep, goats, and chicken in their houses. It was estimated that one-third of the households in Atbara kept domestic animals.[51]

One of the most important and cherished objectives for workers was the education of their children. Education was considered a major vehicle for social mobility. Railway workers did not want to see their children go through the same difficulties they had gone through. As Hashim al-Sa`id put it, "you don't want your child to grow up and become like you."[52] Workers believed that education would enable their children to have better careers so that they would help them in their old age. In other words, children's education was an investment, tantamount to pension. It was also a source of prestige. According to `Awadalla Dabora, "when people enter your house and see that you have many *tarabish* [sing. *tarbush*, or hat] hanging on the wall, you feel proud."[53] In other words, the tarbush became a status symbol that reflected the family's social standing.

In addition to maintaining households, workers from rural areas had several other obligations, one of which was that they were expected to provide financial help to their parents and relatives. A monthly remittance, or *mahiyya*, to one's parents was an important obligation. Failure to fulfill it would seriously damage one's social standing both within his immediate family and within his community at large. The importance of remittance was expressed in songs, poetry, and proverbs, and was an integral part of popular culture in the northern region. A popular Shaiqi song was in the form of a letter from a woman to her son who had been absent for a long time. After expressing her deep affection, the mother goes on to tell him of her sadness for his long absence and neglect of family obligations. She then talks about how crop failures and falling prices of dates had caused tremendous hardships and pain to the family. At the end of the song, the mother pleads with him, in the name of God, to send her a few pounds. Although the song is about a breach of expectations, it also underscores the social and cultural significance of home remittance. Urban workers were also expected to give presents to relatives and neighbors when they visited as well as on religious and other social occasions.

The concept of male breadwinner among the railway workers of Atbara was reinforced by the rural notions of domesticity, honor, and respectability. While in other Sudanese urban centers workers' wives engaged in various forms of economic activities, such as selling food to supplement their husbands' incomes, the railway workers of Atbara viewed this with disdain. According to Hashim al-Sa`id,

> With the exception of old women, you would not find a worker's wife selling things in the market. In addition to the fact that it is disrespectful, it is against our religious and cultural values. To maintain the dignity of their families, many workers took second jobs, for instance, in the Industrial Area where they worked as mechanics, blacksmith, etc.[54]

In the northern region, the selling of food in particular was considered ignominious. The provision of food to guest and strangers was considered a sign of honor and generosity. According to Dabora, "we used to laugh at the people of Khartoum because they were selling *kisra* (Sudanese bread).[55]

Although wives were not wage earners, they did play a leading role in the management of the household budget. With the meager resources of their husbands, wives became responsible for maintaining the family financial stability. It is important to point out that the social values on which families were built were not rooted only in patriarchy. As in the northern region, railway workers' wives upheld the notions of domesticity and respectability. However, these notions began to crumble in the face of growing economic hardships. To supplement their husbands' wage, wives and daughters engaged in various economic activities within the domestic sphere. The most popular of these was tailoring. According to the population survey of 1964–1965, about 23 percent of the households in Atbara had sewing machines.[56] Women were also very active in rotation credit associations, a subject that will be examined later.

The fact that wives did not work did not mean that they were confined to their homes. While their husbands were at work, women went to the market to buy food items and other necessities. They visited one another and engaged in a wide range of social activities. Moreover, single women and widows engaged in various economic activities that ranged from selling food and vegetables in the market to prostitution to brewing local drinks. In the face of economic hardships in the 1940s, it became difficult for workers to keep women in the domestic sphere. Workers' wives made baskets and other handcrafts and sold them in the market. As will be shown in the following chapter, this became one of the principle motives behind workers' agitation for the provision of family wages.

SOCIAL NETWORKS AND COMMUNAL SOLIDARITY

One of the most important traits that characterized Atbara was its strong social bonds and communal solidarity. The following statement by `Abd al-Rahman al-Bashir, a railway worker who still lives in Atbara, amply illustrates the essence of Atbara.

> The Atbarawis are the most sociable and friendly people in the Sudan. When you meet someone in Atbara for the first time, you feel that you have met him twenty times previously. If you ask him about someone's house, he wouldn't give you directions, but he would take you to the person's house.[57]

As mentioned in the preceding chapter, the great majority of railway workers in Atbara were rural immigrants.[58] In order to face the challenges of wage labor and urban life, these immigrants reproduced many elements of their rural culture in the city. They used village, ethnic, and family connections and developed extensive social networks and support institutions. Among the most important support institutions were charitable organizations, rotational credit societies, and village associations.

Mutual aid associations were indeed a major part of urban life throughout colonial Africa. Early literature on this subject advanced the adaptation theory, which stressed that these associations represented immigrants' effort to "adjust" to urban life. According to this thesis, regional and kin-based associations illustrate the persistence of rural culture in the city. Recent writings, however, have argued that beyond the coping strategy, mutual aid societies and village associations reflected the multifaceted world of African urban dwellers, a world that encompassed both the town and the countryside. By incorporating their rural culture into the urban cultural milieu, rural immigrants created a new model and thereby shaped the city itself.[59]

Mutual aid and charity organizations flourished in the Sudan, particularly during the depression of the early 1930s. One of the oldest urban-based charity organizations was *Malja' al-qirish* (The piastre shelter), which was founded in Omdurman in 1931, and later established branches in other towns such as Atbara, al-Ubayyid, Wad Medani, Sinnar, and Port Sudan.[60] The committee of the Atbara branch included Ahmad Hasan Khalifa, Hasan `Abd al-Hafiz, Muhammad al-Sayyid Lubodi, Qasim Babikir, `Umar Salih Siwar al-Dahab, and Hussain Marjan.[61] In addition to giving financial help to the poor, Malja' al-Qirish provided shelter to orphans, the elderly, and other displaced people.

Of all Sudanese towns, Atbara had the largest concentration of mutual aid, charity, and village associations. In addition to helping individual members, one of the primary goals of these organizations was to improve material conditions in rural areas and provide financial assistance to relatives at home in emergencies such as flood, fire, or crop failure. Rotational credit associations in particular helped their members save money and borrow against future contributions to meet unexpected expenses.

The formation of voluntary associations and clubs reflected the development of an urban identity that had many dimensions. Although these institutions were organized on the basis of village, ethnic, and communal links, they also encouraged values that had industrial functions, such as time consciousness, saving, thrift, and hard work. The response of colonial officials was ambivalent. On the one hand, they considered civic institutions signs of "modernity." On the other hand, these officials were apprehensive of autonomous organizations that could become sites of political mobilization.

The formation of societies and clubs in the Sudan came under the Public Order Ordinance. The ordinance stipulated that a society would not be legal unless it had known premises in a specific location. Each society had to have a written constitution, which provided for annual elections of committees and officers.[62] Moreover, each society had to inform authorities about its officers, constitution and by-laws, and financial activities.[63] Requests for establishing a society or a club had to be submitted to the provincial governor for his approval. The civil secretary encouraged provincial governors to maintain an open attitude toward the formation of societies and clubs. According to him, the governor should maintain, "a detached attitude of neither encouragement nor discouragement."[64] The civil secretary went on to urge governors to report to his office not only the formation of new societies but also changes in the personnel and officeholders of existing ones. In short, in line with official policy, mutual aid societies had been transformed into bureau-cratized and systematized institutions.

Among the oldest cooperatives in Atbara was Umbakol Cooperative Society. It was established in 1933 by immigrants from the villages of Umbakol and al-Ghorayba in Meroe District. The society's president was Muhammad Hasan Abu Sham, a merchant in Atbara, and the secretary was Sa`id Muhammad Ahmad Rahma. Other officers included `Abdalla Medani, treasurer; al-`Ubaid Hamid, assistant treasurer; Bashir Ahmad Kandai; `Abdalla al-Hasan; Muhammad Malik; Tahir Muhammad Hamid; and Khidir al-Hajj Muhammad.[65] The main function of the society was to provide financial help to its members in times of need. The monthly subscription was ten piastres. After one year, members would be eligible to apply for a loan, which would be decided by the committee.[66]

Another society with similar goals was the Kuri People Society. It was established in 1934 by people from the villages of Hussain Narti, Kuri, al-Takar, Moura, al-Rikabiyya, and al-Naf`ab. This cluster of villages was part of the Kuri `omodia (a native administration unit). The most prominent members of the society were Ibrahim al-Shush, an eminent merchant in Atbara and president of the society; al-Tayyib al-Malik; `Uthman Ahmad `Abd al-Rahim; and Hasan Sorketi.[67]

In 1936 immigrants from the town of Kosti established the Kosti Youth Association. Despite its name, its efforts were directed mainly at helping the poor in Kosti. By World War II there were fourteen other regional and village associations in Atbara. They included the Nubian Cooperative Society, Berber Boys' Society, Dongola Men's Society, Mahas People's Society, Kordofan and Dar Fur Society, Mograt Cooperative Society, and al-Bawga Men's Society.[68]

Other important institutions of communal support were the religious *zawias*, which were associated with the various Sufi tariqas. As mentioned earlier, the majority of Atbara's residents belonged to various Sufi brotherhoods. The most popular brotherhoods in Atbara were the Khatmiyya, Qadiriyya, Burhaniyya, and Tijaniyya.[69] Each Sufi order built its own zawia, where followers congregated for prayers and religious ceremonies. People also gathered in the zawias to mark deaths, for naming ceremonies, and so forth.

These associations fostered development of communal bonds in the city and strengthened links with rural areas. It was through these institutions that railway workers were linked to the larger community and found common language, familiar cultural symbols, and support. Old residents of Atbara still reminisce about the simple way of life in the city. They report that the overwhelming majority of Atbara residents lived on credit. Workers obtained everything from groceries to newspapers on credit. Typically, a worker would maintain accounts with retail traders, butchers, barbers, and tailors, and would pay them at the end of the month.[70] The first week of the month was, therefore, the busiest time for businesses in Atbara.

Communal organizations and mutual aid societies were also prevalent among foreign communities in Atbara. Among the most important of these was the Egyptian community. As mentioned previously, the majority of Egyptians in Atbara were Coptic Christians. Of all the Coptic communities in the Sudan, the one in Atbara was the best organized. They were conspicuous in the accounting, administration, and stores sections of the Sudan Railways, while a few of them owned small businesses.

Since their settlement in Atbara in the early years of the twentieth century, the Copts had taken the lead in establishing communal organizations, most of which revolved around the Church. As mentioned in chapter 1, the Coptic Orthodox Benevolent Society was established in 1912 and was affiliated with the Coptic Orthodox Patriarchate in Cairo. The society ran a Coptic school, a Bible society, a Sunday school, and a Christian girls' school.[71] Although the primary function of the society was religious, it also provided important social services. One of its most important contributions was the establishment of a blood bank.[72]

Although most Copts in Atbara were immigrants from Egypt, they gradually adopted Sudanese cultural norms. But, as a Christian minority in a predominantly Muslim society, the Copts strove to maintain their distinctive identity. At the core of this identity was Christianity. The Copts clustered in particular residential neighborhoods and formed a close-knit community.[73] They resisted intermarriage with Sudanese for fear that their sons and daughters would be converted to Islam. Old residents in Atbara recall that when a Coptic woman married a Muslim man against the wishes of her parents, there was a big uproar among the Coptic community, which boycotted the woman.[74] Nonetheless, the Coptic community was not monolithic. In addition to Orthodox, there was a small group of Coptic Evangelical Christians, who were affiliated with the American Presbyterian Church. They numbered about twenty-three people in the late 1940s.[75] Moreover, there were major cleavages within the community along occupational and social lines. It was reported that there was major tension between the artisans and the educated elite who occupied senior posts in the railway department.[76]

Another important foreign community in Atbara was the Greek. Since their early settlement in Atbara, the Greeks had established a local branch of the Hellenic Society, which was based in Khartoum. However, with Sudanization of the railway posts, the number of Greeks declined sharply. In the mid-1940s, the Hellenic Society in Atbara had about eighteen members, the most eminent of them Savas Marketto, Christo Antoniadis, John Diamandopulos, and Nicolas Mavrikious.[77]

Atbara was the home of a small but significant European community. In addition to the British and the Greeks, there were Yugoslavs, Czechs, Austrians, Italians, Poles, Armenians, and Turks. Most of the Central and Eastern Europeans were artisans. Some of them had interesting backgrounds. Joseph Lukavsky was an Austrian-Czech who fought in World War I on the Allied side. He was taken as prisoner during the war. After his release, he came to Egypt and was hired by the British to work in the Sudan Railways. Another was Oshood, a Turkish locksmith who was taken to Egypt by the British after World War I and then came to the Sudan.[78] By the late 1930s, most Central and Eastern European artisans had left Atbara.

It was reported that Atbara had an active Masonic Society. The exact number and the identity of its members are not known. The Masons became a major source of controversy in the 1960s, when the Muslim Brothers denounced them as "Zionists" and demanded their dissolution. In response, the society's president in Khartoum wrote an article in one of the newspapers defending it as a civic association whose activities did not violate any law.[79]

Mutual aid organizations continued to play a pivotal role in Atbara's social and economic life. The postindependence era witnessed a proliferation of cooperative societies, which were encouraged by the railway department. In the 1960s there were at least nineteen societies in Atbara, with a membership of 14,000 people. The largest of these was the Sudan Railways Cooperative Society, which was administered by the Social Services Division. The society established three pharmacies—one in Atbara, one in Kareima, and one in Babanusa. The pharmacies sold to workers in these stations for 10 percent less than the market price.[80]

LEISURE AND SOCIAL LIFE

The topic of leisure and recreational activities in African cities during the colonial period has attracted considerable attention in recent years.[81] Most studies have stressed the fact that leisure activities were closely linked with the official attempt to inculcate African workers and urban residents with industrial concepts of time and discipline. Leisure and recreational activities, these authors have argued, were used as instruments of social control and were closely supervised by colonial officials. The provision of this "supervised" leisure was designed to counter political mobilization and to check development of autonomous social and cultural activities among colonial subjects. But as was so often the case, colonized people reshaped and refashioned these new forms of recreation to suit their own needs.

Social and recreational activities in Atbara reflected its highly regimented industrial environment. The tight discipline and control of the railway department also permeated every aspect of life in Atbara. Daily life in the city was organized by the *suffara* (sirens) that were blown several times during the day, to signal the beginning and end of the working day, meal times, breaks, and so forth. The suffara signaled not only when people went to and left work, but also how they organized their social activities.

The fact that the working day in Atbara began very early in the morning had a great impact on how people spent their leisure time. For instance, municipal laws regulated everything from vagrancy to the opening and closing hours of clubs, cafés, and beer houses. These regulations limited the evening hours of coffeehouses, restaurants, cinemas, parties, and so forth.[82]

Atbara had limited public parks, casinos, and other entertainment venues. Until the mid-1970s there were only three public parks for a population of approximately 66,000 people. It is not surprising that leisure activities revolved around coffeehouses and sport clubs. In this regard, Atbara had no rival among Sudanese towns. By the mid-1940s it had about thirty registered clubs. The proliferation of these clubs became Atbara's hallmark. Nearly every resident belonged to a club.[83]

Social and sports clubs reflected the socioeconomic status and interests of their members. The most elitist clubs in the town were the Atbara Club and the Atbara

Sports Club, for their membership was restricted to senior British officials.[84] However, members of the Atbara Sports Club included junior officials, many of whom were members of the Hammer and Sickle Club. Little is known about this club except that it was established by European artisans who had socialist leanings.

Some clubs had purely religious functions. These included the Catholic Mission Club and the Evangelical Club. The former had about forty members in 1945, most of whom were Italians. Its main function was to provide Christian education to youth. The Evangelical Club was affiliated with the Evangelical Church, and its main function was to provide a venue for young men to study and socialize.

Other venues for leisure activities in Atbara were bars and *anadi*. There were seven bars that sold imported liquor. Bar owners were mainly Greeks and Copts, and the main customers were senior railway employees and well-to-do citizens. The majority of low-income workers attended the anadi, where less expensive, locally made drinks were sold. As in other Sudanese towns, the bars and anadi continued to exist until the early 1980s when Ja`far Nimeiri imposed the so-called September Laws, which made the selling and consumption of alcohol illegal. In December 1982, a mob led by the Muslim Brothers set fire to the bars in Atbara. One of these bars was owned by Bushra Bahna `Abd al-Malik, a Coptic resident in the city.[85]

It is important to point out that leisure and social activities in Atbara remained a male domain, reflecting the masculine culture of railway employment. While women were relegated to domestic chores in the home, there were very limited venues for young children.

Football in a Railway Town

A number of studies have stressed the link between athleticism and colonial service.[86] Imperial governments considered athletic abilities an essential quality for competent administrators, and believed that athleticism would enhance responsibility, initiative, and integrity. Sport activity was particularly important for railway work; it was considered an essential ingredient for molding railway employees and helping them internalize the norms and values of the industry.

The oldest football team in Atbara was organized within the Atbara Sports Club. Its rival was the Egyptian Club, established in 1911. However, football began to take hold in Atbara in the 1920s, when the railway department established the Parker's Cup, for which teams representing various railway divisions competed. These teams included Management, Engineering, Stores, Carpenters, and Workshops. Tournaments were organized by the Parker's Cup Committee, which included senior officials from the railway department.[87] Heads of divisions led their teams, and tea parties were held after the games. These interdepartmental tournaments were seen as a means of promoting esprit de corps among the railway employees. According to one official, these internal competitions would lead to understanding:

> Understanding means sympathy and appreciation, and mutual appreciation is the keystone of departmental life. These inter-departmental meetings will re-act in

no uncertain manner an office and workshop, and it is by such means that we can best foster and maintain that ideal of which we are all proud. The Atbara spirit.[88]

Hence, railway employees were to view themselves as a team, and reproduce workplace connections in the outside world.

As elsewhere in Africa, sport fields became arenas where European colonizers and their African subjects mixed. In her recent book on football in Zanzibar, Laura Fair observes that this interaction created a sense of equality and "symbolically undermined colonial hierarchies that placed Europeans at the top of the racial scale."[89] During the 1920s, Sudanese, British, and Egyptians played together on the soccer field of the Atbara Club. But this was highly resented by British members, who asked the general manager of the SR to either find another soccer field for Sudanese and Egyptians or abolish the tournaments altogether. Realizing the growing popularity of soccer, the general manager and the Parker's Cup Committee decided to establish a new stadium. The construction of what came to be known as Parker Stadium began in 1927 and was completed in 1928. It was the first soccer stadium in the Sudan.[90]

The opening of the stadium gave soccer a tremendous impetus and spurred the establishment of several teams in Atbara. In 1927 some Sudanese employees of the SR organized a team, which played twice a year against Gordon Memorial College. However, the team had been absorbed into the newly founded Dibble Team, which was named after Captain Harry Dibble, the first commandant of the Sudan Railways Police Force.

Another trophy for which teams competed was the Shield of the Egyptian Emirs, which was given by the Egyptian government to the Sudan Railways in 1927. However, British officials saw this as another form of Egyptian propaganda in the Sudan, and did not permit competition for the cup until 1939.[91]

Football spread rapidly in Atbara and generated great enthusiasm among the city's residents, which was attested by the proliferation of teams in the 1930s and 1940s. Football clubs had many sociological and political implications. The organization of these clubs reflected existing social patterns in the city. Clubs became important symbols of communal identity and provided avenues for the expression of neighborhood, regional, ethnic, and occupational loyalties. Football clubs remained an exclusively male domain. They provided male workers with places to interact in the public sphere as well as avenues to socialize and develop lifetime friendships. In addition to leisure, clubs played myriad functions. They became sites of political mobilization, particularly during the nationalist struggle in the late 1940s and 1950s.

One of the oldest neighborhood teams in Atbara was *al-Watan* (The Nation), which was formed in 1927 by a group of youth from the eastern part of the city. However, over the next four years, the club's name changed to *al-Hayyia al-Raqta* (the Black Snake), to *al-Liwa*, and to Thomas Team. It was reported that the latter was adopted following a dispute among the team members over changing the name. When they presented the matter to Thomas, the district commissioner of Atbara, they admired the way in which he settled the dispute and decided to name the team after him. In 1947 the name was changed again, to *al-Nisr* Team (the Eagle).[92] In 1948 al-Nisr obtained a piece of land to build its premises, but owing to financial difficulties, they could not hire construction workers. In the end, the club had to be built by the members themselves, who took advantage of the 1948 railway strike and completed the project. Al-Nisr emerged as a leading football club in Atbara in the 1940s and 1950s and played against national teams from Port Sudan, Khartoum, and Kassala. In addition to football, al-Nisr had one of the strongest basketball teams in Atbara.

Another team whose history goes back to 1929 was al-Dakhla Team, which was established by the youth of al-Dakhla. In 1936 the club was formally registered with the district authorities, and Sirour al-Saflawi, the Shaykh of al-Dakhla, became president of the club. In 1944 the club built its premises and changed the name to al-Watan Sport Club. Al-Watan became well known for its cultural activities. In addition to organizing adult education classes for men and women, the club invited students from Gordon Memorial College to organize lectures and debates. During the height of the anticolonial struggle in the late 1940s, al-Watan organized political rallies to which it invited nationalist leaders from various political parties.

Football clubs often underscored political, ethnic, and regional conflicts. For instance, in 1947 a group of members, whose original home was the town of Berber, left al-Watan and established a new club called *al-Hilal* (the Crescent). Al-Hilal remained an exclusive club whose membership was limited only to people from Berber. A group called the Berber Town Revival Committee used the club's premises to hold meetings and present demands to provincial authorities. These demands included the building of a hospital and the supplying of electricity to the town of Berber. In 1948 they sent a petition, bearing the signature of the general secretary of al-Hilal, to the province governor. The governor's office was also flooded by telegraphs from the people of Berber, residing in different parts of the country. The governor was incensed and threatened to close down al-Hilal Club unless the Berber Town Revival Committee was dissolved. The club's committee complied and al-Hilal was saved. It remained a viable football club and won the local championship in the 1949–1950 season.[93]

In 1932 Sudanese railway workers and junior officials, living in the railway cantonment, formed a team called *Team al-Arba`iyn* (the Forty Team). They used the number forty as a rejection of the European football rule, which limited the number of players on each team to eleven. However, the name was later changed to *al-Nil Club* (the Nile Club). In 1934 al-Nil played against the British Army Team, which resulted in a draw. In the jubilation that followed the match, several Nil players, who were still members of Dibble Team, withdrew and became full-time members of al-Nil Club. In 1942 the team rented a house and converted it into a club for its social activities. Membership continued to grow, and by the early 1940s, the team had more than thirty members. In 1945 al-Nil played against al-Hilal of Omdurman, which resulted in a draw. During the same year, the club formed a cheering band. Al-Nil became one of the most important football clubs in Atbara. It had many prominent players such as Zaki Salih, Shambi, and ʿAbd al-Baqi al-Jizuli, who were well known at the national level. The club won the 1959–1960 local championship.[94]

Another neighborhood team was *al-Shabiba* (the Youth), which was formed in 1936 by a group of young people from al-Gaygar neighborhood and the railway hostels. Al-Shabiba became one of the most prominent clubs in Atbara and performed well in the 1954–1955 annual tournament.

One of the most important neighborhood clubs was *al-Amal Club* (the Hope), which was established in 1946 by the youth of al-Mawrada. At the beginning the team had no building of its own, and the players held meetings in their homes. As mentioned earlier, the majority of al-Mawrada residents were people of West African origin, former slaves, and other marginal groups. As an expression of their African identity, al-Amal players called their team the Mau Mau, the anticolonial movement in Kenya. Among its most prominent players were ʿAwad Jabbar, Shambi, Lubodi, and Baʿosh. Al-Amal won the local championship in the 1958–1959 season. Besides football, the club had several social and cultural activities, which included a newspaper and adult-education classes for women.[95]

As mentioned earlier, some football clubs expressed ethnic and regional loyalties. For instance, in 1936 a group of people from Dar Fur Province who were living in the railway cantonment formed a football team called *al-Najm al-Ahmar* (the Red Star). Some members were called *al-Umara* (the Emirs) because they belonged to the families of the Khalifa ʿAbdullahi—successor to al-Mahdi—and Ali Dinar, the sultan of Dar Fur who was defeated by the British in 1916. It was not surprising that the team's name was soon changed from the Red Star to *al-Amir*. To raise funds for building the club, al-Amir established a drama society that performed in Atbara, al-Damer, and neighboring towns. The proceeds were used to rent a small house in the market area until the team was able to obtain a piece of land and build its premises in 1955. Al-Amir had some of the most prominent players in Atbara. One of them was ʿAbu ʿAbd al-Raziq, who was "borrowed" by al-Marrikh Club of Omdurman when it visited Egypt in the late 1950s.

In 1938, Nubians from the Wadi Halfa region who were residing in Atbara formed a club. However, the organizers split over the name of the club and two teams were formed. The first was called the Nubian Union Club, and the second was the Northern Peoples' Club. To resolve the dispute, the two teams decided to hold a match to show which one would get the support of the Nubian community in Atbara. The Northern Peoples' Club won the match and attracted a large number of members. In 1942 the Nubian Union Club was dissolved and its members joined the Northern Peoples' Club. However, in 1951 the name was changed to al-Marrikh, after the al-Marrikh Club of Omdurman.

One of the most important occupational clubs that played a pivotal political and social role in Atbara was the Old Boys of the Technical School Club. It was founded in 1934 by the Sudanese artisans of the railway department. Initially, the club had been established for social and recreational purpose. However, some members were active football players on other teams such as Thomas, al-Nil, and al-Shabiba. In 1936 these artisans withdrew from other clubs and formed their own team, which they named *al-Dar*. This was followed by the introduction of a new rule, which prohibited al-Dar players from playing on other teams and limited the team membership to graduates of the technical schools of the SR.[96] The club's committee included many artisans who later played a leading role in the railway workers' movement. The club devoted great energy to social programs such as adult education and literary activities. It offered classes in technical subjects in both English and Arabic. However, the exclusive nature of the club was a source of conflict between leftist artisans and other members. The former strove to open membership to all workers, regardless of skill level, while the latter opposed the idea of socializing with unskilled and uneducated workers.[97] This was the reason behind the establishment of a separate Workers' Club in the late 1940s.

As elsewhere in Africa, sport activities were supervised and controlled by colonial officials. Until 1942 the main governing body of football in Atbara was the Parker's Cup Committee, which consisted mainly of railway senior officials. However, with the proliferation of clubs, the Parker's Cup Committee was replaced in 1942 by a local football league, chaired by the general manager of the SR. With the exception of three Sudanese, the league's executive committee consisted of British railway officials.

In the late 1940s and 1950s, enthusiasm for football in Atbara had reached a new height. In 1945 the Parker Stadium was expanded and admission charges were instituted. But football activity had become more regulated as players and clubs were required to register with the league. Moreover, clubs were classified on the basis of their performance during tournaments into first- and second-class divisions. The number of trophies for which teams competed increased considerably in the 1950s; these included the Northern Province Cup, the Workers Cup, and the Dabora Cup, to name a few.

The success of football in Atbara can also be attributed to the sustained support it received from various institutions and individuals. The Sudan Railways remained the leading advocate and sponsor of football activities in town. In addition to building the Parker Stadium, the SR continued to give donations and loans for the expansion and renovation of football fields. Another major supporter of football was the Atbara Municipal Council, which exempted the local league from the payment of municipal dues and fees. Moreover, football became a major part of the local schools' activities, as special tournaments were regularly held for primary and secondary schools in Atbara, Berber, and Damer.

There were also a number of individuals who played a pivotal role in the promotion of football in Atbara. Some of them were prominent players who later became team managers or referees, and held positions in the local football league. They included Muhammad Ahmad Rahma, Amin Muhammad Ali, Muhammad Karrar, Ahmad Zaki, and Hassan `Arabi. Rahma was born in al-Dakhla and joined the SR in 1943 as an accountant. In the 1940s he played for al-Amir and al-Nil, and in 1953 he retired as a football player and became a referee. A year later, Rahma was elected as president of the executive committee of the Atbara Football League, a position he held for five years. It was Rahma who invited foreign teams to come and play against Atbara teams. Amin Muhammad Ali studied engineering at Gordon Memorial College and joined the SR in 1927. In 1954 he became the general secretary of the Atbara Football League and officially opened the new football stadium in 1955. In addition to his sustained financial contributions, he donated two trophies.

Atbara football teams attained great notoriety locally, nationally, and internationally. On November 16, 1951, al-Hilal Club of Omdurman visited Atbara and played against al-Amir Club for the Sudan Cup. This was considered a landmark in the history of football in the city. The match drew the largest number of spectators in the history of Atbara stadium (1,600 people) and generated the highest income (LS 100,810).[98]

In August 1954, al-Trasana of Egypt visited Atbara and played against Atbara Team, which consisted of the best players from different clubs in town. Atbara Team won the match, one goal to nil. In the following year, the Ethiopian Air Force Team visited Atbara and defeated Atbara Team three goals to one. However, the biggest test for Atbara Team came in 1958 when they played against a visiting team from Poland, which resulted in a tie. A year later, the Red Star of Czechoslovakia visited Atbara and defeated Atbara Team, five goals to three.

Football generated great excitement among Atbara's residents. Each team had a hard core of dedicated fans who cheered during matches and paraded through the streets when it won. Players and supporters were integrated into a dense social network.

As in other African towns, football in Atbara played a vital role in the town's social life. The sport gave individuals from poor and socially marginal backgrounds an opportunity to achieve social status, titles, and fame. Most of these players were railway workers and junior officials. Among the most well-known player in Atbara, who attained national notoriety, was Mahmoud Ibrahim Luboudi. He was born in Atbara in 1933, and after completing his education at Comboni School, he joined the Sudan Railways as an accountant. Luboudi began his football career in 1949 when he joined the al-Mawarada Club in 1949. In 1953 he joined al-Amal Club, where he remained until his retirement in the early 1960s. In 1959 Luboudi became a member of the Sudan national team, which played against the Ethiopian national team. Another famous Atbarawi player was Yusuf Muhammad Ahmad, who was nicknamed *Iqriqi* (the Greek). He was born in Nuri in the Northern Province, and after completing his elementary education, he joined SR's workshops. He joined al-Marrikh in 1947 and moved to al-Amir in 1949, where he spent the rest of his career. Another well-known player was Muhammad Nur al-Din, nicknamed *al-Usta* (the artisan), who completed his education at the Atbara Technical School in 1955 and joined the railway workshops division. In 1957 he joined al-Shabiba Club and was chosen for the Sudan national team in 1959. Atbara produced many outstanding players who later joined the big clubs in Khartoum.

In addition to football, several other sports flourished in Atbara. They included basketball, which began in 1940 in the Egyptian Club and gradually spread to other clubs. However, one of the oldest sports in Atbara is tennis. In the beginning, tennis was limited to British residents in Atbara, and thus was considered an elite sport. It was only in the 1950s that it began to appeal to some segments of Sudanese residents. Bicycle racing became a highly popular sport in Atbara, following the establishment of a club and organized competitions.

Clubs and Political Activism

During the height of labor unrest and nationalist agitation in the mid-1940s, social and sport clubs became a major site of political activities. Realizing the strategic importance of railway workers, various nationalist organizations established branches in Atbara and tried to rally workers' support. Club premises became major centers for political rallies and public debates. In response, colonial officials began to pay considerable attention to club activities. They gathered detailed information on the activities of various clubs and associations, and compiled reports on the background and political affiliations of club members.

One of the oldest nationalist organizations in the Sudan from which the various political parties emerged was the Graduates' Congress. The congress was founded in the late 1930s by the small class of Sudanese intelligentsia, who established branches in Sudanese towns such as Khartoum, Wad Medani, Port Sudan, and Atbara. In 1938 the Sudanese Club in Atbara became the main center for the Graduates Congress. The executive committee of the club at the time included Muhammad Hassan Zayn Al-`Abdin, a junior railway official; Muhammad Magdhub al-Bahhari, vice president; Muhammad Fathi `Abd al-Ghaffar, secretary; and Muhammad Idris, treasurer. Other members included Mirghani `Ageed; `Abd al-Raziq Hammad, a railway artisan; al-Tayib Hussein; Majdhoub Ali Hassib, a district judge; and Muhammad Kheir Khojali.[99]

Owing to internal conflicts, the Graduates' Congress split and several political parties emerged, the most important of which were the Ashiqqa and Umma parties. The former demanded Sudan's independence and unity with Egypt, while the latter was patronized by the Mahdist religious sect and opposed unity with Egypt.

In 1945 the Umma party founded a club in Atbara. The president of the club was `Abd al-Fattah al-Dawi, vice president was Abdalla Muhammad Salih, and treasurer was Muhammad Mahmoud Ibrahim. Other committee members included Muhammad Ahmad al-`Abbadi, Mansour al-Tijani, Muhammad `Uthman Idris, `Abdalla al-Awad Salih, Haroun Ibrahim, Yassin Uthman, and Muhammad `Umar Idris.[100] However, it was the Ashiqqa Party that had the strongest influence in Atbara. The party's patron was Sayyid Ali al-Mirghani, leader of the Khatmiyya. As mentioned earlier, the vast majority of Atbara's people were followers of the Khatmiyya. The main venue for the Ashiqqa Party in Atbara was the Ahli Club. The club's membership included such prominent figures as Sirour al-Saflawi, al-Rayyah al-Faki, Ahmad Hasan Bayram, Muhammad Hasan Abu Sham, Khidir Khojali, Babikir Ahmad al-Shaykh, Mansour al-Tijani, and Sulayman Musa—a railway artisan who became a prominent trade-union leader in the late 1940s. By the mid-1940s, the club had 210 members.[101] The Unionist and the Ashiqqa parties had great influence in Atbara, but it was the Old Boys of Technical School Club that took the center stage of political life in Atbara. It was in this club that the Workers' Affairs Association (WAA), which led the struggle for trade unions, was established. This subject will be examined in the following chapter.

An important movement that took advantage of clubs in Atbara in the 1960s and 1970s was the Republican Brotherhood. This was an Islamic reformist movement that advocated a new interpretation of the Quran and the Prophet Muhammad's tradition and called for the reformation of Muslim jurisprudence to suit the realities of the modern age. Although they were small in number, the Republican Brothers were effective in propagating their ideas through an intensive campaign of publications, lectures, and public debates. By using the numerous social and sport clubs in Atbara as venues for their activities, the Republican Brothers managed to establish a stronghold in the city, particularly among the students of Atbara Secondary School.

Literary Activities

The obsession with strike actions and confrontations, which characterized most writings on labor and working-class history, portrayed workers as people who were totally consumed with militancy and activism and ignored the human and creative elements of working-class culture. Not only did workers exhibit keen interest in literature, poetry, music, and theater, but many of them were accomplished artists who used these idioms to express their experiences and celebrate their struggle. Literary activities played a vital role in the development of working-class culture in Atbara.

As in other Sudanese towns, literary activities in Atbara were pioneered by the small class of intelligentsia, most of whom were junior government employees. They included railway employees, teachers, army officers, and civil servants. As mentioned in chapter one, these groups played a leading role in the development of early Sudanese nationalism following World War I. Their activities culminated in the 1924 uprising, which was crushed by the colonial regime. Following the defeat of the uprising, the colonial regime tried to marginalize the intelligentsia and promote traditional authorities such as tribal heads and religious leaders. However, this policy was reversed in the mid-1930s, when the colonial government began to co-opt the western-educated class to counter sectarian influences. This strategy was associated with Sir Stewart Symes, who became the governor-general of the Sudan in 1934 and adopted a more liberal policy toward the intelligentsia. Moreover, since the defeat of the 1924 uprising, the educated elite focused their attention on literature, poetry, theater, and music, and established literary societies and social clubs in various Sudanese towns.

As a cosmopolitan town, with a highly diverse and relatively educated population and numerous clubs, Atbara created an environment conducive to cultural activities. A cadre of Sudanese, Egyptian, and Syrian railway employees, administrators, and teachers took the lead in the development of a vibrant cultural life in the city.

One of the most influential Sudanese to have a huge impact on literary activities in Atbara was al-Tayyib al-Sarraj (1894–1963), an Arabic language teacher who taught at the Atbara intermediate school in the 1930s. Al-Sarraj was an accomplished linguist, translator, and poet, who wrote in classical Arabic as well as in Sudanese colloquial Arabic. While in Atbara, al-Sarraj educated and influenced a whole generation of young Sudanese artists such as Abu Sharaf, Muhammad `Umar Idris, Khalifa `Abbas, Muhammad `Abd al-Rahim, and Hasan Muddathir.[102]

Another prominent intellectual in Atbara was Ibrahim Hasan Mahlawi (1898–1977). Mahlawi's ancestors migrated from Egypt in the nineteenth century and settled in Swakin and Kassala in the Red Sea region, where they became leading merchants. After completing his intermediate education in Atbara, Mahlawi joined the Sudan Railways in 1916. At an early age, he developed a keen interest in European languages and literature. It was reported that he spent one-third of his six-pounds monthly salary on a private tutor to learn French. He also learned English through correspondence with a college in London and obtained a diploma in economics from Columbia University.[103]

By the 1920s, Mahlawi had become a prominent figure in Atbara's social and cultural circles. He was a leading member of the Literary Society and gave a series of lectures on the development of Arabic poetry from the pre-Islamic era to the modern period. He also published several articles in *Hadarat al-Sudan* and was a regular reader of the *London Times*, the *Manchester Guardian*, and Egyptian newspapers and magazines. In the 1930s, Mahlawi began to learn German and developed a strong interest in socialist ideas, particularly the Fabian strand. His lecture on the Italian invasion of Ethiopia in 1936 at the Sudanese Club drew the attention of British officials and prompted the general manager of the SR to entrust him with the task of training new accountants. However, Mahlawi was replaced in 1939 by a British expert. From then on, Mahlawi devoted his attention to the study of Fabian and socialist ideas. Following a series of lectures he gave during World War II on fascism and Communism, Mahlawi received a letter from the civil secretary, commending him for his vast knowledge and intellectual abilities.[104]

After the war, Mahlawi adopted a more radical and activist stand as he began to advocate for the establishment of trade unions and played a key role in organizing the railway workers. In 1948 he led a demonstration to protest the establishment of the Legislative Assembly, which had been introduced by the colonial administration in the same year and been opposed by many nationalist groups. Consequently, Mahlawi was dismissed from the SR and imprisoned. Following his release, he became heavily involved in the anticolonial struggle and joined the unionist groups.[105] In 1954 he joined the first nationalist government as the minister of mineral resources, but he resigned as a result of disagreements with unionist leaders. Mahlawi devoted the rest of his life to the exploration of mineral resources in the Red Sea region and the promotion of education in Atbara and Sinkat. In his final years, he lived a modest life and continued to pursue his interests. Neither age nor economic hardships could hamper Mahlawi's quest for knowledge and learning. He began learning Italian when he was in his sixties. He died in 1977 at the age of eighty-three.

Another prominent literary figure in Atbara was Joseph Latif Sabbagh, a Syrian Christian who was born at al-Nuhud in Kordofan Province. His grandfather came to the Sudan in the nineteenth century; after a brief stay in Omdurman, he moved to Kordofan, where he became a trader. Sabbagh's parents went to Atbara when he was a child. He attended Atbara intermediate school and the Coptic School, then went to Egypt to study at Cairo University. Sabbagh returned to the Sudan in 1939 and settled in Atbara, where he taught Arabic at the Anglican School for Girls, and later English at the Coptic School.[106]

At an early age, Sabbagh exhibited keen interest in poetry and music. His poems were published in such magazines as *al-Sudan, al-Nil, al-Fajr*, and *Omdurman*. His companions in Atbara included al-Tayyib al-Sarraj, Mahmoud Abu Bakr, Muhammad `Utham Mahjoub, Muhammad `Abd al-Rahim, and Mustafa Abu Sharaf. His first collection of poems, titled *al-Khatwa al-Ula* (The First Step), was published in 1938. It was filled with romantic themes and gained great notoriety, particularly among Egyptian literary critics. However, his second collection, *dhaura al-Zikrayat* (dispersed memories), had more political and nationalistic overtones. In addition to poetry, Sabbagh was a talented musician.[107]

Sabbagh played a major role in promoting literacy among the railway workers. He held English classes at the workers' club and encouraged those who had an interest in literature and poetry. He was also a political activist who became heavily involved in the political activities of the Graduates' Congress. In 1944 Sabbagh delivered an anticolonial poem in Atbara, resulting in his banishment to Wadi Halfa. However, owing to growing factionalism within the nationalist movement, Sabbagh became disillusioned with politics and moved to al-Ubayyid, where he established a business.

Literary activities in Atbara received strong support and encouragement from the railway department. As mentioned earlier, in addition to departmental news, the *Sudan Railways Bulletin* was a major forum for creative writing. The bulletin's editorial board included such figures as `Abd al-Majid Maher, `Ali Hamu, Shatir al-Busayli `Abdel Jalil (a prominent Egyptian historian), Khalifa `Abbas, Muhammad Sinada, and Muhammad Siddiq. As an incentive to contributors, the editorial committee offered prizes for the best four articles. The scope of articles ranged from history and literature to railway work and international affairs.

However, the railway bulletin was primarily designed to promote the railway work culture among employees. For instance, in the September 1948 issue, a whole page was devoted to the train. A few articles celebrated the train as a symbol of modernity and contrasted it to the camel, which was considered a sign of backwardness. Another article spoke about the train as a source of grief because it separated children from parents, husbands from wives, and lovers from one another.[108] The editors reprinted a lengthy poem about the train by the famous Egyptian poet Hafiz Ibrahim, in which he expressed great fascination with the train's speed, comparing it to lightning.

Besides these official publications, there were several other popular avenues for literary activities. In addition to clubs and bookstores, magazines and newspapers were widely circulated. One of the oldest bookstores in Atbara, which still exists, was Dabora Bookstore. According to `Awadalla Dabora, the current owner, the bookstore was established by his father in 1923. In its initial phase, the bookstore specialized in Muslim religious texts. However, after finishing his education, `Awadalla took over the responsibility of running the bookstore and brought a wide range of books, magazines, and newspapers. Dabora Bookstore is located in the central market and has become a meeting place for artists, poets, and singers.[109]

In 1955 the municipal council of Atbara opened a public library. Within two years, the library had a collection of seven hundred books, both in English and in Arabic, and an array of magazines and daily newspapers.[110]

Other arenas for cultural and literary activities were social and sport clubs, where public lectures, drama, and performances were regularly held. Atbara clubs attracted prominent Sudanese poets and writers, such as Muhammad `Umar Idris, Muhammad al-Amin Musa, Mubrak Zarruq, Muhammad `Uthman Mahjoub, Salih Mustafa al-Tahir, Mustafa Muhammad Hasan Sharaf, Khalifa `Abbas, Makki al-Sayyid, and Mahmoud al-Fadli, as well as singers such as Ahmad al-Mustafa, Ibrahim al-Kashif, and Hasan `Atiyya. For instance, on June 28, 1945, the Sudanese club invited a speaker from Khartoum to lecture on the relationship between science and religion. Two days later the Coptic Bible Society held a lecture on gender equality. The lecture was followed by a very lively debate.[111]

There was a great deal of interest in drama and poetry. Most clubs had dramatic societies. In 1944 a drama society known as Atbara Native Actors Society was established. It was headed by `Ali `Uthman and included Bashir Muhammad Bashir, Muhammad Mahjoub, Ali Salih, Ahmad Wida`a, and `Abdalla Adam.[112]

The railway workers themselves played a pivotal role in the cultural life of Atbara. Many artisans, who became prominent labor activists, were gifted poets and writers. The most eminent of these were al-Tayyib Hasan al-Tayyib, al-Hajj `Abd al-Rahman, and Hashim al-Sa`id. For instance, the Old Boys of Technical School Club also had an active drama society. Although the railway management encouraged this form of leisure, it also felt threatened by the development of autonomous cultural activities. For instance, on July 26, 1945, the Old Boys society produced the play of `*Antra ibn Shaddad*. A descendant of an Ethiopian slave mother in pre-Islamic Arabia, `Antara appeared as the hero of a famous romance play of chivalry, involving wars against Persia, Byzantium, the Crusaders, and so forth. According to al-Tayyib Hasan al-Tayyib, when the society tried to perform this play in 1945, it was prevented by the railway manager who viewed it as politically enticing. The cast performed the play in Omdurman and the proceeds were given to malja' al-Qirish, the charitable association.[113]

These activities laid the groundwork for the development of a vibrant urban popular culture that has become the hallmark of Atbara. It is important to point out that Atbara witnessed the production of the first Sudanese movie, *Amal wa Ahlam* (Hopes and dreams). The film was produced in the summer of 1970 at Studio al-

Rashid, the oldest studio in Atbara. The film is a story of loyalty and betrayal, involving a husband who turned against his loyal wife by trying to marry a second wife. Al-Tayyib Hasan, who had by then attained great notoriety as a veteran railway activist and writer, played the main character in the film.

Atbara also had one of the best known musical bands in the country. The musical band of the Northern Province Police, stationed at Atbara, was one of the most outstanding musical groups in the Sudan in the 1960s and 1970s. The band consisted of forty-three members who specialized in brass instruments. About twelve members formed a jazz band, with `Awad Marajan and Salah Taj al-Sir as lead singers. But the best-known member of the band was `Abdalla Deng, who was considered the best saxophone player in the Sudan. `Abdalla was a Dinka from southern Sudan, who sang in Arabic and wrote many musical pieces that were regularly broadcast by the national radio station in Omdurman. It was because of `Abdalla that the SR police band became popular throughout the country.

CONCLUSION

During the interwar period, Atbara had become the home of a large and dynamic community of railway workers, most of whom were rural immigrants. These workers drew upon elements of their rural culture to face the challenges of city life and constructed a new urban identity, with multiple dimensions. They developed a vibrant urban popular culture that revolved around clubs, sport, coffeehouses, and literary activities. Through their activities and communal solidarity, the railway workers of Atbara tamed the city and made it the "sustainer of orphans and hub of spinsters."

NOTES

1. The term `azabat refers to a wide range of unmarried women including divorcées, widows, and those who had never been married. It does not, however, refer to prostitutes. The verse is taken from a popular poem, related to the author by `Awadalla Dabora and `Abdalla `Abd al-Wahid, 11 October 1999.

2. NRO, NP 2/29/312, Governor, Berber Province to General Manager, Sudan Railways, 5 May 1927; one *feddan* = 1.038 acres, or 0.420 hectares.

3. NRO, NP 2/29/312, Petition by 25 natives of Al-Dakhla to the Governor, Berber Province, 20 January 1928.

4. SAD 759/13/1-3, Petition by the People of Al-Dakhla to the District Commissioner, Atbara, 7 February 1929.

5. Hasan Ahmad al-Shaykh and Muhammad `Ali Mustafa, interview by author, Atbara, 13 October 1999.

6. Following the departure of British railway staff after independence, this quarter was occupied by senior Sudanese employees and was renamed Hay al-Sawdana.

7. It was so named because many of the prostitutes were Ethiopian immigrants.

8. NRO, NP 2/30/313, Minutes of the Town Planning Board, 6 March 1939.

9. The term *Native Lodging Area* referred to informal settlements that fell outside official classification.

10. Muhammad Idris Ahmad, "Madinat Atbara: dirasah fi gughrafiyat al-mudun" (Master's thesis, Cairo University, 1978), 80.

11. NRO, NP 2/29/312, DC Atbara to Governor, Northern Province, 7 June 1941.

12. Ibid., DC Atbara to Governor, Northern Province, 12 March 1947.

13. Ahmad, "Madinat Atbara," 81.

14. Hasan Ahmad al-Shaykh and `Ali Mustafa, interview see also "Atbara," *Al-`Arabi* 154 (September 1971): 106.

15. NRO, NP 2/2/21, District Commissioner to Governor, Berber Province, 23 February 1932.

16. NRO, NP 2/2/21, DC Atbara to Governor, Berber Province, 3 May 1933.

17. NRO, NP 2/2/21, Acting Civil Secretary to Governor, Berber Province, 14 March 1933.

18. NRO, NP 2/2/21, DC Atbara to Governor, Berber Province, 7 July 1939.

19. `Awadalla Dabora, interview by author, Atbara, 11 October 1999.

20. NRO, NP 2/3/26, DC Atbara to Governor, Northern Province, 12 August 1953.

21. Ibid.

22. Ibid.

23. Kamal Hamza, *Murshid Baladiyat Atbara* (Guide to Atbara municipality) (Khartoum: Tamadun Press, 1958), 70.

24. *Sudan Railways Annual Report*, 1938, appendix 35.

25. NRO, NP 2/30/315, Notes on the Status of Atbara Cantonment, 14 September 1944.

26. NRO, NP 2/3/26, Note on the Institution of the Municipal Council in Atbara, by DC Damer, 10 June 1946.

27. Ibid.

28. Ibid.

29. Ibid.

30. Hamza, *Murshid Baladiyat Atbara,* 19–49.

31. Ibid.

32. Ibid.

33. Ahmad, *"Madinat Atbara,"* 116.

34. Hamza, *Murshid Baladiyat Atbara*, 59.

35. Ahmad "Madinat Atbara," 118.

36. Ibid., 123.

37. Hamza, *Murshid Baladiyat Atbara*, 44–45.

38. NP 2/57/588: Governor, Northern Province to Acting Civil Secretary, 26 July 1926.

39. NP 2/57/588: Director of Education to Acting Civil Secretary, 16 August 1926.

40. NP 2/57/586, Extract from Atbara Interim Intelligence Report, 20 March 1948.

41. *Sudan Railways Bulletin*, February 1945, 2.

42. Hamza, *Murshid Baladiyat Atbara*, 55.

43. Ahmad "Madinat Atbara," 71.

44. *Sudan Railways Bulletin*, September 1945, 5.

45. Ibid., 51.

46. Ahmad "Madinat Atbara," 73.

47. Louise White, *The Comforts of Home: Prostitution in Colonial Nairobi* (Chicago: University of Chicago Press, 1990); Lisa A. Lindsay, "Domesticity and Difference: Male Breadwinners, Working Class Women, and Colonial Citizenship in the 1945 Nigerian General Strike," *American Historical Review* 104 (June 1999): 783–812.

48. Hayder Ibrahim, *The Shaiqiyya* (Wiesbaden: Franz Steiner Verlage, 1979), 111–12.

49. Sudan Government, *First Population Census of the Sudan, 1955/56* (Khartoum, April 1960), 43–44.

50. Republic of the Sudan, Department of Statistics, *Population and Housing Survey, 1964/65: Atbara* (Khartoum, 1966), 16.

51. Ibid., 18.

52. Hashim al-Sa`id, interview by author, Khartoum, 23 August 2001.

53. Dabora, interview. The tarbush was part of the uniform that civil servants and other government employees wore.

54. Al-Sa`id, interview.

55. Dabora, interview.

56. Republic of the Sudan, Department of Statistics, *Population and Housing Survey*, 18.

57. `Abd al-Rahmanal al-Bashir, interview by author, Atbara, 11 October 1999.

58. According to the 1955 population census, about 84.7 percent of Atbara's population had come from the Northern Province. See Muhammad Idris, "Madinat Atbara," 53.

59. Kenneth Little, "The Role of Voluntary Associations in West African Urbanization," *American Anthropologist* 59 (1957): 579–96; A.L. Epstein, *Politics in an Urban African Community* (Manchester: Manchester University Press, 1958). For a critique of this literature, see Frederick Cooper, ed., *Struggle for the City: Migrant Labor, Capital, and the State in Urban Africa* (Beverly Hills: Sage, 1983).

60. NRO, NP 1/12/68, History of Clubs and Societies in Atbara.

61. NRO, NP 1/12/68, DC Atbara to Governor, Northern Province, 3 September 1936.

62. NRO, NP 2/34/385, Acting Civil Secretary to Governors, 20 September 1930.

63. Ibid.

64. NRO, NP 1/12/68, Petition to District Commissioner Atbara, 13 November 1933.

65. Ibid.

66. NRO, NP 1/12/68, Committee of Kuri Society to DC Atbara, 1 January 1934.

67. NRO, NP 2/34/401, Societies Functioning in Atbara, 1945.

68. Dabora, interview.

69. Ibid.

70. Ibid.

71. Louis Nashid, interview by author, Atbara, 13 October 1999.

72. Most Copts lived either in the railway cantonment or near the central market.

73. Dabora, interview.

74. NP 2/57/586, Evangelical Church Atbara to Director of Education, 7 February 1947.

75. NRO, NP 2/34/384, Societies Functioning in Atbara.

76. Ibid.

77. C.R. Williams, *Wheels and Paddles in the Sudan, 1923–1946* (Edinburgh: Pentland Press, 1986), 34.

78. Abdel Rahim El-Rayh, "Political Processes in Atbara Town" (B.A. diss., University of Khartoum, 1970), 33.

79. *Al-`Ummal*, 7 (1973): 3.

80. Phyllis M. Martin, *Leisure and Society in Colonial Brazzaville* (Cambridge: Cambridge University Press, 1995); Frederick Cooper, "Urban Space, Industrial Time and Wage Labor in Africa," in *Struggle for the City: Migrant Labor, Capital, and the State in Urban Africa*, ed. Frederick Cooper (Beverly Hills: Sage, 1983), 7–50. See also William Baker and James A. Mangan, eds., *Sports in Africa: Essays in Social History* (New York and London: Africana Publishing Company, 1987); Remi Clignet and Maureen Stark, "Modernization and Football in Cameroun," *Journal of Modern African Studies* 12, no. 3 (1974): 409–21.

81. Hasan Ahmad al-Shaykh and `Ali Mustafa, interview.

82. Ibid.

83. All oral informants stressed the exclusiveness of European clubs.

84. Bushra Bahna `Abd al-Malik, interview by author, London, 26 February 2000.

85. Terence Ranger, "Pugilism and Pathology: African Boxing and the Black Urban Experience," in *Sports in Africa: Essays in Social History*, ed. William Baker and James A. Mangan, (New York and London: Africana Publishing Company, 1987), 196–213. See also in the same volume Anthony Kirk-Greene, "Imperial Administration and the Athletic Imperative: The Case of the District Officer in Africa," 81–113.

86. SAD, APK 1500, *Atbarabian*, Vol. 1, July 1927, p. 12.

87. Ibid., vol., 2, August 1927, p. 3.

88. Laura Fair, *Pastimes and Politics: Culture, Community, and Identity in Post-Abolition Urban Zanzibar, 1890–1945* (Athens: Ohio University Press, 2001), 236.

89. Muhammad Ahmad Rahma, Isma`il Ahmad Sulayman, and `Umar al-Mubarak al-Hasan, *Al-riyada fi Atbara* (Sport in Atbara) (Khartoum: Tamaddun Press, 1961), 8.

90. Ibid., 11.

91. Ibid., 35.

92. Ibid., 44–45.

93. Ibid., 25–26.

94. Ibid., 28.

95. Ibid.

96. Al-Hajj `Abd al-Rahman, interview by author, Khartoum, 23 August 1995.

97. Rahma et al., *Al-riyada fi Atbara*, 18.

98. NRO, NP 2/33/384, DC Atbara to Governor, Northern Province, 5 May 1945.

99. Ibid.

100. Ibid.

101. Mahjoub `Umar Bashari, *Ruwwad al-Fikir al-Sudani* (Khartoum: Dar al-Fikr, 1981), 88–90.

102. Ibid., 15–18.

103. Ibid.

104. Those who called for unity with Egypt.

105. Ibid., 114–18.

106. Ibid.

107. Ibid., September 1948.

108. Dabora interview.

109. Hamza, *Murshid Baladiyat Atbara*, 52.

110. *Sudan Railways Bulletin*, September 1948.

111. NRO, NP 2/23/384, Clubs and Societies Functioning in Atbara, 1945.

112. Al-Tayyib Hassan al-Tayyib, *Mudhakirat `an al-Haraka al-`Ummaliyya* (Khartoum: Khartoum University Press, 1989), 5.

113. *Al-Iza`a wa al-Talvizion*, (Radio and Television Magazine), July 1970, 24–25.

4

LABOR PROTESTS, TRADE UNIONS, AND NATIONALIST POLITICS, 1940–1955

During the post–World War II period, the Sudan witnessed an unprecedented wave of labor unrest involving various groups of workers in response to economic hardships and deteriorating social conditions. These labor protests were spearheaded by the railway workers of Atbara, who used their numerical strength and pivotal role in the colonial economy to win major concessions from the colonial government, including pay increases and legalization of trade unions. The railway workers of Atbara, whose protests were replicated in other Sudanese towns, laid the foundation for the development of one of the most militant labor movements in Africa and the Middle East, and transformed Atbara into a major center of labor activism and radical politics.

The events of the late 1940s and the development of the Sudanese labor movement have been examined in numerous studies.[1] The main aim of this chapter, therefore, is to highlight some of the salient features of these labor uprisings, particularly the pattern of mobilization; leadership and ideology; the role of social networks and communal support; and the link between the labor movement and the decolonization process. The principal argument here is that railway strikes of the late 1940s did not happen suddenly, but were deeply rooted in workplace struggles that had been simmering for many years. Moreover, the manner in which the strikes were conducted and sustained underscored the strong bond between railway workers and the communities in which they lived. The high level of mass participation transformed these strikes into a popular movement that provided the social base for anticolonial struggle.

The strikes of the Sudanese railway workers were part of a continent-wide trend. Large-scale labor uprisings occurred in British and French colonies in East and

West Africa as well as in the mining towns of southern Africa. As several authors have noted, these protests became a catalyst for the introduction of a series of labor and social reforms in African colonies.[2] After several decades of neglect, colonial governments were forced to rethink their labor policies and develop new strategies to contain the militancy of African workers. The post–World War II colonial discourse emphasized the development of a stable, efficient, and disciplined African working class. The cornerstone of the new strategy was provision of a family wage, decent housing, and social services. Colonial policy of labor stabilization was premised on European notions of gender and domestic life, which presupposed the male worker as primary breadwinner, responsible for his wife and dependent children.[3] Moreover, the legalization of trade unions and collective bargaining institutions was intended to create a more malleable and docile working class, and to keep labor disputes within legal boundaries.

In the Sudan, the Anglo-Egyptian officials had no intention of introducing such social reforms in what they considered "a predominantly agricultural country," where the working class constituted a "negligible element" of the population. Moreover, colonial labor policy in the Sudan was marred by several stereotypes related to the country's heritage of slavery. British officials believed that slavery had made the Sudanese indolent and averse to manual labor. For instance, when the idea of forming trade unions was discussed in 1946, J.W. Robertson, the civil secretary, wrote:

> Trade unions will not change the traditional "Arab" contempt for manual labor: shop stewards and workers' committees will not make sense in the conditions which are permitted and encouraged by popular opinion and the teaching of Islam.[4]

However, the outbreak of World War II and the growing labor unrest in the late 1940s forced the Anglo-Egyptian administration to reverse its policies. It was the railway workers of Atbara who took the lead in bringing about this change.

WORLD WAR II AND ITS IMPACT

It is commonplace that World War II was a turning point in the history of colonialism in Africa. More than ever, colonial empires had become dependent on their African colonies for the supply of raw materials and manpower. Despite economic hardships, African workers and rural producers were expected to increase productivity to meet the increasing needs of the metropolitan countries.

In view of its strategic location, Sudan had become involved in the war in a major way. The Italian occupation of Ethiopia in 1935 brought the country into direct confrontation with the Axis powers. The Sudan became a supply center for the Allied forces in North Africa and the Middle East. The Sudan Railways in particular played a vital role in the war efforts. Traffic increased sharply, as the SR carried 78,000 troops, 5,000 motor vehicles, and 80,000 tons of military equipment between Sudanese ports and Eritrea.[5] Moreover, the war prompted the railways to make many innovations in machinery and techniques. For example, owing to the shortage of imported building materials, railway engineers used local material such as *jalous* (mud) for construction purposes. Atbara workshops built all coach bodies, different types of wagons, and even aircraft components and some military equipment.[6] Austerity measures and lack of raw material induced the artisans in the workshops to make various innovations. Owing to the shortage of high-speed steel, the artisans collected the scrap from the workshops and reconditioned it into tip tools of various types. In addition to saving time in workshop production, the use of such composite tools did not require frequent grinding as in the case of ordinary steel.[7] It is not surprising that the Sudan became the prime target of the Italians, whose main goal was to cut this line of supply to the Allied forces in the Middle East.

In the beginning, British authorities were very slow in taking defensive measures. In 1940 the Italians had over 215,000 troops in Libya and more than 200,000 in East Africa, while the British had 85,000 troops in the same regions. The Sudanese army had no tanks, no artillery, and no aircraft.[8] Sudanese towns such as Khartoum, the capital; Atbara, headquarters of the railways; and Port Sudan, the harbor, remained vulnerable to enemy attacks.

On July 4, 1940, about 8,000 Italian troops occupied the towns of Kassala and Gallabat in the eastern part of the Sudan. Kassala was about 270 miles from Khartoum. Instead of launching a ground campaign, the Italians, who enjoyed heavy air superiority, mounted probing air attacks. On the morning of July 7, 1940, three Italian aircrafts raided Atbara, dropping twenty bombs that injured one person and caused slight damage to buildings. The bombing led to widespread panic among the city's residents. Compounding the problem was the arrival of many refugees from Kassala, who told frightening stories to local residents. Within 48 hours about 4,000 people, mostly women and children, left Atbara.[9] Railway workshops and the market closed. A month later, the Italians launched a second raid on Atbara and dropped between twenty and thirty bombs, killing one policeman and slightly damaging the railway headquarters. The final raid on Atbara was launched on September 10, during which fifty bombs were dropped, with no casualties.[10] Italian raids not only caused panic but led to widespread anger among Atbara's residents. People were asking such questions as, Where were the British aircraft? and Why were the Italians allowed to fly over Atbara without being attacked by the British? When the British Chief Air Warden met with one hundred leading figures in Atbara to reassure them, they expressed their indignation about the lack of defensive measures and told him that if no action was taken, the remaining population of the city would leave.[11]

Khartoum was bombed on August 23, and the next day two Italian aircraft bombed Omdurman, killing three children. On September 10 bombs were dropped on the outskirts of Khartoum. These raids exposed the weakness of the Sudanese defense. For several months the defense of the eastern frontier fell on Sudanese irregular forces, which consisted mainly of Beja and other ethnic groups in the area. Despite their poor equipment, they were able to hold 1,200 miles of frontier against

Italian tanks, aircraft, and artillery. It was only toward the end of 1940 that the British were able to mount an offensive, forcing the Italians to evacuate Kassala on January 18, 1941. The city was occupied by Sudanese forces the following day. Two days later, Emperor Haile Selassie returned to Ethiopia from exile in Khartoum. Within the next three months, Keren, Addis Ababa, and Massawa had fallen at the hands of British and Sudanese troops, and by May 20 the Italians were defeated. In addition to East Africa, Sudanese soldiers played a major role in the North African campaign.

The war had an enormous impact on the Sudan. Despite British fears of enemy propaganda, Sudanese public opinion remained loyal. Leaders of the main religious sects and the nationalist movement expressed their strong support for the Sudan Defense Force and the Allies. During the war, the Omdurman radio station regularly broadcasted patriotic songs, and leading Sudanese singers such as Ahmad al-Mustafa, Ibrahim al-Kashif, and `Aisha al-Fallatiyya visited the front and performed for the troops. The end of the war sparked off a wave of celebration in different Sudanese towns. Government employees were given a two-day holiday. In Atbara, for instance, following the news of Japan's capitulations, the Atbara Club held a big ceremony to which it invited members of various clubs in the city. A few days later the Sudanese Club organized a big celebration to which the general manager of the SR and members of the Egyptian Club and the Old Boys of Technical School Club were invited. After refreshments a play was performed. One of the play's scenes was a court-martial in which Hitler and Mussolini were tried. Following the play, al-Tayyib Hasan al-Tayyib read a poem celebrating the German defeat in North Africa.[12] In short, the war and the direct attack on Atbara created a strong sense of internationalism among its residents and stimulated their interest in world politics.

The war affected the railway department in other ways. Many discharged and retired soldiers were absorbed into the railway workforce.[13] Some of them enlisted in the railway police, while those with technical skills found employment in various technical divisions. Mahjoub Jadallah was born in a small village called al-Magal in Meroe District. As a young man, Mahjoub enlisted in the Engineering Corps of the Sudan Defense Force and spent several years in North Africa during the war. He was still young at the time of his discharge, and consequently enlisted in the railway police force in 1945.[14] Another ex-serviceman from the same village, Ahmad Muhammad Salih, also served in the Sudan Defense Force and participated in the North African campaign. After his discharge from the army, he enlisted in the railway police and lived in Atbara from 1949 until his retirement in 1977.[15] While Mahjoub remained in Atbara and became a taxi driver, Ahmad Muhammad Salih returned to his village and became a farmer.

One of the most important consequences of the war in the Sudan and elsewhere in Africa was the intensification of the anticolonial struggle. As mentioned previously, the various political organizations that led the nationalist movement in the Sudan grew out of the Graduates' Congress, which was established in the late 1930s. The largest of these were the Ashiqqa and the Umma. The former was patronized by the Khatmiyya sect and called for Sudan's unity with Egypt; the latter represented the Mahdist sect and opposed unity with Egypt.

The post-war era witnessed a dramatic growth of the Sudanese left. As discussed in chapter 1, Communist presence in the Sudan in general and the railways in particular goes back to the 1920s. However, the establishment of a well-organized Communist movement in the country took place in 1946, when the Sudanese Movement for National Liberation (SMNL)—the predecessor of the SCP—was founded. It was reported that several British officials and teachers who were members of the British Communist Party managed to recruit some Sudanese students, particularly at Wadi Sayyidina Secondary School and Gordon Memorial College. Another Communist cell was established by a group of Sudanese students studying in Egypt who were heavily influenced by the Egyptian Communist movement. It is not surprising that the SMNL was named after the Egyptian Movement for National Liberation (EMNL).[16] The first SMNL cell in the Sudan was established in Omdurman in 1946, and the first executive committee included Muhammad Amin Hussain (advocate and journalist), `Abd al-Wahab Zayn al-`Abdien (physician), Ahmad Zayn al-`Abdein (teacher), `Uthman Mahjoub (teacher), Ahmad Muhammad Khayr (teacher), `Abd al-Rahman Hamza (civil servant), `Abd al-Rahim Ahmad (worker), Adam Abu Sinain (student), and `Abd al-Qayum Muhammad Sa`ad (student).

From the beginning the SMNL was marred by ideological conflicts and divisions over its program and direction. These conflicts led to the departure of Muhammad Amin Hussain, the secretary, and Ahmad Zayn al-`Abdein, who later became a prominent member of the pro-Egyptian Ashiqqa Party. But the SMNL continued to attract a dynamic group of young men such as `Awad `Abd al-Raziq and Mirghani `Ali Mustafa.[17]

Under the leadership of `Abd al-Wahab Zayn al-`Abdein and `Awad `Abd al-Raziq, the SMNL adopted a nationalist posture, emphasizing self-determination and solidarity of workers, peasants, and marginal groups. At the same time, the movement adopted a gradual approach to the principles of socialist transformation. The SMNL also established strong links with the Graduates' Congress, and some of its members held prominent positions within the congress. SMNL members such as Hasan Abu Jabal and Mirghani `Ali Mustafa were elected to the congress's executive committee, while `Abd al-Wahab Zayn al-`Abdein became the congress's general secretary for a brief period in 1946.[18]

Although the SMNL regarded the principle of socialist revolution a long-term goal, it had nonetheless directed its effort to mobilization of workers, peasants, and other marginal groups. To achieve this goal the SMNL sent some of its best cadres to Atbara, the Gezira, and the Nuba Mountains. In 1946 Mustafa al-Sayyid was sent to Atbara to mobilize railway workers. He was a native of Atbara who had studied medicine at Gordon Memorial College in Khartoum but was dismissed for organizing protests. After his tenure as party organizer in Atbara, al-Sayyid completed his medical studies in Cairo and Britain, then returned to the Sudan and established a private clinic.[19]

There were major ideological and personal differences among the SMNL leadership, particularly between its members in Egypt and their counterparts in the Sudan. A radical group led by `Awad `Abd al-Raziq was sharply critical of `Abd al-Wahab Zayn `Abdein's leadership and his close association with the Ashiqqa Party. Zayn al-`Abdein was finally replaced by `Awad `Abd al-Raziq.[20]

Under `Abd al-Raziq's leadership the SMNL hoped to transform itself into a truly revolutionary movement with a distinctive identity. This was reflected in the movement's strong emphasis on the study of Marxism by its members and its sharp criticism of sectarian parties. The movement also devoted great attention to the rank and file of railway workers.[21] The movement was determined not only to establish a constituency among workers but also to influence the ideological orientation of the labor movement. There was a marked increase in the frequency of leaflet distribution in Atbara and other urban centers. However, by the late 1940s there were signs that `Abd al-Raziq was reverting to the political line of his predecessor, which emphasized a gradual rather than a revolutionary approach. `Abd al-Raziq and his faction advocated the two-stage revolution theory and argued that given the Sudan's socioeconomic structure, the establishment of a socialist system must be preceded by a strengthening of the "national" bourgeoisie. This would entail encouraging local industry and boycotting imported goods. `Abd al-Raziq also emphasized the need to mobilize the educated middle class. It is not surprising that his moderate approach had come under sharp criticism by younger and more radical SMNL members who had just returned from Egypt. The most prominent of these was `Abd al-Khaliq Mahjoub, who returned to the Sudan in 1948 after completing his studies in Egypt. Mahjoub and his faction criticized `Abd al-Raziq for what they described as his excessive preoccupation with theory and his links with sectarian parties.[22] There was also a fear that the labor movement, in which the SMNL had great hopes, was about to be co-opted by the government, particularly after the introduction of the 1948 labor legislation. During a conference in 1949, in which a major ideological battle was fought between the two factions, `Abd al-Raziq was replaced by Mahjoub as the general secretary of the party. Despite his ouster, `Abd al-Raziq remained in the party and returned to Port Sudan where he worked as a teacher. However, following another confrontation during the SCP conference in 1951, `Abd al-Raziq and his faction left the SCP.[23]

The departure of `Abd al-Raziq and his faction marked the beginning of a new phase in the history of the SCP. Under Mahjoub's leadership, the SCP audaciously expressed its commitment to the principles of Marxism-Leninism. But to avoid the alienation of the conservative Muslim establishment in the Sudan, the SCP adopted a cautious approach toward the subject of religion. Following its general congress in 1956, the SCP announced its program, stressing that the socialist revolution could only be accomplished by an alliance comprising workers, peasants, the intelligentsia, and the national bourgeoisie. By appealing to peasants, the party hoped to undermine the traditional base of support of sectarian parties. The SCP launched a vigorous attack on the two sectarian leaders, Sayyid `Abd al-Rahman al-Mahdi of the Umma Party and Sayyid `Ali al-Mirghani, dubbing them exploiters of Sudanese masses and agents of British and Egyptian imperialism.[24]

LABOR ACTIVISM AMONG THE RAILWAY WORKERS

The railway strikes in Atbara were spurred by a convergence of economic hardship and workplace grievances, and intense political activities associated with the anticolonial struggle. As mentioned previously, the rigid job hierarchy in the railway department and its wage system were a major source of grievance among various categories of Sudanese workers.

One of the most disaffected groups of railway employees were the Sudanese artisans, most of whom were graduates of Atbara Technical School.[25] These artisans developed a distinctive occupational identity based on their education and technical skill. They considered themselves elite, a cut above the rest of the workers. Sudanese artisans resented the manner in which railway management favored foreign skilled workers in terms of pay and other benefits. According to Musa Mitay, local artisans were paid less despite the fact that many of them had better skills than some of their foreign counterparts.[26] Sudanese artisans took great pride in manual labor and considered it more valuable than that of office employees. They were indignant about the fact that a clerical employee working in an office was paid four or five times the wage of a skilled worker who performed his job in the "intense heat of the workshops."[27] Sudanese artisans themselves were differentiated according to education and skill levels.[28] They were classified into first-class and second-class artisans. The second-class artisan was one who rose from the rank of general laborer and did not receive technical training.[29] The first-class artisan, on the other hand, was one who had completed the technical school and joined the SR as an apprentice. After further training he would be employed as an artisan, usually at the age of twenty-two. After several years of practice he would be promoted to first-class artisan. Despite this lengthy period of training, Sudanese railway artisans were paid less than their counterparts in other government departments. For instance, while the artisan in the SR was paid about LE 10.00 per month, the wage of his counterpart in other government departments was between LE 12.00 and LE 15.00.

Another cause of disaffection among railway workers was the condescending manner in which they were treated by British supervisors. The following statement by the late al-Shafi` Ahmad al-Shaykh, a railway artisan and a prominent trade-union leader, illustrates the racist attitudes of colonial officials:

> Those were difficult circumstances. For instance, whenever the British supervisor wanted to fill a form or write something he would use the back of one of the workers as a writing desk. Also, there was the problem of the rest rooms, a worker could not go there without permission and they had a clerk at the door to check on workers. Another humiliating thing was the search of workers at the gate at the end of their shift.[30]

However, the primary factor that sparked off labor unrest in the late 1940 was difficult economic conditions. With their precarious income, wage laborers could not cope with a sharp rise in the cost of living and deteriorating economic conditions in urban centers. During World War II the government had enforced a strict policy of price control and rationing of consumer goods. These policies led to serious shortage of basic commodities such as sugar, tea, grain, and flour. A rationing board was established in Atbara as well as in other towns to supervise distribution of these commodities. In the case of sugar, there was one wholesale trader in Atbara who received his consignment from the railway stores and sold it to about seventy-five retail traders. Rationing cards were given to government employees by their department heads. The monthly allotment for one person was one kilogram of sugar, one-and-a-half ounces of tea, one pound of cooking oil, one pound of coffee, and one-and-a-half *rub*˙[31] of *dhura* (sorghum).[32] Similarly, there was a serious shortage of imported cloth. In response, the government tried to encourage local textiles by promoting the slogan of "make your own *damour*."[33] According to this policy, wholesale traders would purchase bales of ginned cotton from the government at a reduced price and would in turn sell them to spinners, who sold cloth to consumers.

Government policy of price control and rationing led to widespread black marketers. For instance, wholesale traders often diverted their grain quotas to rural areas where they could get much higher prices. Meanwhile, the cost of living continued to rise during the war years, affecting both the highest- and the lowest-paid workers. In 1942, for instance, the cost of living in Atbara rose by about 30 percent from the previous year.[34] Compounding the problem was the poor harvest and the Nile floods of 1946.[35] The flood had a devastating effect on many villages in the northern region, prompting large-scale migration to Atbara and other towns.

Signs of unrest among the railway workers had begun to emerge as early as 1940. In that year the carpenters presented a petition to the railway management. The petition contained a list of demands, including pay increases and shorter working hours. After a great deal of persuasion and threats, the railway management was able to split the petitioners. One faction decided that they would launch a strike if the management did not respond to their demands, while the other opposed the idea of strike action. Those who supported the strike were dismissed immediately.[36]

Strikes occurred even among nongovernment workers. In 1942 taxi drivers in Atbara went on strike and demanded an increase in the monthly quota of gasoline. During the same month, workers at the Sawiris Mahrous and Tsakigroglous Button Factory went on strike, demanding a 100 percent wage increase.[37] In short, during the war years, the labor movement began to move beyond informal coping strategies toward a more direct and organized challenge to employers.

THE STRIKES OF 1947 AND 1948

The failure of the 1940 strike convinced railway workers of the need for collective actions.[38] In this regard, the artisans took the lead. In 1946 the Sudanese artisans submitted a petition to the railway management demanding wage increases and the creation of a uniform system of pay for skilled workers. At the time their total number was 113. When the management asked them to name three representatives to meet with the general manager, they insisted that he must meet with the whole group. The management responded by suspending all second-class artisans. But this action had a negative impact on the railway operation and the management was forced to reinstate them after one month. According to al-Hajj `Abd al-Rahman, "this experience taught us that when we act collectively, we will succeed."[39]

During a meeting in 1946, members of the Old Boys of Technical School Club decided to form a Workers' Affairs Association (WAA), to act as a liaison between railway employees and management. The establishment of the WAA received wide support among railway workers.[40] The first provisional committee included Sulayman Musa, president; al-Tayyib Hasan al-Tayyib, vice president; Muhammad `Abeidi Bardaweil, secretary; and Qasim Amin, assistant secretary. Other members included Dahab `Abd al-`Aziz, al-Hajj `Abd al-Rahman, and Qasmalla Sabah al-Khair.[41] Most executive committee members were artisans, representing various railway divisions. They were chosen because of their age, organizational ability, and charisma. Sulayman Musa was a chargeman who had joined the SR in 1926. Al-Tayyib Hasan was a pattern maker who had joined the service in 1928, and Bardaweil was a fitter who had begun his railway career in 1938.[42]

At the beginning, the WAA adopted a rather cautious and nonconfrontational approach. Its program emphasized mutual help and promotion of education and literacy among railway workers. Membership was open to all railway workers provided that they were Sudanese citizens.

The WAA emerged at a time when the colonial government was considering the introduction of labor legislation that would give workers some form of representation. In 1944 the government appointed a labor officer, and a year later it revived the Labor Board that had been dormant for many years.[43] The government also sought advice from the labor attaché at the British Embassy in Cairo on the question of workers' representation and related matters. In 1945 the Labor Board held a series of meetings during which it discussed British laws of industrial relations. In the end, the board concluded that the Sudan was not ready for trade unions owing to the lack of literacy among workers.[44] Instead, it suggested the formation of works committees—joint consultative bodies that would include employers and employees.[45]

The Labor Board made it clear that works committees were not intended to become representative bodies for negotiating with the central government and would not concern themselves with wages and working conditions.[46]

The formation of works committees received mixed reactions from various government departments. When this proposal was presented to the railway employees, the WAA vigorously opposed it and insisted that it should be recognized as the sole representative of the railway workers, a demand that was rejected by the railway management. The railway workers felt that the works committees would seriously compromise the autonomy of their movement. As al-Hajj put it, "as workers, we did not want government representatives to attend our meetings because we did not want to reveal our strategies and secrets."[47] The WAA launched a campaign to rally the support of the rank and file.

In response to the intransigence of the railway management, the WAA decided to take a bold step. On July 12, 1947, it led a peaceful march to the railway headquarters to present a petition to the general manager. It was reported that about five thousand workers participated in the march.[48] When they arrived at the railway headquarters, they were confronted by the district authorities and a contingent of armed police. The district commissioner asked the WAA leaders to hand him the petition and to disperse, but they insisted on meeting the general manager to present him with the petition. During these negotiations a scuffle broke out between police and demonstrators. According to eyewitness accounts, when the police attacked the demonstrators with sticks and tear gas, they responded by throwing stones and bricks. The clash lasted for about forty minutes and resulted in the injury of eighteen policemen and several hundred workers including Sulayman Musa, president of the WAA. Leaders of the WAA immediately declared a general strike.

The news of the strike spread rapidly throughout the railway network and the entire system was shut down. Anticipating the arrest of the executive committee, leaders of the WAA held a meeting in the evening and elected a shadow committee headed by Babikir `Abdalla and Hashim al-Sa`id. The WAA also sent telegrams to the leaders of the main nationalist organizations—the Independence Front and the Nationalist Front.[49]

On the following day, a detachment of the Sudan Defense Force arrived in Atbara to reinforce the railway police. On the same day about sixty strike organizers were arrested, including Sulayman Musa, al-Tayyib Hasan al-Tayyib, and other WAA leaders. They were charged with organizing an illegal demonstration, which made them liable for prosecution under Local Government Regulations. They were transferred from the railway police headquarters to the provincial prison at al-Damer. On the way to al-Damer, the detainees shouted anticolonial slogans and were cheered by a large crowd of men, women, and children.[50]

On July 17 a delegation from Khartoum, representing the main nationalist organizations and members of the local press, arrived in Atbara. They included Muhammad Ahmad Mahjoub, a prominent lawyer who later became prime minister, `Abdalla`Abd al-Rahman Nugdalla, and Amin al-Tom of the Independence Front. The pro-Egyptian Nationalist Front was represented by Muhammad Nur al-Din, `Abd al-Rahim Shadad, Hasan Taha, and Muhammad Amin Hussain. Members of the press included Ahmad Yusuf Hshim, Isma`il al-`Atabani, and `Abd al-Rahim al-Amin. Following their arrival, the delegation contacted the local authorities and bailed out the detainees.[51] When the delegation met the WAA leaders, the latter insisted that they would not end the strike unless the government legalized trade unions and dropped all charges against them. In the end, a compromise was reached in which the WAA would be recognized as the representative of railway workers, subject to a systemwide referendum. Another condition was that the WAA should incorporate works committees from various railway divisions. In exchange, the WAA withdrew its demand for a dropping of charges. The strike, which lasted for ten days, ended on July 23.

The results of the referendum and the election of a new executive committee were a resounding victory for the WAA. The overwhelming majority of railway workers approved the WAA as their sole representative and reelected members of the existing executive committee.[52]

The trial of the WAA leaders was held in August 1947. In their attempt to win workers' support, Muhammad Ahmad Mahjoub of the Umma Party and Mubarak Zarruq of the Ashiqqa Party volunteered to represent WAA leaders. At the end of the trial each defendant was fined fifty piastres and put on probation.

The strike of July 1947 was a remarkable historical event that has been embedded in the memory of Atbara's residents.[53] This labor uprising represented the most serious challenge to the Anglo-Egyptian government since 1924. The success of the strike was due in large part to workers' solidarity, the leadership of the WAA, and support of the local community. Commenting on these events, the district commissioner of Atbara at the time wrote:

> The success of the strike showed unmistakably how strong an influence Sulieman [sic.] Musa and his Workers Affairs Association had over the men. There is no doubt that a strike would have been called in any case as soon as their demands were refused.[54]

The high level of mass participation transformed the strike into a powerful popular movement. The unprecedented moral and material support given to the strike revealed the extent to which railway workers were integrated into the communities among which they lived. In his published memoir, al-Tayyib Hasan al-Tayyib relates numerous stories that illustrate the high level of communal support. For instance, in addition to being cheered on their way to prison by al-Damer residents, the WAA detainees were sent food, tobacco, tea, sugar, and other daily needs by residents of Atbara and al-Damer. Leading merchants such as Ahmad ʾAbdalla and Mahmud Barsi also provided the detainees with their daily needs.[55] According to al-Tayyib Hasan al-Tayyib, even prison inmates expressed their sympathy by cheering the WAA leaders and giving them tobacco, tea, and food. A prisoner from the Batahin tribe, imprisoned for stealing a camel, told the WAA detainees that since he had nothing to offer, he could entertain them by singing. The Batahin were known throughout the Sudan as excellent *dobait* singers.[56] According to al-Tayyib Hasan al-Tayyib; the man sang for them until the early morning hours.[57]

Throughout their detention, WAA leaders received generous donations from the people of Atbara and the neighboring villages. This communal support alarmed the authorities, prompting the district commissioner to summon the leading merchants in Atbara and threaten to punish them if they continued to support the striking workers. The DC's suspicion of collusion between the merchants and workers stemmed from the fact that on July 10, two days before the strike, about fifteen shops in the central market did not open until ten o'clock in the morning.[58] Indeed, shopkeepers had many grievances pertaining to the government's price controls.

The strike also gave workers the opportunity to develop creative ways to combat government repression. For instance, the WAA formed eight "reserve" committees to succeed one another in case the leadership was arrested. Throughout the ten days, al-Shafi` Ahmad al-Shaykh was coordinating the strike from his hideout despite the intensive police hunt for him. According to al-Hajj `Abd al-Rahman, "throughout the strike al-Shafi` was hiding in the building of the Old Boys of Technical School Club. When the police come and ask for him, the workers would rap him in a prayer's mat and put it in the corner. In this way, al-Shafi` evaded police for several days."[59] These innovative ways proved to be useful—particularly during the postcolonial period, when workers struggled against increasingly repressive regimes.

The success of the July strike and the recognition of the WAA gave the railway workers a sense of empowerment and led to further militancy. Following its recognition, the WAA pressed ahead with its demand for wage increases, reduction of working hours, traveling privileges, and housing. The next several months witnessed a series of negotiations with railway management that produced no result. The management considered the WAA's demand for wage increases and reduction of working hours extravagant.[60]

In December 1947 the government established a Committee of Inquiry to report on the conditions of railway workers at Atbara, Port Sudan, and Khartoum North. The deadline for submitting the committee's report was February 1948. While the committee was conducting its investigation, railway workers became frustrated because of what they considered government evasion. The WAA sent letters to the governor-general and the prime ministers of Britain and Egypt, informing them that it would launch a two-day strike in January 1948 and that it would take further action if its demands were not met. The strike took place as scheduled and had the full support of railway workers.

In February, the Committee of Inquiry went to Atbara and held several meetings with leaders of the WAA, after which it proceeded to Port Sudan. The deliberations of the committee revealed a great deal about workers' strategy as well as their perspective on various issues. The WAA leaders argued that in comparison with workers in Africa and Europe, Sudanese workers lagged far behind in terms of pay, housing, leave, workload, and other benefits. They pointed out the marked differences between the wages of skilled and unskilled workers and demanded the abolition of the prevailing job hierarchy in the SR.[61]

As the Committee of Inquiry continued its work, the rank and file of railway workers, particularly in the outlying stations, became frustrated and began to pressure the WAA by sending telegrams calling for a strike.[62] Consequently, the WAA announced that it would launch an indefinite strike if the committee's report was not submitted by March 16. The deadline passed and the WAA announced a general strike.

The strike of March 1948 was different from that of July 1947 in terms of duration and intensity. The March strike lasted over a month and proved to be more challenging to the workers. One of the main problems that faced the WAA this time was provision of food and water to workers in outlying stations. Ten days into the strike, the WAA received telegrams from workers in these outlying stations, complaining about shortage of supplies. Apparently the train service it organized to these stations could not meet the demand. The WAA then sought help from private citizens such as Muhammad Hasan al-Basili, who had been very helpful during the July 1947 strike. Al-Basili put all his lorries at the WAA's disposal. Similarly the `Ababda nomads volunteered to carry supplies on their camels to railway stations. Prominent families in Atbara such as the Dabora donated vegetables and other food supplies to workers' families.[63] The WAA also set up committees in other towns such as Khartoum, Kosti, al-Ubayyid, and Gedarif to supervise the distribution of supplies in these districts.

Another issue that concerned the WAA was the payment of tuition for workers' children attending private schools. Since the WAA did not have enough resources to cover this cost, some members of the executive committee, including Sulayman Musa, borrowed money from a local merchant using their houses as collateral.[64]

In the meantime merchants and nonwage workers in Atbara as well as farmers from neighboring villages continued to send donations both in cash and in kind. Of particular significance was the contribution of women in the informal sector such as petty traders, beer brewers, and venders. It was reported that a beer brewer named Sabila donated fifteen pounds, which was a large sum at that time.[65] Another woman, called Had al-Zayn, donated money, which she borrowed by putting her house as collateral. The wife of Isma`il al-Azhari, the nationalist leader and future prime minister, contributed twenty-one pieces of gold. The donations of market women ranged from jewelry to meat and grain.[66] Women's support for the striking workers was particularly significant. It reflected a continent-wide pattern and underscored the notion of the male worker as the head of the household and the primary breadwinner. For instance, during the Nigerian general strike of 1945, women contributed to the strike funds despite the fact that many of them were economically independent.[67] The concept of the male breadwinner formed the basis for workers demand for wage increases and family allowances. The contributions and the mass support for the strike reflected the deep social bonds that people of Atbara had developed and sustained for many years.

The struggle of Atbara's railway workers gained notoriety outside the Sudan. In addition to generous contributions from Egyptian labor unions, which amounted to three thousand pounds, Sudanese in Cairo contributed ninety-one pounds, while an anonymous Egyptian gave one thousand pounds.

In addition to financial contributions, railway workers received critical support from several groups and individuals in Atbara. For instance, Ibrahim al-Mahallawi, the chief accountant of the railway department and president of al-Ahli Club, provided WAA leaders with vital information about railway finance, which helped them in their negotiations with the management. Similarly, Sudanese civil servants in Atbara such as Khalifa `Abbas, Mirghani `Aqid, Ahmad Mukhtar, and `Uthman Ahmad `Umar helped the WAA write petitions and gave them invaluable advice. The reports of `Awadalla Dabora, who was the correspondent of *al-Ra'y al-`Am* newspaper, played a major role in publicizing the strike and workers' grievances.[68]

WAA leaders used various forums to mobilize public support. During the strike, they held evening rallies outside their club. These rallies attracted large crowds and generated great sympathy for the workers' cause. The WAA also used various mosques and zawias in the town. For instance, on Friday, April 2, 1948, Sulayman Musa gave a fiery speech at the Atbara mosque in which he attacked the authorities. He was subsequently accused of engaging in "subversive activity," arrested, and taken to Khartoum, where he was fined LE 5 and sentenced to fifteen days in prison.[69]

In response to Musa's arrest, the WAA organized a demonstration in Atbara and sent a letter to the government demanding his release. By that time the strike had become a heavy burden on the rank and file whose morale had declined. Realizing this, the railway management and district authorities began to pressure the WAA to end the strike. For instance, the WAA was prevented from holding rallies outside the premises of its club. Moreover, police informants infiltrated workers' gatherings and reported to the railway management.

Before his release, Sulayman Musa sent a telegram to the WAA in Atbara threatening that he would go on a hunger strike if it insisted on making his release a condition for ending the strike.[70] After completing his sentence, Sulayman was released and returned to Atbara, where he received a hero's welcome.

On April 10, 1948, the Committee of Inquiry finally submitted its report. The report reflected opposing views within the committee on wages, job scales, working hours, and other workers' demands. Nonetheless, the committee unanimously recommended a 100 percent increase in the cost of living allowance for the lowest-paid workers, a basic minimum wage of LE 2.100 per month, rising by biennial increments to LE 2.550.[71] However, when these recommendations were submitted to the financial secretary, he made drastic modifications. Moreover, it took the government three years to introduce a comprehensive system of wages and job scales, a subject that will be examined later in this chapter.

Despite its dissatisfaction with many aspects of the report, the WAA ended the strike on April 18, 1948.[72] The decline of workers' morale and intensive pressure of politicians and other prominent figures played a major role in ending this strike. Mediators included representatives from the Workers' Union in Khartoum, the Atbara municipal council, and the Ahli Club. Several politicians and journalists such as Mubarak Zarouq, Isma`il al-`Atbani, and Ahmad Yusuf Hashim also intervened.

Although the strike ended, the WAA vowed to continue its struggle until workers' demands were fully met. One month after the strike, the WAA clashed with the government. The clash involved the establishment of the Legislative Assembly and the Executive Council, introduced by the government as part of constitutional reform. While these institutions received the full support of the Umma Party, they were opposed by the Nationalist Front and the Sudanese Movement for National Liberation (SMNL). On May 14, 1948, leftist members of the WAA organized a protest against these reforms. The demonstration turned into a big riot in which the police used tear gas and arrested Qasim Amin and `Abd al-Qadir Salim. They were tried and sentenced to four years in prison. In response, the WAA called for a general strike but failed to gain workers' support for it. The authorities took this opportunity to dismiss Sulayman Musa, Qasim Amin, and `Abd al-Qadir Salim from their railway jobs. By that time workers had become exhausted and were in no mood to wage another battle with the government. With the dismissal of these people, the WAA lost some of its most dynamic leaders. At the annual elections of the executive committee, held in August 1948, only four of the fifteen outgoing members were reelected. Al-Tayyib Hasan decided not to run for health reasons. The new committee was headed by Muhammad `Ali Mahdi and included leftist members such as al-Shafi` Ahmad al-Shaykh and Dahab `Abd al-`Aziz. This marked the end of an important phase in the history of the railway workers movement.

The events of the late 1940s transformed Atbara into a center of labor activism, prompting a British official to lament the fact that the city had

> Ceased to be a tranquil town in the tradition of the province. It has potentially turbulent elements consisting of semi-organized railway workmen in addition to the usual urban law-breakers and hooligans. Atbara is liable to both political and labor unrest.[73]

In addition to labor activism, Atbara had also become a focal point of nationalist agitation, a subject that will be examined later. In the late 1940s, political rallies were held in different clubs such as al-Ahli, al-Wadi, and Graduates' clubs. Three labor leaders in Atbara—al-Tayyib Hasan al-Tayyib, al-Hajj `Abd al-Rahman, and `Abdalla Bashir, were renowned poets who evoked patriotic themes. Atbara was also the home of well-known Sudanese singers of whom the best known was Hasan Khalifa al-`Atbarawi, who was also a railway worker. Al-`Atbarawi's patriotic song *Ya gharib yalla lay balladak* inspired the nationalist movement and became one of the most popular songs in the country. When al-`Atbarawi performed it at a public gathering in al-Damer in 1949, he was imprisoned for three months.[74]

LABOR LEGISLATION AND WAGE STRUCTURE

As mentioned previously, the Condominium government was reluctant to establish full-fledged trade unions in the Sudan. But the strike of July 1947 and the recognition of the WAA accelerated the legalization of trade unions. In 1947 the labor attaché at the British Embassy in Cairo prepared a memorandum on trade unionism and labor laws for the Sudan. A year later an expert from the British ministry of labor was sent to the Sudan. By the time of his departure in April 1948, several pieces of labor legislation had been drafted, and these became law in subsequent years. This legislation dealt with employment conditions and the formation of trade unions, and included the Trade Union Ordinance, Workmen's Compensation Ordinance, Workshops and Factories Ordinance, Wage Tribunal Ordinance, and Employment Exchange Ordinance.[75]

Details of this legislation have been examined elsewhere.[76] It is worth mentioning, however, that Sudanese labor laws were not dissimilar from those in other

British colonies in East and West Africa. All these laws were based on British models of industrial relations, designed to discourage politicization of trade unions. For instance, the Sudanese Trade Unions Ordinance required compulsory registration of unions and prohibited government employees from joining unions outside their particular department. The ordinance also made it illegal for unions in government departments to federate with nongovernment unions.

Application of these laws became the primary responsibility of the Labor Department, which was established in 1947 and later came under the Ministry of Social Affairs. The department was established initially as an employment agency for demobilized soldiers after the end of the war, but its function expanded in 1949 to embrace all labor matters. It had several sections that dealt with such issues as factory inspection, formation of trade unions, workers' training, wage tribunals, and housing. By 1954 the department's staff included a commissioner of labor, his deputy, fourteen inspectors, and nine clerks.[77]

Among the most important tasks of the Labor Department was wages. As mentioned earlier, the majority of the Committee of Inquiry's members were convinced that the wages of railway workers were inadequate; however, the WAA and the Committee of Inquiry could not agree on an appropriate wage system. The WAA demanded a 40 percent increase in the wages of employees earning between LE 1.800 and LE 4.200 per month. These figures were based on a housing survey the WAA had conducted in Atbara.[78] One of the most intriguing aspects of the negotiations between the WAA and the Committee of Inquiry was the way in which the question of wages was linked to household structure and marital status. As noted earlier, the provision of family wage, housing, and health service was an integral part of the post-war strategy of labor stabilization.[79] Unfortunately, little is known about household structure and marital status among the railway workers of Atbara. As mentioned in the previous chapter, the 1955–1956 census showed that the total population of Atbara was about 36,298, of whom 19,948 were male and 16,350 female.[80] The number of people over the age of puberty was 11,875, of whom 7,110 were married and 4,765 unmarried. In other words, 59 percent of Atbara's population over the age of puberty were married.[81]

Regardless of the social profile of railway workers, the provision of family wage remained a cardinal principle in the WAA strategy. In contrast, colonial officials insisted that wages should be linked to labor-market conditions and productivity. They argued that Sudanese wage workers were nothing more than parasites. According to a Labor Department officer, "there is no true labor market in the Sudan. What is the value of a month spent nursing the sick, or repairing telephones or motorcars?"[82] He went on to state that "town-dwelling and wage-earning are too atypical in the Sudan to have created a proletariat."[83] In other words, the oscillation between wage and nonwage employment, which was considered an anathema in the earlier years of colonial rule, was turned into an argument against wage increases in the postwar era. The statement of the labor officer underscores the slow death of the "native" African worker paradigm that dominated the thinking of the early generation of colonial officials.

The WAA struggle for wages continued to drag on until 1951, when the Unclassified Staff Wage Commission, known as the Wakefield Commission, was established. The old grade system was replaced by a "group system," involving seven scales in a single job ladder. The new system was supposed to reflect various skills and job responsibilities. It ranged from group 1 for general laborers to group 7 for highly skilled artisans.[84] The Wakefield Commission determined the minimum wage on the basis of subsistence needs of various categories of workers. The commission estimated that a single worker would require LE 3.820 per month to subsist, while a married man with no children would need LE 5.835. The monthly upkeep of a married man with one child was estimated at LE 6.488, and the cost of a married man with two children was projected at LE 7.652. Table 4.1 illustrates the wage structure that was recommended by the commission for railway workers.

The Wakefield Commission's wage structure was based on a dietary survey conducted among Gezira farmers. According to this survey, an unmarried man would require 13 pounds of rice, 13 pounds of flour, and 4 ½ pounds of meat each month. The survey did not include such items as milk and vegetables. The railway workers were incensed by the use of a survey of rural farmers to determine the cost of subsistence. As Hashim al-Sa`id, a prominent trade-union leader, put it, "we felt extremely insulted by the way in which the cost of living was determined. Government calculations were based on low quality food items that were common in the rural areas but had never been part of our diet."[85]

The railway workers also rejected the technocratic solutions of the cost of living contained in the recommendations of the Wakefield Commission. As mentioned previously, workers wanted to invest in education for their children and fulfill various

Table 4.1 Wakefield Commission Wage Structure

Group	Min./ Max. Wage (in Egyptian pounds)	
1	5.700	7.800
II	6.500	9.200
III	8.500	12.100
IV	10.700	16.100
V	13.500	23.500
VI	14.750	26.500
VII	23.500	36.000

social obligations. Another thorny issue was the slow pace of promotion from one grade to another, which amounted to ten years in some cases. The railway workers also resented the marked distinctions between their wages and those of expatriate officials. In short, the wage structure that was implemented in the early 1950s continued to provoke workers' protests during the postcolonial period until the system was reformed in 1968.[86]

LEADERSHIP, IDEOLOGY, AND POLITICS OF TRADE UNIONS

During the period 1949–1952, a large number of trade unions emerged, in both government departments and private firms. Among the first registered unions were the Sudan Medical Association, the Sudan Builders' Trade Union, the Post-Elementary Schoolmasters' Union, the Municipalities Workers' Union, and the Bahr al-Ghazal Mill Workers' Union. The number of unions increased from 5 in 1949 to 123 in 1954.[87] The Trade Union Ordinance, which legalized formation of trade unions, was criticized by the WAA because the ordinance prohibited the federation of labor unions. The right to form a federation of trade unions was one of the main objectives of the leftist elements who dominated the WAA. This issue triggered another round of confrontation between the WAA and the government.

In August 1949 the WAA organized a conference in Atbara attended by several trade unions to form a Workers' Congress. Initially, the congress was an informal organization that supported individual unions in their struggle with employers. From the beginning, the congress was dominated by railway workers who controlled its executive committee. In November 1950 the congress held a general meeting attended by forty-eight unions. The delegates decided to transform the congress into the Sudan Workers' Trade Union Federation (SWTUF). Within three years the SWTUF membership reached about 150,000 workers, and its headquarters were moved from Atbara to Khartoum.[88]

In 1950 the WAA became the Sudan Railways Workers' Union (SRWU), the largest and most influential trade union in the country. By 1951 the SRWU had 20,000 members, and it reached about 25,000 in the mid-1950s.[89] The transformation of the WAA into the SRWU also entailed a change of leadership. The old WAA leaders were succeeded by younger and more radical elements. Prominent among these were `Abd al-Qadir `Ali Hamid, president; al-Shafi` Ahmad al-Shaykh, secretary; and `Ali Muhammad Bashir, assistant secretary.[90] Only three of the WAA executive committee were reelected to the same positions in the SRWU. These were al-Shafi` Ahmad al-Shaykh, `Abdalla Nur al-Din, and Ahmad Muhammad Daoud.

The Ashiqqa had a strong interest in the railway workers' movement, owing to the fact that the vast majority of railway workers in Atbara had come from the northern region, the stronghold of the Khatmiyya sect. Muhammad Nur al-Din, the prominent Ashiqqa leader, had kept close contact with leaders of the WAA during the strike of July 1947. According to official reports, shortly before the strike, Nur al-Din urged some railway employees in Atbara to form a pro-Ashiqqa organization to disseminate the party's ideas and to organize anti-British protests.[91] Whatever the merits of these allegations, it was evident that Nur al-Din played an important role in channeling Egyptian donations to the WAA during the events of 1947. Some of the most prominent leaders of the WAA such as al-Tayyib Hasan and Sulayman Musa were known to be Ashiqqa supporters. On the other hand, the Umma Party had few followers in the northern region and could not establish a strong influence among Atbara workers.

It was the SCP that had the greatest influence on the railway workers' movement. From the beginning, the party paid great attention to Atbara, where it sent its best and most dynamic leaders such as Ahmad Shami. Shami was a native of Tengasi in Meroe District. After completing his intermediate education in Berber, he attended Wadi Sayyidna Secondary School, where he was recruited into the SCP in the late 1940s. After completing his education, Shami was briefly employed as a government civil servant, and then became a full-time SCP organizer in Atbara from 1953 until 1964. Following his expulsion from the SCP in 1964, Shami and Yusuf `Abd al-Majid, another prominent SCP leader, established a pro-Chinese Communist organization known as *Al-qiyada al-thawriyya* (Revolutionary command).[92] This organization advocated armed struggle and emphasized the mobilization of peasants, agricultural laborers, and other rural folk.

In Atbara the Communists focused their attention on railway artisans, particularly in the mechanical division. From their perspective, the artisans were the most educated and enlightened group of workers. Moreover, unlike other railway employees in the traffic and engineering divisions who traveled frequently, workshop artisans were stable and, therefore, easy to organize. The first Communist recruits among railway artisans included al-Shafi` Ahmad al-Shaykh, Qasim Amin, Ibrahim Zakariyya, Dahab `Abd al-`Aziz, Taj al-Sir Hasan Adam, and Qurashi al-Tayyib, many of whom were prominent WAA leaders.

The SCP developed several strategies for recruiting workers. Informal personal contacts played a major role: SCP members within the railway department identified potential recruits among fellow employees and gave them copies of the party's magazine, *Al-liwa al-ahmar* (The red flag), and other Marxist literature. If the potential candidate, after reading and discussing this literature with SCP members, became interested in joining the SCP, he would be nominated to become a party member. New members went through a probationary period during which they were required to acquaint themselves with the party's internal rules and bylaws. During this phase, they were assigned to perform such tasks as distributing leaflets. At the end of the probationary period, they became full-fledged party members.[93]

The SCP tried to establish grassroots organizations outside the formal institutions of trade unions by setting up committees in factories and residential neighborhoods. In addition to the workplace, SCP cadres were active in social and sport clubs. Communist figures such as al-Jinaid `Ali `Umar—a renowned writer and translator—and Mirghani Khalid played a prominent role in the cultural life of Atbara. Al-Jinaid translated literary works from European languages and organized cultural events in various clubs.

By the early 1950s the SCP had created an impressive cadre in Atbara. In addition to the early recruits such as Qasim Amin and al-Shafi` Ahmad al-Shaykh, there were Ibrahim `Uthman, al-Hajj `Abd al-Rahman, and Hashim al-Sa`id. Because of their experience and organizational skills, these leaders enjoyed considerable influence among the railway workers. An intelligence report described Qasim Amin as follows:

> He is generally spoken of as the brain of the workers and their real leader. It was said that he used to draft all the proclamations and press statements of the WAA, and he continued to do so even when he was in jail.[94]

Qasim Amin became known as a fierce, dedicated trade-union leader who gained the respect of his comrades. Qasim faced increasing prosecution by the postindependence Sudanese governments as a result of which he lived in exile in the former Soviet Union. He died shortly after his return to the Sudan in the late 1970s. Following one of Qasim's numerous arrests, Hashim al-Sa`id, his close friend, wrote the following poem:

> Salute leadership in its most noble qualities
> Salute those who hold and guard it
> Salute Qasim, the brave lad who was cheered by millions, near and distant,
> the rebel whose forearms never worn from raising the banner.[95]

Al-Shafi` and al-Hajj were regularly elected to represent their divisions in the SRWU and became its most dominant figures. When the SWTUF was formed in 1949, al-Shafi` became its first general secretary and moved to Khartoum, which became the federation's headquarters in 1950.

The Sudan Workers' Trade Union Federation, in which over one hundred unions were represented, became a formidable political force in the Sudan and a powerful wing of the SCP. The federation established close contact with the World Federation of Trade Unions (WFTU), which represented leftist labor organizations from Eastern Europe and elsewhere. It regularly sent delegations to the WFTU conventions; both al-Shafi` and Muhammad Salam held leadership posts in the WFTU.

To a large extent the SWTUF adopted the SCP's perspective on the question of national liberation and social transformation. In 1951 the SWTUF, the SCP, and pro-Egyptian unionist parties formed a United Front for the Liberation of the Sudan, which launched a large-scale campaign against the Anglo-Egyptian government. But in 1953 the front split in response to the Anglo-Egyptian Agreement for self-government. While sectarian and unionist parties hailed the agreement, the SCP and trade unions opposed it, arguing that self-government at that stage would lead to domination by sectarian parties and the perpetuation of the existing socioeconomic structure. But in view of the euphoria over self-government, the position of the SCP and leftist organizations gained little support, and the SWTUF failed to organize a general strike against the agreement.[96] Moreover, the SWTUF's attitude toward the issue of self-rule caused a major rift with its former allies, namely the unionist parties. It is not surprising that when these parties took power in the postindependence period, they adopted a hostile attitude toward the SWTUF and other radical trade unions and social movement despite their role in the anti-colonial struggle.

Sectarian hostility toward the labor movement had become clear during the transitional period that preceded Sudan's independence. Yahya al-Fadli, the first Sudanese minister of social affairs, whose ministry was responsible for all labor matters, was a leading figure in the National Unionist Party (NUP) and an ardent anti-Communist. To undermine the SWTUF, al-Fadli tried to create a wedge between the federation and its largest constituency, the SRWU. At the same time, the NUP made relentless efforts to overtake the SRWU.

Competition between the NUP and the Communist party over leadership of the SRWU began in the days of the WAA. During the 1949 elections for the WAA executive committee, the unionist parties tried to oust al-Shafi` Ahmad al-Shaykh and other Communists. Their effort did not succeed owing to the organizational skills and strong support these leaders had among the rank and file.[97] But in the 1953–1954 SRWU elections, sectarian parties did succeed in electing an anti-SWTUF and anti-Communist executive committee, headed by Musa Ahmad Mitay, Ahmad Muhammad al-Faki, and Hashim al-Sanusi.[98]

The anti-Communist campaign in the labor unions gained momentum in the postindependence era. In the mid-1950s Yahya al-Fadli seriously considered introducing legislation to ban Communist activities in trade unions. During his official visit to Britain in December 1954, al-Fadli complained to the British minister of labor about what he described as Communist domination of trade unions in the Sudan, and sought his advice on how to curb this influence. He also informed the British minister that the Sudan government was in fact preparing anti-Communist legislation.[99] But the British minister discouraged him from introducing such legislation, arguing that it might actually increase Communist popularity. In the British minister's view, it was better to leave it up to unions themselves to fight Communist elements. Al-Fadli received similar advice from the Trades Union Congress (TUC). According to the TUC's leaders, anti-Communist legislation would affect the credibility of non-Communist union leaders. They argued that Communist influence in labor unions could be curtailed through an "enlightened social policy" that would "diminish" the appeal of Communism by showing the workers that their demands could be achieved by "democratic" means. Furthermore, the TUC leaders advised al-Fadli to strengthen the link between Sudanese trade unions and anti-Communist labor unions in Western countries such as the TUC itself and the International Confederation of Free Trade Unions (ICFTU).[100] In fact, in 1951 the ICFTU sent a delegation to the Sudan but failed to establish any link with the SWTUF, which continued its close contacts with the leftist World Federation of Trade Unions.

The intensive campaign by the minister of social affairs resulted in the election of an anti-Communist executive committee of the SRWU in 1955.[101] The new committee supported the government in its effort to dismantle the SWTUF. At the core of government policy was the establishment of multiple federations of trade unions in government departments and private firms.[102] Although the government had failed to establish viable anti-SWTUF federations, it did succeed in creating a major rift between railway workers and the SWTUF. In 1956 the SRWU broke away from the SWTUF.[103]

The breakaway of the SRWU was indeed a major blow to the SWTUF. Realizing the fact that it could not afford to lose such an important constituency, the SWTUF launched a vigorous campaign to win back the SRWU, particularly during the annual election for the executive committee in 1956–1957. Within two years, the rift between the SRWU and the SWTUF was bridged. Realizing the danger of fragmentation and the looming government threat of reducing the cost-of-living allowance, the SRWU decided to adopt a more conciliatory attitude toward the federation.

In 1958 the coalition government headed by `Abdallah Khalil faced serious political and economic crises, emanating from crop failure and decline of exports. These crises led to widespread labor unrest. In October 1958 the SWTUF launched a general strike, which received strong support from organized labor and opposition groups. The strike was followed by the formation of a National Front comprising the SWTUF, the SCP, opposition parties, and tenant and student unions, which sought to force a vote of no confidence in Khalil's government. Realizing the inevitable outcome of the vote, Khalil "invited" General Ibrahim `Abboud, general commander of the armed forces, to take power. On the morning of November 17, 1958, the date for the vote of confidence, the army staged a bloodless coup and placed the Sudan under a military dictatorship that lasted for six years. The impact of this regime on the railway workers' movement will be examined in the following chapter.

CONCLUSION

The period between World War II and Sudan's independence was perhaps the most crucial in Atbara's history. This era witnessed the development and the radicalization of the railway workers' movement. Atbara railway men linked their struggle with the broader issues of social justice, democracy, and national liberation, thereby transforming the strikes of the late 1940s into a popular movement that formed the social base for the nationalist struggle. These workers established a tradition of militancy and working-class solidarity that formed the basis of the struggle of future generations of workers.

NOTES

1. The pioneering works on the labor movement in the Sudan are those of Saad ed Din Fawzi, *The Labor Movement in the Sudan, 1946–1955* (London: Oxford University Press, 1957), and "The Wage Structure and Wage Policy in the Sudan," *Sudan Notes and Records*

36 (1955): 158–80; Abdel Rahman El-Tayib Ali Taha, "The Sudanese Labor Movement: A Study of Labor Unionism in a Developing Society" (Ph.D. diss., University of California, Los Angeles, 1970).

2. On the postwar strikes and colonial labor reforms, see Frederick Cooper, *Decolonization and African Society: The Labor Question in French and British Africa* (Cambridge: Cambridge University Press, 1996), and *On the African Waterfront: Urban Disorder and the Transformation of Work in Colonial Mombassa* (New Haven: Yale University Press, 1987).

3. Lisa A. Lindsay, "Putting the Family on Track: Gender and Domestic Life on the Colonial Nigerian Railway" (Ph.D. diss., University of Michigan, 1996); Frederick Cooper, "From Free Labor to Family Allowances: Labor and African Society in Colonial Discourse," *American Ethnologist* 16 (November 1989): 745–65.

4. P.R.O FO 371/53254, Note by J.W. Robertson, June 4, 1946.

5. Ibid., 109.

6. Ibid., 110.

7. *Sudan Railways Bulletin*, October 1945.

8. M.W. Daly, *Imperial Sudan: The Anglo-Egyptian Condominium, 1934–1956* (Cambridge: Cambridge University Press, 1991), 130–31.

9. N.R.O., Dakhlia 15/3/9, Chief Air Warden to Governor, Northern Province, and General Manager of the Sudan Railways, 11 July, 1940.

10. N.R.O., Dakhlia 15/3/9, Kaid Aam to Mideast, 12 September 1940.

11. Ibid.

12. *Sudan Railways Bulletin*, September 1945.

13. Historically, the Shaiqiyyia were known for their propensity for military service. During World War II, many of them were enlisted in the Sudan Defense Force.

14. Mahjub Jadalla, interview by author, Atbara, 11 October 1999. Mahjub was in his seventies at the time of the interview.

15. Ahmad Muhammad Salih, al-Magal, interview by author, 29 September 1999.

16. Mohammed Nuri El-Amin, "The Sudanese Communist Movement, Part 1," *Middle East Studies* 32 (July 1996): 22–40.

17. Ibid., 34–35.

18. Mohammed Nuri El-Amin, "The Sudanese Communist Movement, Part 2," *Middle East Studies* 32 (October 1996): 251–63.

19. Ibid., 262.

20. Ibid.

21. Muhammed Nuri El-Amin, "*The Sudanese Communist Movement*, Part 3," *Middle East Studies* 33 (January 1997): 128–51.

22. Ibid., 137–45.

23. Ibid.

24. Ibid.

25. Al-Haji `Abd al-Rahman, interview by author, Khartoum 23 August 1995.

26. Musa Mitay, interview by author, Atbara, 12 October 1999.

27. PRO, FO 371/69236, Report of the Committee of Inquiry on the Sudan Railways Employees, Khartoum, 14 April 1948.

28. `Abd al-Rahman, interview.

29. PRO, FO 371/69236, Report of the Committee of Inquiry on the Sudan Railways Employees.

30. Quoted in Taha, "The Sudanese Labor Movement," 67.

31. One quarter of a kayla, a measure of capacity of about 15 liters.

32. SAD 403/9/1-38, Tour of Rationing Officer in Northern Province, 8 February 1946. Rub` is a local measurement of capacity.

33. SAD 763/5/5: Atbara Monthly Diary, January 1942. Damour refers to a particular type of locally made cloth.

34. Ibid.

35. Fawzi, *The Labour Movement*, 23–24.

36. Al-Tayyib Hasan al-Tayyib, *Mudhakirat `an al-Haraka al-`Ummaliyya* (Khartoum: Khartoum University Press, 1989), 5-7; al-Tayyib was one of the main leaders of the Society of the Old Boys of Technical School and was a leading member of the WAA.

37. SAD 763/5/5: Atbara Monthly Diary.

38. `Abd al-Rahman, interview.

39. Ibid.

40. Al-Tayyib, *Mudhakirat `an al-Haraka al-`Ummaliyya*, 6–7.

41. Ibid.

42. NRO, NP 2/70/693: Sudan Railways, Workers' Affairs Association, July 1947.

43. The Labor Board was originally established in 1921 to control wages but lapsed. It revived in 1936 as an advisory body concerned mainly with the Gezira Scheme; see M.W. Daly, *Imperial Sudan*, 318.

44. PRO, FO 371/63088, Communiqué by the Sudan Government, February 1947.

45. Ibid.

46. Fawzi, *The Labor Movement*, 26–27.

47. `Abd al-Rahman, interview.

48. Mitay, interview.

49. Al-Tayyib, *Mudhakirat `an al-Haraka al-`Ummaliyya*, 27–29.

50. Ibid.

51. The bail of LE 100 for Sulayman Musa, al-Tayyib Hasan al-Tayyib, Qasim Amin, and Qasmalla Sabah al-Khair, and LE 50 for the rest of detainees, was paid by Muhammad Ahmad Mahjoub and Muhammad Nur al-Din; al-Tayyib *Mudhakirat `an al-Haraka al-`Ummaliyya*, 37.

52. Fawzi, *The Labor Movement*, 66.

53. Such as Musa Mitay and al-Hajj `Abd al-Rahman.

54. NRO, NP 2/70/693, District Commissioner Atbara to Governor, Northern Province, 31 July 1947.

55. Ibid., 35.

56. Dobait is a form of chanting that is very popular among the Batahin and the Shukriyya.

57. Al-Tayyib, *Mudhakirat `an al-Haraka al-`Ummaliyya*, 34.

58. NRO, NP 2/70/693, District Commissioner Atbara to Governor, Northern Province, 31 July 1947.

59. `Abd al-Rahman, interview.

60. For instance, the WAA proposed a 40 percent increase for unskilled laborers at the bottom of the pay scale and the reduction of the working day to 6 ½ hours; Fawzi, *The Labour Movement*, 67–68.

61. PRO, FO 371/69236, Sudan Government, Report of the Committee of Inquiry, Khartoum, 14 April 1948.

62. Al-Tayyib, *Mudhakirat `an al-Haraka al-`Ummaliyya*, 62.

63. Ibid., 64.

64. These were Sulayman Musa, al-Tayyib Hasan, Qasmalla Sabah al-Khair, Husayn al-Sayyid, and Muhammad Ahmad Hamad.

65. Hasan Ahmad al-Shaykh, interview by author, Atbara, 13 October 1999.

66. Al-Tayyib, *Mudhakirat `an al-Haraka al-`Ummaliyya*, 65.

67. Lisa A. Lindsay, "Domesticity and Difference: Male Breadwinners, Working Class Women, and Colonial Citizenship in the 1945 Nigerian General Strike," *American Historical Review* 104 (June 1999): 783–812.

68. Ibid., 84–85.

69. Fawzi, *The Labor Movement*, 76.

70. Al-Tayyib, *Mudhakirat `an al-Haraka al-`Ummaliyya*, 74.

71. Fawzi, *The Labor Movement*, 77.

72. Ibid., 75.

73. NRO, NP 2/29/308, L.M. Buchanan to Commissioner of Prisons, January 1949.

74. Hasan Khalifa al-`Atbarawi, interview by author, Atbara, 12 October 1999.

75. Fawzi, *The Labor Movement*, 79–80.

76. Ibid., 79–102.

77. Ibid., 90–91.

78. Ibid., 68.

79. Cooper, "From Free Labor to Family Allowances," 745–65. See also Lisa A. Lindsay, "Putting the Family on Track," 1–20.

80. *Sudan Government: First Population Census of Sudan, 1955/56*, vol. 1, (Khartoum: April 1960).

81. Ibid., 44.

82. PRO, FO 371/102930, Civil Secretary's Office, Labor Branch, Annual Report, 30 June 1953, 2.

83. Ibid.

84. Fawzi, *The Labor Movement*, 137.

85. Hashim al-Sa`id, interview by author, Khartoum, 23 August 2001.

86. `Abd al-Rahman `Abbas Malik, *Adwa `ala al-ujur wa mustawa al-ma`isha* (Khartoum: Sudan Workers' Trade Union Federation, 1968), 39–41.

87. Ibid.

88. Fawzi, *The Labor Movement*, 100.

89. Ibid., 96.

90. Other members were Musa Muhammad Mitay, `Abdalla Muhammad Nur al-Din, Isma`il Matran, `Uthman al-Rufa`i, Khidir Muhammad al-Husayin, Ahmad Muhammad Ali al-Tom, Mahjoub Sulayman Shora, Ahmad Muhammad Da'oud, and `Uthman al-Misri; see SRWU, *The Silver Jubilee* (Atbara: SRWU; July 1997); 4.

91. NRO, NP 2/70/693, DC Atbara to Governor, Northern Province, 31 July 1947.

92. Ahmad Shami, interview by author, Khartoum, 1 September 1996.

93. Ibid.

94. NRO, NP 2/70/693, Notes on the WAA Elections, 1949, Yousef Mustafa Tinay, 29 September 1949.

95. Narrated to author by Hashim al-Sa`id, Khartoum, 23 August 2001.

96. Taha, "The Sudanese Labor Movement," 87–89.

97. NRO NP 2/70/693, Notes on the WAA elections, 1949, Yousef Mustafa Tinay.

98. SRWU, *The Silver Jubilee*, 11.

99. PRO, FO 371/108348, A Note by D.C. Barnes, 2 December, 1954.

100. Ibid.

101. Ibid.

102. The idea was to form three federations of trade unions: one for government employees, one for the private sector, and one for independent crafts. See Taha, "The Sudanese Labor Movement," 98–101.

103. Ibid.

5

The Making
of a Militant Town:
Atbara, 1956–1969

The postindependence period in the Sudan was marked by political instability, exemplified by vacillation between military and parliamentary rule, social inequalities, a destructive civil war, economic decline, and labor protests. As we have seen in chapter 4, the decolonization process brought to power two sectarian parties: the Umma Party and the Democratic Unionist Party (DUP). Both parties represented the interests of religious and economic elites, who were threatened by the political assertiveness of the labor movement and its close links with the Sudanese left. It is not surprising that sectarian governments exhibited great hostility toward trade unions and marginalized them. Sectarian rule ended with the military takeover of General Ibrahim `Abboud in November 1958. The period of military rule (1958–1964) witnessed increased repression, during which the activities of political parties, trade unions, and independent organizations alike were suppressed. In spite of this, labor unions and professional associations led a popular uprising in October 1964, which brought down the junta and restored parliamentary rule. But the "second democracy" was dominated by sectarian parties, whose policies paved the way for the return of military rule in May 1969 under Ja`far Nimeiri.

Throughout the period covered by this chapter, the railway workers of Atbara were in the spotlight, as a target of government repression and a center of popular resistance. Using their vast experience, Atbara railway men continued to both lead the Sudanese working class in its struggle for better working conditions, and defend the autonomy of the labor movement. Their struggle transformed Atbara into a major center of labor activism and radical politics. In short, the tradition of militancy that characterized Atbara in the post–World War II period became more pronounced during the 1950s and 1960s. This chapter will focus on the strategies the railway workers of Atbara invented in order to survive and to wage battles under extremely repressive conditions. Of particular importance in this discussion are workers' initiative, strategies, and creativity in combating repressive governments.

THE SUDAN RAILWAYS IN THE POSTINDEPENDENCE PERIOD

In the postindependence period, the Sudan Railways remained the main means of transportation and continued to play a vital role in the country's economy. Several railway lines were extended in the 1950s and 1960s. With the exception of the Sinnar-Rusayris line, which was completed in 1964, most of the new extensions were in the western and southern parts of the Sudan. Railway expansion in the western parts of the country recommenced in 1955. A track was laid from `Aradeiba to Abu Zabad in 1956 and reached al-Di`ein in 1957. In 1959 the railroad reached Nyala in southern Darfur, 689 kilometers from `Aradeiba.[1] The line linking Babanusa in Kordofan and Wau in Bahr al-Ghazal Province began in 1959 and was completed in 1962. By that time the Sudan Railways operated a route line of 4,751.8 kilometers.[2]

The railroad system in the Sudan used a wide variety of steam locomotives, most of which were imported from Britain. The use of diesel locomotives began in the 1950s, and by 1964 the main lines had been dieselized. By that time, there were 67 diesels and 133 steam locomotives. In general, steam power was used on the light traffic 50-pound rail lines. As will be discussed later, these technical improvements required the creation of a more skilled labor force.

The volume of freight traffic rose from 2,675,000 tons in 1961–1962 to 3,327,000 tons in 1963–1964, but declined to 2,666,000 tons in 1967–1968.[3] Revenues increased from SL 5,716,176 in 1950 to LS 12,140,846 in 1957–1958, reaching LS 19,18,239 in 1963–1964. Operating costs during the same period remained relatively low, ranging from LS 4,534,913 in 1950 to LS 8,930,867 in 1957–1958 to LS 12,630,292 in 1963–1964. The ratio of operating cost to gross revenue was 68 percent between 1957 and 1965, but soared to 89 percent between 1964 and 1969.[4]

On the organizational level, the Sudan Railways was a government agency until 1967, when it became an independent organization, administered by a board. This arrangement continued until 1969, when the military government of Ja`far Nimeiri dissolved the board and reorganized the SR, a subject that will be discussed in the following chapter.

The most visible change in the railway labor force in the postindependence era was the fact that it was completely Sudanized. With the exception of a few Egyptians, most of whom had become Sudanese citizens, all administrative and technical posts vacated by Britons were filled by Sudanese. The first Sudanese general manager of the SR was Muhammad al-Fadl, formerly chief engineer. He was succeeded by Abu Bakr `Ali Rida in 1962, who had also been chief engineer.[5] The number of workers rose from 24,615 in 1957–1958 to 31,531 in 1963–1964, while the size of managerial, technical, and clerical staff increased from about 1,971 in 1956–1957 to 3,230 in 1963–1964.[6] The staff fell into three broad categories. The upper strata consisted of senior administrative and technical personnel, such as heads of divisions and engineers. Their number rose from 130 in 1955–1956 to 211 in

1965–1966. Below them was the junior technical staff, whose number had risen from 1,030 to 1,575 during the same period. At the bottom of the hierarchy were clerical personnel, who grew from 1,115 in 1955–1956 to 1,443 in 1965–1966.[7]

The expansion of the railway workforce had a direct impact on the demographic, economic, and spatial growth of Atbara; it created employment opportunities and attracted a growing number of immigrants to the town. Moreover, the growth of administrative, technical, and clerical personnel and their concentration in the headquarters had many sociopolitical consequences that will be discussed in the following section.

ATBARA: A SOCIOECONOMIC PROFILE

Atbara's population rose from an estimated 36,298 in 1955–1956 to about 48,250 in 1964–1965–a 33 percent increase within a period of nine years.[8] Of the 48,250 residents, 30,110 (62% of the total) had actually been born in Atbara and 18,140 were classified as immigrants, of whom 13,310, or 73.3 percent, were from the northern region. The rest were from Khartoum, Kordofan, Kassala, and Blue Nile provinces. In other words, Atbara continued to attract a large number of people from the northern region, who remained the vast majority of the town's immigrant population.[9] The number of foreigners declined from 1921 in 1955 to 1,100 in 1964. Of those classified as foreigners, 440 were West Africans and 310 Egyptians. Compared with the 1955 census, the number of Egyptians had declined by 749.[10] This decline was due in large part to the Sudanization of railway posts. Moreover, many Egyptians who had resided in Atbara for many years had become Sudanese citizens. In short, northern Sudanese groups—Nubians, Shaiqiyya, Rubatab, and Ja`liyyin—remained the overwhelming majority of Atbara's population.

Moreover, Atbara had a relatively young population, of whom 40 percent were under the age of thirteen and 50 percent under eighteen.[11] The gender ratio was 117 males to 100 females. About 66.3 percent of people who were eighteen and older were married. These figures show that Atbara had a relatively young, stable urban population.

The labor force in Atbara remained overwhelmingly male. According to the survey, the labor force was estimated at 13,830 people, of whom 13,110 were male and 720 female.[12] The bulk of this labor force (about 10,000) consisted of railway employees.[13] The rest of the labor force in the city was employed in other government departments, such as education, health, and municipal offices; private firms; and the informal sector of the economy.

The growth of administrative, clerical, and technical personnel in the railway and other government departments led to the emergence of a small but dynamic middle class, which played a major role in Atbara's social and political life. Many senior railway administrators and engineers were graduates of Khartoum University and Khartoum Polytechnic. Expansion of junior administrative, accounting, and clerical posts created employment opportunities for the graduates of Atbara

Secondary School, the Coptic School, the Angelical School, and other secondary schools in the town. Most of these were sons and daughters of railway workers. In addition to using personal connections to find employment, railway management had traditionally given preference to the sons of its employees because of their familiarity with the railway environment.

In comparison to other Sudanese towns, Atbara had a relatively high literacy rate. According to the 1964 population survey, more than half of the adult population in Atbara had some school education. However, there was a remarkable disparity between males and females; about 74 percent of males and only 26 percent of females had some formal education.[14] While a few educated women found opportunities in the accounting and management divisions of the SR, the majority were employed as teachers, civil servants, and nurses.

SPATIAL GROWTH AND RESIDENTIAL PATTERN

The growth of Atbara's population during the 1950s and 1960s entailed an enormous expansion in the city's physical layout. The old residential neighborhoods of al-Mawrada, al-Faki Medani, al-Dakhla, and al-Murba'at swelled, and new quarters were established in the eastern and northern parts of town. Atbara may be broadly divided into five residential areas. The western area included the former British Quarter, which became known as Hay al-Sawdana; the railway cantonment, Hay al-'Ummal, or the Workers' Quarter; al-Dakhla al-Jadida, New Dakhla; al-Dakha al-Qadima, Old Dakhla; and Sayyala. The population of the western area was estimated at 14,140 in 1964, most of whom were concentrated in al-Dakhla and Sayyala.[15] The central part of town included al-Faki Medani, the market area, al-Murba' at al-Jadida, al-Murba'at al-Shariqiyya, and al-Hilla al-Jadida. The population of these quarters was estimated at 11,400. The southern area consisted of Umbakol, Mawrada West, Mawrada East, and al-Tilayh, with a population of 10,180. The eastern area, where most of the new expansion took place, consisted of Faki Medani East, al-Hasa extensions, al-Anadi, and al-Gala'a, with a population of 11,050.[16] The northern part of town consisted of the military area, which was the home of 1,250 soldiers and officers from the artillery division of the Sudanese army.

As in other Sudanese towns, home ownership in Atbara was based on leasehold, according to which municipal authorities allocated plots of land to tenants in exchange for a nominal fee. Tenants were required to build their houses according to certain guidelines, which varied from one residential area to another. As mentioned previously, colonial urban policy classified residential neighborhoods in Sudanese towns into first-, second-, and third-class areas, each with specific building regulations. Owing to the fact that the overwhelming majority of Atbara's residents were low-income workers, many did not own houses. According to the 1964 survey, 58 percent of households in the town were paying rent that averaged LS 3.2 per month.[17]

Unlike Khartoum and other Sudanese towns where residential patterns reflected class and social status in terms of building material, plot size, and modern amenities, the housing pattern in Atbara was relatively homogeneous. However, there was a sharp contrast between Hay al-Sawdana (formerly the British Quarter) on the one hand, and the rest of the city on the other. According to the 1964 survey, about 74 percent of houses in Atbara were built of mud material and 18 percent of red brick. The rest used grass, wood, and other such materials. With regard to modern amenities, houses in the western and central parts of town had running water, electricity, and modern sewage, while those in the rest of the city used either pit latrines or buckets.[18] Until the mid-1960s, about 66 percent of houses in Atbara had electricity, 43 percent had their own bathroom, 14 percent shared bathrooms, 50 percent had their own toilet, 45 percent shared toilets, and the rest used public toilets in the neighborhood.[19] It is worth mentioning that with the exception of a few buildings in the market area, Atbara had no buildings more than seven stories tall.

With the exception of Hay al-Sawdana and the Railway Quarter, where senior railway personnel lived, residential patterns in Atbara did not reflect the occupational distinctions among the city's population. Various segments of the city's population—workers, civil servants, teachers, petty traders, and merchants—lived in the same neighborhoods and participated in similar social activities.

REPRESSION AND RESISTANCE: ATBARA DURING `ABBOUD REGIME, 1958–1964

As noted in chapter four, the postcolonial history of Atbara had begun with large-scale repression focusing mainly on the trade-union movement in general and railway workers in particular. The hostility of sectarian governments toward the labor movement escalated under the military regime of General Ibrahim `Abboud. Realizing the strength and potential threat of organized labor, the military regime moved swiftly to suppress trade unions. Two weeks after taking power, the junta dissolved trade unions, political parties, and other independent organizations. It also announced its intention to amend the Trade Union Ordinance of 1948. The first confrontation with the government was initiated by the Sudan Workers' Trade Union Federation (SWTUF), which sent a petition to General `Abboud, demanding that it should be allowed to resume its activities and participate in the review of the Trade Union Ordinance. The government responded by arresting several members of the SWTUF as well as Communist leaders such as al-Shafi` Ahmad al-Shaykh, the federation president; Shakir Mursal; Taha Muhammad Taha; and Muhammad Ibrahim Nugud.[20] They were charged with holding an unlawful meeting and having links with such Communist organizations as the World Federation of Trade Unions (WFTU). They were subsequently tried in a military court and received prison sentences reaching five years for al-Shafi` Ahmad al-Shaykh, Shakir Mursal, and Taha Muhammad Taha.[21] The arrest of al-Shafi`, who held the post of vice president of the WFTU, was condemned by leftist labor organizations including the WFTU itself, which launched a large-scale campaign for his release. In conjunction with the International Confederation of Arab Trade Unions, the

WFTU filed a complaint with the International Labor Organization (ILO) accusing the Sudanese government of violating the basic rights of workers.

In its effort to contain the labor movement, the military regime focused its attention on Atbara. The intelligence division of the Northern Province Police closely monitored the activities of trade-union leaders and Communist elements in town, and gathered detailed information about their daily movements.

Following the government decision to dissolve trade unions, the premises of the SRWU and the Workers' Club in Atbara were closed. In December 1958 local officials allowed the Society of the Old Boys of Technical School to resume its activities but refused the same right for the Workers' Club because they believed that it was dominated by Communist elements.[22] During the same month, al-Hajj `Abd al-Rahman, the secretary of the SRWU, sent telegrams to the prime minister and the editor of *al-Ray al-`Am* newspaper calling for the restoration of trade unions. In response, al-Hajj, Taj al-Sir Hasan Adam, and other labor activists were arrested, questioned by the police, and released.[23]

In 1959 the junta stepped up its anti-Communist campaign in Atbara. For instance, in January the police confiscated the property of the Atbara branch of the Sudanese Youth Union. Leaders of the branch included Ibrahim `Izz al-din, Taha Hasan Taha, and Bushra `Abd al-Malik, all of whom were railway employees. Government repression forced several SCP leaders such as Ahmad Shami to hide.[24]

Despite increased repression and persecution, the SCP branch in Atbara continued to maintain contacts with railway workers, distribute leaflets, and write on buildings. Moreover, the SCP publications *Al-shyu `i* (The Communist) and *Al-liwa al-ahmar* (The red flag) were frequently distributed in residential neighborhoods. But owing to continuous police surveillance and lack of equipment, most of the SCP literature was sent from Khartoum.[25]

Meanwhile, trade-union activists in the railway department continued to press the government to reopen the Workers' Club and to lift the ban on trade unions. With regard to the former, local authorities agreed to reopen the club, provided that a new non-Communist committee was elected. The club's secretary agreed in writing to these conditions and promised to hold elections within three weeks. Despite official intervention, the new committee included some Communist elements. Local authorities reluctantly accepted the results but insisted that Muhammad Ahmad Salim, a trade-union activist and the treasurer of the club, be removed, arguing that he might use his position to channel funds for political activities.[26]

During the summer of 1959, the SCP increased its activities after joining other political parties to form a broad front against the military government. The junta responded by launching a massive campaign of arrests, particularly in Atbara. In May, several trade-union leaders such as al-Hajj `Abd al-Rahman and `Abd al-`Azim Yusuf, a railway accountant, were arrested. Al-Hajj was taken to Khartoum, from where he was sent to a remote prison in southern Sudan. This was followed by the arrest of other trade-union leaders such as Ibrahim `Uthman, Yusuf Hamad, Hashim al-Sai`d, Khidir Mabrouk, and Muhammad Ahmad Salim.[27] On June 29 Yusuf Jadalla, a prominent Communist activist, was arrested for allegedly distributing a leaflet asking for donations to support the families of detained union leaders.[28] But these arrests did not deter Communists and union activists from distributing leaflets and demanding the return of the labor unions. The government launched another round of arrests, which included the leading Communist cadre in the city. But the most serious blow to the Communists occurred on August 18, 1959, when the police captured Ahmad Shami, leader of the SCP branch in Atbara, who had been hiding for several months.[29] In October 1959 the detainees were tried in a military court, fined, and released. Upon returning to work, they resumed their political activities among workers. The constant surveillance on roads and bridges had forced the Communists to develop new ways of distributing leaflets, such as putting them on roofs and allowing the wind to blow them around.[30]

In early November 1959 a number of trade-union activists in Khartoum submitted a petition to the government demanding the release of their fellow union leaders and the legalization of trade unions. Their petition was refused, and they were subsequently arrested. In response, railway workers in Khartoum went on strike and were joined by students of Khartoum University and Khartoum Polytechnic. But lack of support among workers in Atbara and other railway divisions led to the failure of the strike. The junta responded by dismissing 228 railway workers in Khartoum and detaining many Communists and trade-union activists. Despite its failure, the strike was the first organized action by workers against the military regime.[31]

In 1960 the junta took steps to implement its new Trade Union Ordinance, which allowed the establishment of trade unions but placed serious restrictions on their freedom. For example, the ordinance limited the right to form trade unions to blue-collar workers, completely excluding white-collar employees. It also prohibited formation of federated trade unions. Moreover, the ordinance denied workers the right to strike and imposed heavy penalties for violating these regulations.[32]

The new ordinance received a mixed reaction from the leadership of the SRWU. One faction, led by Musa Ahmad Mitay, supported it. This faction argued that workers would be better off with limited representation than with none at all. The other faction, representing the Communists and led by al-Hajj `Abd al-Rahman, rejected the new ordinance and demanded reestablishment of the SRWU on the basis of the 1948 Trade Union Ordinance. A third faction, led by `Ali Muhammad Bashir, opposed the ordinance but was not willing to ally itself with the Communists. Competition among these factions intensified in early 1960. To defeat the new ordinance, the Communists began to mobilize the railway workers by distributing leaflets in the workshops.[33] But owing to the deep divisions among the leadership, the new Trade Union Ordinance was adopted and became law in February 1960.

Faced with this reality, workers turned their attention to the election of the union's executive committee. During the following months, various factions, particularly the Communists, intensified their activity to rally workers' support, but their effort was seriously hampered by police surveillance and harassment. Elections were held between December 1960 and early January 1961 and witnessed stiff competition between the Communist faction, led by al-Hajj `Abd al-Rahman, and the conservative faction, led by `Ali Muhammad Bashir. The latter won six-teen seats while the former won nine. Consequently, `Ali Muhammad Bashir be-came the president of the SRWU and al-Hajj `Abd al-Rahman its general secretary.[34] However, a few weeks later, al-Hajj was detained and dismissed from his job for leading a protest against the government plan to transfer the people of Wadi Halfá to Khashm al-Girba following the signing of the Nile water agreements between the Sudan and Egypt. The political crises in the neighboring Congo and the assassination of Patrice Lumumba in early 1961 gave the railway workers an opportunity to protest al-Hajj's detention and other repressive measures. Large-scale demonstrations took place in Atbara and other Sudanese cities. The Com-munists in Atbara played a major role in organizing large demonstrations, demanding that the military government cut off diplomatic relations with Belgium and withdraw Sudanese peacekeeping forces from the Congo. They also distrib-uted leaflets condemning `Abboud's regime and its foreign policy. The Commu-nists used this opportunity and launched a campaign for the release of al-Hajj `Abd al-Rahman, collecting signatures from workers for this purpose.[35] Al-Hajj was fi-nally released.

In the meantime, the SRWU concentrated its effort on working conditions, wages, and other workplace issues. In May 1961 it submitted a petition to the rail-way management, demanding a 45 percent wage increase and cost-of-living al-lowance. The general manager accepted the petition but refused to meet with union leaders. In mid May the union notified management that it would take drastic ac-tion if its demands were not met. In response to the invitation of the railway man-agement, the commissioner of labor in Khartoum decided to intervene. On June 1 the SRWU announced that it would call for a general strike after fifteen days. The labor commissioner and the minister of transport issued several statements con-demning the strike, describing it as illegal, and warning railway workers not to take part in it.

There were serious disagreements among the SRWU leadership with regard to the timing and objectives of the strike. The leftists opposed the strike, arguing that it would give the junta an excuse to destroy the railway workers' movement.[36] De-spite the leftists' objection, the strike was announced. However, on June 13, four days before the strike date, the government dissolved the SRWU and closed down its premises in Atbara. Nonetheless, the strike was carried out as scheduled on June 17, 1961, and continued for seven days. The Communists accused `Ali Muham-mad Bashir and his faction of disappearing after the announcement of the strike and leaving workers without leadership.[37] Official response was swift and severe, particularly against the leftists. Dozens were arrested, including once again al-Hajj `Abd al-Rahman, the general secretary of the SRWU. He was tried in a military court, which sentenced him to six months in prison. The rest of the SRWU lead-ers were dismissed from their jobs and faced other disciplinary measures.

Although the strike did not achieve its objectives, it nonetheless raised the con-fidence and morale of the opposition movement against the junta. Most important, the unsuccessful strike stimulated broader protests. Leaders of political parties sent a petition to the government demanding the return of parliamentary democracy. They were immediately arrested and detained in remote parts of the country.

As in the strikes of the late 1940s, the 1961 strike received strong communal support. Workers, merchants, and various segments of Atbara's population donated money and looked after the families of detained union leaders. They sent food, cigarettes, and magazines to the detainees and kept them informed about political developments.[38]

Continuing repression and harassment forced the Communists in Atbara to go underground and develop new strategies for mobilization. The leadership of the SCP branch in Atbara included Ahmad Shami, Yusuf Jaddala, and `Abdalla `Ibaid. According to Shami, they rented two adjacent houses in the central part of town. They lived in one house and used the other as an office. Shami related that with the help of a female postal employee who was a party member, they linked their telephone to that of the railway manager so that they could listen to conversations between the manager and the central government in Khartoum.[39] However, during the campaign of arrests that followed the strike of June 1961, the police raided this Communist "center." Although Ahmad Shami and his comrades were able to escape, police seizure of important documents and printing equipment was a serious blow to the SCP branch.[40] Following the discovery of this center, the Communists moved to another house in al-Faki Medani, but this was soon discovered and searched by police.[41]

Despite these setbacks, the Communists continued to produce leaflets and distribute their publications. The relatively high literacy rate among Atbara residents made it possible for the Communists to produce radical publications. Communist magazines such as *Al-shamaliyya* (The Northern Province) and *Al-liwa al-ahmar* (The red flag) were distributed frequently in the railway workshops. In June 1962 several SCP publications were found in the workshops. They included *Lamahat min tarikh al-hizb al-shiu `i al-Sudani* (Glimpses from the history of the Sudanese Communist Party), *Al-istiqhlal al-rasmali lil tabaq al- `amila* (Capitalist exploitation of the working class), and *Al-ijur wa al-istiqlal al-rasmali* (Wages and capitalist exploitation).[42]

As mentioned earlier, the Communists were also active in the student movement. Atbara Secondary School, the Technical School, and the Coptic School were major centers of mobilization. In November 1962 police arrested eleven people, including four students, for writing Communist slogans on the walls. During the same month, the students of Atbara Secondary School as well as those of the Technical School refused to take part in the celebration of the fourth anniversary of the junta's takeover. On December 2, 1962, the students of Atbara Secondary School went on strike and occupied the school premises for several days.[43]

Rather than alienating the workers' movement, the government decided to win it over. From the government's perspective, the development of a loyal trade-union movement would require purging. Anticipating the restoration of the union and the holding of new elections, the Communist elements began to mobilize railway workers. They established secret committees in different workshops to gather signatures for the purpose of submitting a petition to the minister of transport. For instance, in May 1963, fifty-one leftist labor leaders in Atbara submitted a petition to the military commander of Northern Province, demanding the restoration of the SRWU. The commander refused to accept the petition and ordered their arrest.

In August 1963 the labor office in Khartoum organized a conference, to which it invited various labor unions, to discuss its measures for reestablishing a trade-union federation. However, the conference turned out to be an embarrassment to the junta, for it quickly turned into an antigovernment forum. Delegates demanded the return of the SRWU and lifting of the state of emergency.

Two months later, pro-government leaders within the SRWU, including Musa Mitay and `Ali Muhammad Bashir, asked the junta to lift the ban on the SRWU. The junta welcomed their request and announced the restoration of the union and the formation of a trade-union federation.

In November 1963 a delegation of trade-union leaders from Khartoum visited Atbara to make plans for the establishment of the SRWU. A meeting was held at Musa Mitay's house on November 21, 1963, attended by fifty-two pro-government labor leaders. They formed a preparatory committee of the SRWU consisting of sixteen members, with Musa Mitay as president. Other members included `Abd al-Rahman Hussain Mustafa, `Uthman `Ali Fadl, al-Sir Mirghani al-Boub, Mirghani `Abd al-Rahman, and Sidahmad `Abdalla.[44] Within a few weeks, the SRWU building was reopened, and the committee began to hold its meetings there. This pro-government committee launched a campaign against Communists and other leftist labor leaders. A series of meetings were held in December 1963, in which the committee discussed the principals and the objectives of the new union. The committee argued that the union should put the "country's interest above all other considerations"; strive to strengthen employer-employee relations; remain politically neutral; and purge "destructive elements."[45]

Apart from their anti-Communist stance, members of the preparatory committee had little in common. According to official reports, some members were apprehensive about Musa Mitay's leadership ability to the extent that some of them wanted to withdraw from the committee. Moreover, it was reported that the majority of rank and file among railway workers had similar views and distrusted both Mitay and `Uthman `Ali Fadl.[46]

In January 1964 the committee announced its intention to hold "fair and democratic" elections. To prepare for the elections, the Communists stepped up their mobilization campaign by distributing leaflets in the residential areas in which they told railway workers that they would not be served by "the opportunists from Khartoum." The Communists also used the split of the preparatory committee and launched a campaign against Musa Mitay and his group, describing them as traitors. They also focused their effort on sport clubs such as al-Wadi and al-Ahli.[47] They held a meeting in early January and formed a committee, headed by al-Hajj 'Abd al-Rahman, to organize their campaign, particularly in the railway workshops. Al-Hajj immediately contacted Hasan Hamid, president of the Workers' Club, asking him to revive the club's activities through the collection of membership dues and to encourage workers to attend regularly.[48] In March the Atbara branch of the SCP distributed an internal memo to its members, who were active in sport clubs, in which it urged them to enlighten club members about the current political developments in the country and the danger of government attempts to divert the attention of the youth from "national issues."[49]

Approach of the election heightened the competition between the Communists and the preparatory committee. The Communists nominated fifty-three candidates in various railway divisions. In response, the preparatory committee asked Abu Bakr Ali Rida, the general manager of the SR, to transfer some Communist candidates from their posts in Atbara. The general manager replied that such an action would create a backlash among the workers.[50] Shortly before the elections, which were scheduled for May 26, 1964, the police launched a campaign against the Communists in town. Roadblocks were set up throughout Atbara and residents of al-Mawrada, al-Dakhla, and Umbakol were subjected to personal searches. For several days, Atbara's residents lived in what amounted to a state of emergency. Communist and leftists candidates in various railway divisions were intimidated and forced to withdraw from election lists. Moreover the government used native administrators such as Sirour Muhammad al-Saflawi—the Shayleh of al-Dakhla and Ibrahim al-Shoush—another shaykh—to persuade workers not to vote for Communist candidates.[51] As a result of this campaign, the number of Communist candidates dropped from fifty-three to thirty-five.

Elections were held as scheduled on May 26. Each of the railway divisions (engineering, traffic, mechanical, headquarters, harbor, steamers, and catering) would elect seventeen representatives to the general assembly. As expected, Musa Mitay's faction swept the elections. The Communists elected a total of 22 candidates: eight in the workshops, eight in the management division, four in the engineering division, and two in the stores.[52] Officers of the new executive committee consisted of Musa Mitay, president; Muhammad `Uthman al-Mudir, secretary; Muhammad al-Hasan `Abdalla, treasurer; and Sa`id `Abdalla, assistant secretary.[53] The government received the election results with gratification. After the announcement of election results, Mustafa `Uthman Hasan—the military governor of Atbara—and Muhammad `Abd al-Halim—director of the labor office—visited the SRWU headquarters and congratulated the winners.

Having failed to takeover the SRWU, the Communists took advantage of their control of the workshop committees and pressed the union to adopt the demands of workers in this vital railway division. As a result of workers' pressure, the executive committee of the SRWU sent a petition to the district commissioner of Atbara in August 1964 demanding a reduction in the price of basic commodities.[54]

At the end of the summer of 1964, the political situation in the Sudan had taken a serious turn as the opposition to military rule had begun to gain momentum. The events that led to the downfall of the military regime in October have been described elsewhere and therefore will be outlined briefly here. On October 21 the students of Khartoum University defied the junta's ban on public gatherings and held a meeting on campus to discuss government policy in the south. In an attempt to disperse the crowd, the police opened fire, injuring eight students and killing one. This incident sparked a popular uprising of unprecedented scale. The whole country was engulfed in demonstrations and mass protests in which different segments of the population participated. Three days after the incident, a hastily organized National Front of Associations composed of the Judiciary, the Bar Association, the Medical Association, the staff of the University of Khartoum, student unions, farmers' unions, and labor unions called for a general strike and demanded that the military government step down. On October 26, a group of army officers known as the Free Officers Organization joined the uprising and refused to carry out orders to suppress the demonstrations. The general strike and the fear of bloodshed prompted the junta to resign. On October 31, a civilian government was formed and charged with the task of preparing the country for general elections to be held no later than March 1965. In recognition of their vital role in organizing resistance against the junta, peasant and workers' unions were given two cabinet posts in the transitional government. These were held by al-Amin Muhammad al-Amin, representing the Gezira Tenant Farmers Union, and al-Shafi` Ahmad al-Shaykh, representing the SWTUF. Al-Shafi`'s appointment, however, was complicated by the strong objection of the sectarian parties, who argued that the SWTUF had not yet regained its legal status. Following a legal battle and consultation with various trade unions, al-Shafi` was confirmed to his position as minister of labor. Other leftist elements in the transitional government included Ahmad Sulayman, who represented the SCP.

Under the leadership of the SCP, the SWTUF, and the Gezira Tenant Farmers Union, a Socialist Democratic Coalition was formed, the aim of which was to bring about radical social and political reforms. The coalition demanded that special constituencies be set aside for workers and tenants during national elections. The establishment of the coalition, the growing influence of the left, and the attempt of the government to postpone the elections alarmed the sectarian parties and prompted them to launch a campaign against the transitional government and force it to step down. The SWTUF responded by organizing an unsuccessful general strike. The strike failed because it did not receive the support of many unions—particularly the railway workers' union, which was dominated by anti-Communist elements.

General elections were held in 1965. Once again, the sectarian parties—the Umma and the DUP—came to power. As in the mid-1950s, these parties exhibited great hostility toward trade unions and other social movements. They were particularly threatened by the growing strength and organizational ability of trade unions exhibited during the October uprising.

ATBARA DURING THE "SECOND DEMOCRACY"

In order to understand the role of the labor movement and working-class politics in Atbara during the second period of parliamentary democracy, it is important to briefly examine the main political developments in the country and the relations between the central government and the labor movement.

The removal of the military regime and the return of parliamentary rule opened up a large space for organized labor. Trade unions regained their legal status and resumed activity with great vigor and confidence. Moreover, the influence of the SCP on the labor movement increased significantly. A number of SCP deputies were elected to the Constituent Assembly and used it as a forum to criticize the policies of sectarian parties and to disseminate the SCP program. The growing influence of the SCP and the labor movement became a source of great anxiety for the sectarian parties. Hence, the second parliamentary regime was marred by confrontation between the labor movement and the government.

Sectarian parties found an opportunity to settle their score with the SCP in 1965 when a student at the Teacher's Training Institute allegedly made an uncomplimentary remark about the prophet Muhammad. The Islamic Charter Front and the sectarian parties immediately demanded dissolution of the SCP, arguing that the student was a member. On December 8, 1965, their members in parliament voted to ban the SCP and expelled its deputies from the Constituent Assembly. They also launched a campaign to discredit the SCP and weaken its influence in trade unions, particularly the SWTUF. The government took a series of measures to marginalize the SWTUF and deny its legal status. These included transferring federation leaders from their government posts and amending the Trade Union Ordinance in 1966.[55] In response, the SWTUF called for a general strike scheduled for June 15, 1966. The government made every possible effort to foil the strike by urging labor unions, particularly the SRWU, not to take part in it. A few days before the strike, for instance, the minister of transport dismissed forty-three railway workers deemed sympathizers with the SWTUF. As expected, the strike failed when the SRWU announced that it would not support it.

The SWTUF was able to regain its legal status in October 1966 following the election of al-Sadiq al-Mahdi as prime minister. Al-Sadiq presented himself as a reformer whose intention was to transform the Umma from a sectarian organization into a modern political party. After disagreements with his uncle, al-Hadi al-Mahdi—the leader of the Mahdist sect—al-Sadiq formed his own party. In order to give his new party a progressive image, al-Sadiq adopted more liberal language toward trade unions. But the refusal of his government to abide by the Supreme Court ruling declaring that the dissolution of the SCP was unconstitutional became a source of friction between him and the SWTUF. Al-Sadiq's government accused the SCP of plotting a military coup. Leaders of the SCP and the SWTUF were arrested but released for lack of evidence.

Antagonism between the federation and the government reached a peak in 1968 when the sectarian parties attempted to introduce an Islamic constitution. But the fear of serious repercussions, particularly in southern Sudan, and the vigorous campaign of the SWTUF and other leftist organizations prompted the sectarian parties to abandon this project. During the same year, another round of confrontation between the federation and the government occurred over the question of wage increases and labor reforms. The evasive attitude of the government prompted the SWTUF to announce a general strike beginning August 20, 1968. Although the

federation won the support of several unions, the SRWU decided not to participate. Muhammad al-Hasan ʿAbdallá, president of the SRWU and a DUP supporter,
argued that the strike was illegal and that the federation had not provided con-
vincing reasons for it. Although the pro-federation elements in the SRWU, led by
Hashim al-Saʿid, the union's secretary, vowed to mobilize railway workers to join
the strike, their effort failed. In the end, the strike was staged on the due date. The
success of the strike without SRWU participation was of critical significance; it
meant that the prestige the SRWU had enjoyed since the rise of the labor movement in the 1940s had been seriously damaged. Although the SRWU continued to
be the largest union, with a membership of 25,000 workers, a number of unions
with over 6,000 members had emerged in the late 1960s. Moreover, several developments within the SR had affected the status of the SRWU. The growth of the
railway labor force and the emergence of different occupational groups led to the
emergence of several unions within the department. One of the oldest unions was
the Sudan Railway Staff Union, which had existed since 1950. It represented administrative, clerical, and technical employees in various divisions. In 1963 railway engineers who graduated from Khartoum Polytechnic established their union.
Three years later graduates of Khartoum University's College of Engineering did
the same. In 1967 employees in the administrative and accounting divisions formed
a union, and in 1968 graduates of technical schools established their own unions.[56]
The development of these unions meant the fragmentation of railway employees
along occupational lines.

The success of the strike boosted the confidence of the SWTUF and strengthened its position within the labor movement. With the approach of new elections
and the growing debate on an Islamic constitution, the stage was set for another
showdown between the SWTUF and the government. However, this was halted by
the military coup of Colonel Jaʿfar Nimeiri on May 25, 1969.

LABOR ACTIVISM AND SOCIAL IDENTITY IN ATBARA

Through their persistent struggle against colonial and postcolonial governments,
the railway workers of Atbara created a culture of protest and combativeness that
has become a major component of their identity. Of particular significance is the
way in which these workers transformed their union into an institution that served
myriad social, economic, and political functions. While trade unions in many parts
of Africa and the Middle East have been turned into bureaucratic, unresponsive institutions, the SRWU became an integral part of the social fabric of Atbara. As will
be shown, beyond the demand for wages and better working conditions, the railway workers' union played a pivotal role in Atbara's political and social life. With
a membership of 28,000 in 1968, the SRWU remained the largest trade union in
the country. As a result, various political parties competed vigorously to control
its leadership. It is not surprising that the election of the SRWU became one of the
most contested and closely watched in the country. The competition over the leadership of the SRWU illuminates such vital issues as the struggle between religious

and secular ideologies, class and ethnic identities, leadership and charisma, and the relationship between the labor movement and the state. However, before examining these themes, it would be useful to get a sense of the organizational structure of the SRWU and the manner in which it was governed.

Over the years, the SRWU developed a complex but remarkably democratic organizational structure. At the top of its hierarchy was the executive committee, which consisted of thirty-one members. Below the executive committee was the general assembly, in which the various railway divisions were represented. Four of these departmental committees—mechanical, engineering, stores, and accounting—were located in Atbara. The other three were the Harbor Division in Port Sudan, Catering Division in Khartoum, and Steamers Division in Khartoum North. Each department had between seventeen and twenty-one constituencies spread throughout the country. Each of these constituencies elected a representative to the general assembly of the union. Between three and six of these representatives formed the departmental committee, which represented the division in the executive committee of the union.[57] In other words, the division committees were the backbone of the SRWU. The responsibility of the division committee was to deal with grievances at the local level, collect dues, and act as a liaison between the executive committee and workers in the division. Hence, the effectiveness of the SRWU depended largely on the success of these committees in executing their duties. With the expansion of the railway and emergence of new railway centers, new union branches, with direct connections to the executive committee, were established in such centers as Khartoum, Port Sudan, Kosti, Kassala, and Babanusa.

One of the most important characteristics of the SRWU's leadership was that it had often been drawn from the ranks of unskilled workers. This pattern was set since the emergence of the WAA in the late 1940s. Members of the general assembly and the executive committee were elected at the division level. Even the president of the union had to win elections both in his division committee and inside the executive committee before he could become president.

The SRWU was a site of fierce competition that involved various political organizations and ideological trends. The two political parties that constantly competed for the leadership of the SRWU were the Sudanese Communist Party (SCP) and the Democratic Unionist Party (DUP). As mentioned previously, the latter was patronized by the Khatmiyya sect, to which the majority of the railway workers of Atbara belonged. In spite of this, the Communists have always won seats in the general assembly and the executive committee of the SRWU. For instance, of ten general secretaries of the union between the late 1940s and the late 1960s, four were either SCP members or sympathizers. These were al-Hajj `Abd al-Rahman, Dahab `Abd al-`Aziz, Mahjoub `Uthman, and Hashim al-Sa`id.

Despite the success of the SCP in establishing a strong base among the railway workers, it had great difficulty in steering the railway workers' movement toward its broad political agenda. While railway workers elected Communists to the SRWU leadership, they often voted for sectarian candidates in national elections. From the perspective of the SCP, workers' voting pattern reflected the absence of a true "class consciousness."[58] Indeed, the party's view reflected its theoretical framework, which conceptualized the working class mainly in terms of its location in the socioeconomic structure and presumed that a "truly" proletarian consciousness is essentially "secular" and "socialist." But workers' attitudes underscored the complex ways in which nonclass elements shaped and transformed their politics. The prevalence of religious and sectarian loyalties among workers was not intrinsic to the railway workers of Atbara but existed in both Muslim and non-Muslim societies. In nineteenth-century France, for instance, many workers supported Catholic organizations instead of working-class parties.[59] It is important to point out that when the railway workers elected Communists to their union and voted for sectarian candidates in national elections, they were not necessarily making a choice between "secularism" and religion. Workers' voting pattern had a lot to do with their strategies and goals. To understand the attitude of the railway workers of Atbara, a number of factors have to be taken into account. As mentioned previously, the overwhelming majority of these workers had little understanding of Marxism-Leninism as a tool for analyzing their conditions. Their election of Communists to the union leadership did not reflect a commitment to revolutionary ideology but was motivated by the desire to improve their working lives. Based on their long experience, the railway workers came to believe that Communist trade-union leaders were better organized and more efficient in achieving their goals. As Hashim al-Sa`id put it, "we were few in numbers and had little resources in comparison with sectarian candidates. But we were more persuasive and better organized."[60] According to al-Hajj `Abd al-Rahman,

> Workers came to associate communists with strikes and uprisings. When they had pressing demands, they elected communists. But strikes were usually costly and sometimes workers wanted to avoid them, in which case they would elect non-communist elements.[61]

Moreover, most workers were preoccupied with daily survival strategies and occupational concerns, and were often oblivious to larger political issues. Despite their affiliation with the SCP, some trade-union leaders—such as al-Hajj `Abd al-Rahman and al-Shafi Ahmad al-Shayth—firmly believed that labor unions were democratic institutions and should remain independent from party politics. For instance, when in 1968 al-Hajj `Abd al-Rahman was elected to represent his constituency in the national parliament in Khartoum, he won because of his popularity as a charismatic trade-union leader. By raising the slogan of "Workers' Power," he defeated the DUP candidate and won 5,204 out of 7,410 votes.[62]

At the same time, the allegiance of railway workers to the sectarian parties should not be taken as a given. Sectarian parties, who always held power during the brief periods of parliamentary democracy, exhibited great hostility toward the labor movement. Apart from their effort to establish a constituency among workers, these parties had no place for labor in their programs, and always detested workers' protests and demands for better working conditions. Sectarian parties focused their attention on gaining the loyalty of a handful of trade-union leaders and paid little attention to grassroot mobilization. On the other hand, the Communists, who had always been in the opposition, were able to mobilize workers around the notion that sectarian parties dominated the state and remained oblivious to workers' concerns.

Several developments affected the position of the SCP among the railway workers in Atbara. In 1964 its Atbara branch lost two of its key leaders: al-Hajj `Abd al-Rahman and Ahmad Shami. The former was elected vice president of the SWTUF and moved to Khartoum. Ahmad Shami and several prominent figures in the SCP such as Yusuf `Abd al-Majid were expelled from the party as a result of ideological differences with the party's leadership. Both were sharply critical of the SCP for being an urban-based party that had neglected farmers and rural producers. The two leaders established a new organization called the *al-Qivada al-thawriyya* (revolutionary command), which adopted Mao Tse Tung's strategy of armed struggle, and focused on the agricultural laborers in the Gezira and in the western parts of the Sudan.

With the departure of Shami and al-Hajj, a younger generation of Communist leaders took over in Atbara. Following Shami's expulsion, Muhammad Ibrahim Kabaj, an engineer from Khartoum University, became the leader of the SCP branch in Atbara. Differences over strategy and organization began to emerge between the old and new generations of activists. Some members of the old generation, for instance, viewed Kabaj as a young man who lacked experience and organizational skills. As a result of growing frictions, Kabaj expelled Hashim al-Sa`id from the party, a decision that was overturned by `Abd al-Khaliq Mahjoub, the SCP secretary general. Hashim al-Sa`id recalled,

> A few weeks after my expulsion, I met `Abd al-Khaliq during one of his visits to Atbara. He invited me to a meeting of the SCP branch. When I told him that I have been expelled, he said: no, you are still a party member. I then accompanied him to the meeting. When we arrived at the venue, `Abd al-Khaliq held my hand and walked with me into the meeting room. In doing so, `Abd al-Khaliq wanted to make it clear to Kabaj that his decision was wrong.[63]

However, in the late 1960s, Hashim al-Sa`id suspended his trade-union and political activities, citing age and his differences with the younger generation of party leaders as the main reasons.

By the late 1960s, the SCP had established a large, powerful cadre in Atbara. This new generation of Communists included many sons and daughters of railway workers, who, unlike their parents, had some level of education. They included students, civil servants, teachers, doctors, engineers, and professionals. These people grew up in working-class families and were inspired by the struggle of their parents.

Atbara was the home of many radical organizations. Its secondary school was a major center of Communist activities and produced many eminent SCP leaders. Other leftist organizations included the Sudanese Youth Union and the Sudanese Women's Union. The latter played a leading role in combating illiteracy among women in Atbara. In the early 1970s the women's union had about 350 active members in Atbara.

It divided the town into nine sections, each with a committee of ten members who organized social and cultural activities in their respective divisions. The union organized adult education classes as well as public lectures and debates on various issues confronting Sudanese women.[64] Student organizations included the League of Communist Students and the Regional Union of Atbara Students, formed by Atbara students at Khartoum University.[65]

The fierce political and ideological competition for the leadership of the SRWU resulted in a high rate of turnover in the union's leadership. In twenty years, nine presidents and ten secretaries served on the executive committee. Of those, only four presidents and four secretaries served for more than one term, and only two presidents and one secretary were elected to four terms.[66] The following list illustrates this pattern.

SRWU Leaders, 1947–1968[67]

Year	President	General Secretary
1947	Sulayman Musa	Al-Tayyib Hasan al-Tayyib
1948	Muhammad `Ali Mahdi	Dahab `Abd al-`Aziz
1949	Muhammad Mahmoud Daoud	`Abdalla Bashir
1950	`Abd al-Qadir `Ali Hamid	Al-Shafi` Ahmad al-Shaykh
1951	`Abd al-Qadir `Ali Hamid	`Abdalla Bashir
1952	Khabir Sulayman	`Ali Muhammad Bashir
1953	Musa Ahmad Mitay	Ahmad Muhammad al-Faki
1954	Hussain Al-Sayyid	Mahjoub `Uthman
1955	Hussain Al-Sayyid	Mahjoub `Uthman
1956	Musa Ahmad Mitay	Mahjoub `Uthman
1957	Musa Ahmad Mitay	Mahjoub `Uthman
1960	`Ali Muhammad Bashir	Al-Hajj `Abd al-Rahman
1964	Musa Ahmad Mitay	Muhammad `Uthman al-Mudir
1965	Muhammad al-Hasan `Abdalla	Hashim al-Sa`id
1966	Muhammad al-Hasan `Abdalla	Hashim al-Sa`id
1967	Muhammad al-Hasan `Abdalla	Hashim al-Sa`id
1968	Muhammad al-Hasan `Abdalla	Muhammad `Uthman al-Mudir

The high turnover meant that union leaders could not entrench their power and use it to gain benefits. Moreover, the stiff competition in the SRWU elections forced union leaders to be more responsive to the demands of the rank and file.

SRWU leaders, many of whom were active in the trade-union movement since the late 1940s, gained vast experience and organizational abilities.

One of the most prominent leaders was Musa Mitay, who was elected as SRWU president several times. As mentioned in chapter 2, Musa joined the SR in 1942 as a permanent-way worker in the engineering division. He was an excellent organizer and a dedicated trade-union leader. Although Musa was not affiliated with any political party, he was known as an ardent anti-Communist, a position that was often exploited by sectarian parties in their effort to control the SRWU. Musa later related that just before the strike of 1966, he was contacted by Isma`il al-Azhari, the president of the republic, who urged him as the leader of the SRWU not to participate in the strike—a request that he agreed to.[68]

By far the most popular SRWU leader was al-Hajj `Abd al-Rahman. Al-Hajj was born in Umbakol, Meroe District, in the 1920s. After completing his education at the Atbara Technical School, he joined the Sudan Railways in 1938 as a fitter in the workshops. Al-Hajj joined the SCP in the 1940s and was an active member of the WAA. In the 1950s and 1960s al-Hajj became known as a fierce and dedicated trade-union leader. He was an outstanding orator and poet, whose spontaneous verse in speeches earned him enormous popularity in Atbara. According to contemporaries and fellow workers, al-Hajj had a remarkable ability to rouse the crowd and organize demonstrations.[69] Al-Hajj died in July 2000.

Another SRWU leader was Muhammad al-Hasan `Abdalla. Like al-Hajj, `Abdalla was from the village of Umbakol in Meroe District, and joined the SR in 1948 in the management division. In the early 1950s `Abdalla became involved in the SRWU, and he held the post of SRWU president several times in the 1960s and 1970s. `Abdalla was known as an excellent organizer and shrewd politician, and was a controversial figure. Despite his affiliation with the DUP, `Abdalla often collaborated with military governments, particularly Nimeiri's regime. As a result, `Abdalla lost credibility among the railway workers.

`Ali Muhammad Bashir was also born in Umbakol and joined the Sudan Railways in the early 1940s, after completing his training at Atbara Technical School. He was one of the founders of the WAA and was elected to the executive committee of the SRWU several times. Bashir was dismissed from the SR in 1961 because of his activities against the military government. In 1965 he was elected to the parliament in Khartoum to represent a district in Atbara.[70]

The profiles of these leaders reveal a number of important characteristics of the SRWU. It is obvious that most of them came from the same geographical region, namely Meroe District in the Northern Province. This is not surprising given the preponderance of people from this area in the railway workforce. However, ethnicity and regional origin did not seem to be an important factor in the politics of the SRWU. These leaders were sharply divided along political and ideological lines. Over the years, two factions evolved: the leftist camp, including al-Hajj `Abd al-Rahman, Hashim al-Sa`id, and Taj al-Sir Hasan Adam, and the opposing camp, including Musa Ahmad Mitay, `Ali Muhammad Bashir, and Muhammad al-Hasan `Abdalla. According to Hashim al-Sa`id, the leftists used to call Musa Mitay, `Abdalla, and Bashir "the opportunists" because they had nothing in common except that they were anti-Communist. But political alliances within the SRWU were fluid. For instance, quite often, Musa Ahmad Mitay, al-Hajj `Abd al-Rahman, and `Ali Muhammad Bashir allied themselves against Muhammad al-Hasan `Abdalla, whose collaboration with military governments made his loyalty to the labor movement suspect, Despite their ideological differences, these leaders had an unwavering loyalty to the institution of trade unionism. To them the SRWU was an essential element of their existence as workers, and they were prepared to overcome their ideological differences to defend it. Al-Hajj ʿAbd al-Rahman recalled that Musa Mitay frequently invited him to record the minutes of the executive committee's meetings, even though he was not a committee member.[71]

Over the years, the SRWU became an important social and political force in the country and conceived a role for itself far beyond issues of wages and working conditions. The SRWU developed a discourse that portrayed the railway workers as a coherent, distinct group, with an important social and political role. In 1968 the union published a long document based on a study it had conducted on wages, housing, cost of living, and structure of the SR—its revenue, expenditure, and performance. The document provided important data on various aspects of railway operations and made a persuasive argument for better wage increases. However, the significance of this document lay in the way in which it illuminated the ideological orientation of the SRWU, and its conception of the role of railway workers in the country's economy and their relation with other employees. The SRWU was sharply critical of the rapid growth in the railway bureaucracy, which it considered parasitic and unproductive.[72]

> It is clear that the rate of increase in the number of officials exceeds that of ordinary workers. This indicates a major flaw in the railway department management. It is more sensible for any institution to expand the work force that is directly involved in the production process.[73]

From the SRWU's perspective, the railway department should have increased the more productive technical posts, which would have given the majority of the rank and file greater opportunity for promotion. Throughout the document, the SRWU contrasted the role of office employees with that of workers, and insisted that it was the latter's sweat that generated revenue and produced a surplus for the SR. To support its argument for a pay raise for ordinary workers, the union used official figures on revenue and expenditure in various railway divisions.[74]

The pamphlet reflected a sharp level of consciousness and a sophisticated understanding of the country's political economy and the impact of international capital on their lives. The document went on to say:

> The fact that the Sudan Railway Corporation is a public sector institution does not mean that it is insulated from the perils of the capitalist enterprise. We should not forget the role of neo-colonialism and its unrelenting effort to control public sector institutions in this country.[75]

Throughout the 1960s and 1970s, the SRWU played numerous roles and became the backbone of the community. It built schools both in Atbara and in outlaying railway stations and organized adult education classes and cooperative societies. Owing to the fact that many workers were stationed in remote areas, the SRWU organized mobile clinics and cooperative shops to provide these workers with their daily needs.[76] The SRWU also gave financial help to families of workers who were injured or who died on the job. The SRWU and other SR unions competed with one another in charitable work. For example, in the late 1970s the SR staff union raised funds to solve the problem of power failures that plagued Atbara during that period, and to improve deteriorating conditions in the hospital. Trade unions organized soccer tournaments and used the proceeds to buy medicine for tuberculosis patients. They also raised funds to help sick workers travel abroad for medical treatment.

The railway workers of Atbara took great pride in the tradition of solidarity and militancy that characterized their town, and celebrated these attributes through poetry, theater, and other forms of expression. As mentioned previously, several labor activists were gifted poets and artists. Poetry played a vital role not only in expressing workers' self-image but also in political mobilization and the development of a culture of protest. The following poem by Hashim al-Sa`id is a good example:[77]

Oh Atbara, mother of the masses and the birth place of history
You gave birth to Qasim, al-Shafi`, and many brothers whose words have
    captivated my mind
You are the home of the engineer, the doctor, and the liberated, brave worker,
    who fulfills his promise and marches like a straight arrow
Despite my past sufferings, I never cease revering you.

Perhaps no one has glorified Atbara and its people as has al-Hajj `Abd al-Rahman. Al-Hajj was known for his ability to compose and deliver poetry instantaneously during political rallies and mass meetings. His poems are vivid illustrations of the political and social climate of the period between the late 1950s and the late 1960s. This was a remarkable era that witnessed both repression and triumph. As mentioned earlier, from 1958 to 1964 the Sudan was ruled by a repressive military regime that exhibited great hostility toward the labor movement and imprisoned many trade-union leaders including al-Hajj. During his detention in Malakal prison, al-Hajj delivered the following poem on the occasion of Sudan's Independence Day. The poem depicted workers' struggle against the military junta as a continuation of a long tradition of anticolonial resistance. Al-Hajj invoked the names of national heroes such as the Mahdi, who overthrew Turco-Egyptian rule in the nineteenth century; Abd al-Qadir Wad Habouba, who led an anti-colonial uprising in 1908; and `Abd al-Fadil al-Maz, an army officer who was one of the leaders of the 1924 uprising.

Today aloft is forearms held
And flags on the masts fly
Oh, my brothers, salute them, salute them
Oh Atbara
Fortress of working people

From you arrows shoot forth
Sound reverberating
Today aloft are forearms held
And flags on the masts fly
Oh, my brothers, salute them, salute them
Oh Atbara
Fortress of working people
From you arrows shoot forth
Sound reverberating
No! We will not betray our cause!
Shields for our country we are
A vanguard vigilant
May the cowardly not rest in peace
May he who holds you in contempt not survive
Oh, my brothers, salute them, salute them
Oh my comrades
March forward
Follow in the exalted paths of the struggle
Inspired by May Day
Learn the lessons of centuries past
The wan puppet is on its way to a bottomless pit
Strike your pickaxes into its grave soil!
Bury all tyrants!
No! You won't haul down the flag
Till you see it perish
Oh, my brothers, salute them, salute them
The people won't accept oppression or harsh treatment
How repeatedly they rose up
The Mahdi—a great testimony
And there was Wad Habonba
A giant in the land of Gezira
And Ibn al-Maz, the lion,
Felling the armies of the aggressor with deadly blows
This is history
If it occurs to you that we accept subordination
Oh, my brothers, salute them, salute them
I vow in the name of my people
In the name of [my] principles, of the [people's] struggle
We won't be intimidated by the old prison
Or the clatter of weapons
We will rush into a red battle
Till we ascend the peaks of accomplishment
Long live my country—strong and mighty
Long live the Party—a pinnacle of achievement.

The following poem reflects the sense of triumph and combativeness that prevailed during the period between the October 1964 uprising and the end of parliamentary rule in 1969. Al-Hajj delivered it instantaneously following his victory in the 1968 general elections.

I am Atbara
The color of iron in flame
I am Atbara
The roar of a lion approaching
I am Atbara
Oh, forces of reaction, you may as well burst into wails
I have broken my chains
No longer weighed down by a burden of culpability or guilt
I am Atbara
A voice from a distant past
For the past twenty years
Fixing my gaze in search of a new dawn
Agonizing chains
And tons of promises
Have I time and again experienced
No, no return to the state of backwardness
The era of servitude is over
I am Atbara
I am the fortress of the working people
I have always sheltered the fierce and audacious in my womb
To set the flame of struggle
Those who drop out are not my offspring
No, Never!
I never sowed weakness in my soil
A harvest for mules!

The poetry of these labor activists was a vivid expression of how the railway workers perceived themselves, their work, and their struggle. In addition to presenting their struggle as an act of bravery and heroism, these poems reflected workers' awareness of their status within the Sudanese society, their physical abilities, and masculine identity.

CONCLUSION

The tradition of labor activism and militancy that began in the late 1940s persisted in the postcolonial era and became the defining characteristic of Atbara. Through their struggle against successive postcolonial governments, the railway workers transformed Atbara into a militant, radical working-class town. Despite increased repression, these workers remained a formidable force against the authoritarian postindependence Sudanese regimes. In view of its pivotal social and political role, the railway workers' union became an arena of intense struggle between radical leftist and sectarian parties. The competition over the control of the SRWU impacted the union in various ways; it meant that the SRWU was not just an organization of collective bargaining, merely concerned with wages and working conditions. At the same time, the continuous intervention of political parties in the internal affairs of the SRWU and their effort to manipulate the workers' struggle to suit their agendas seriously undermined the autonomy of the labor movement and, as will be shown in the following chapter, led to its demise.

NOTES

1. Richard Hill, *Sudan Transport* (London: Oxford University Press, 1965), 124.

2. Sudan Railways Corporation, *History of the Sudan Railways* (Khartoum: Sudan Railways Corporation, 1983), 8.

3. *Sudan Railways Annual Report*, 1963–1968.

4. Sudan Government, *Transport Statistics Bulletin*, 1975.

5. Hill, *Sudan Transport*, 145.

6. Sudan Railways Workers' Union, *Mudhakirat nagabat `ummal al-sikah hadid* (Memorandum by the Sudan Railways Workers' Union) (Atbara, 1968), 5.

7. Ibid., 6.

8. Republic of the Sudan, Department of Statistics, *Population and Housing Survey, 1964/65: Atbara* (Khartoum, October 1966), 8, referred to hereafter as *Population and Housing Survey*.

9. Ibid.

10. Ibid., 10.

11. Ibid., 9.

12. Ibid., 13–14.

13. "Atbara," *Majalat al-Arabi* 154 (1971): 107.

14. *Population and Housing Survey*, 11.

15. Ibid., 31.

16. Ibid.

17. Ibid., 16.

18. In the absence of modern sewage facilities in many Sudanese towns during the early years of the twentieth century, waste was gathered in buckets, which were removed from latrines by conservancy workers at night.

19. Ibid., 17.

20. Sudanese Communist Party, *Thawrat sha`b* (People's revolution) (Khartoum: SCP, n.d.), 71.

21. Abdel-Rahman el Tayib Ali Taha, "The Sudanese Labor Movement: A Study of Labor Unionism in a Developing Society" (Ph.D. diss., University of California, Los Angeles, 1970), 108.

22. NRO, 4 NP 2/2/6, Northern Province Police Report, 16 November–15 December 1958 (referred to hereafter as NP Police Report).

23. Ibid.

24. NP Police Report, 16 January–15 February 1959.

25. Ibid., 16 April–15 May 1959.

26. Ibid.

27. All were trade-union leaders.

28. NP Police Report, 16 May–15 June 1959.

29. Ibid., 16 August–15 September 1959.

30. Ibid., 16 September–15 October 1959.

31. SCP, *Thawrat sha`b*, 90.

32. Taha, "The Sudanese Labor Movement," 111.

33. NP Police Report, 16 January–15 February 1960.

34. Ibid., 16 December 1960–15 January 1961.

35. Ibid., 16 February–15 March 1961.

36. SCP, *Thawrat sha`b*, 110.

37. Taha, "The Sudanese Labor Movement," 113.

38. Hasan Ahmad al-Shaykh, interview by author, Atbara, 13 October 1999.

39. Ahmad Shami, interview by author, Khartoum, 1 September 1996.

40. This episode was also confirmed by al-Hajj `Abd al-Rahman, interview, 23 August 1995.

41. NP Police Report, 16 June–15 July 1961, and 16 August–15 September 1961.

42. Ibid.

43. Ibid., 16 November–15 December 1963.

44. Ibid.

45. Ibid.

46. Ibid., 16 January–15 February 1964.

47. Ibid., 16 December 1963–15 January 1964.

48. Ibid., 16 January–5 February 1964.

49. Ibid., 16 February–5 March 1964.

50. SCP *Thawrat sha`b*, 137–38.

51. Ibid.

52. Ibid., 140.

53. NP Police Report, 16 May–15 June 1964.

54. Ibid., 16 July–15 August 1964.

55. For more details, see Taha, "The Sudanese Labor Movement," 129–31.

56. Sudan Railways Workers' Union, *Silver Jubilee of the SRWU* (Atbara: SRWU, July 1997), 15.

57. Sudan Railways Workers' Union, Constitution of the Sudan Railways Workers' Union (Atbara: al-Rashid Press, 1968).

58. Al-Hajj `Abd al-Rahman, interview by author, Khartoum, 23 August 1995.

59. Ronald Aminzade, "Class Analysis, Politics, and French Labor History," in *Rethinking Labor History: Essays on Discourse and Class Analysis*, ed. Lenard Berlanstein (Urbana: University of Illinois Press, 1993), 90–113.

60. Hashim al-Sa`id, interview by author, Khartoum, 23 August 2001.

61. `Abd al-Rahman, interview.

62. Abdel Rahim El-Rayh, "Political Process in Atbara Town" (B.A. diss. University of Khartoum, 1970), 27.

63. Al-Sa`id, interview.

64. Ibid., 118–19. El Rayn "Political Process in Atbara Town"

65. Ibid.

66. See appendix 5.

67. Taha, "The Sudanese Labor Movement," 186.

68. Interview Musa Mitay, October 12, 1999.

69. Shami, interview.

70. SRWU *Silver Jubilee of the SRWU*, 7.

71. `Abd al-Rahman, interview.

72. *Mudhakirat Ithad al-`Ummal*, 1968, 2–4.

73. Ibid., 7.

74. Ibid., 11.

75. Ibid., 16.

76. "Atbara," 115.

77. Al-Sa`id, interview.

6

ATBARA UNDER THE MAY REGIME, 1969–1984

In the preceding narrative we have seen the transformation of Atbara from an obscure military depot into a vibrant railway town and a center of labor activism. The period between 1906 and the late 1960s was indeed an era of remarkable demographic and spatial growth, profound social change, and growing labor militancy and political assertiveness. By the early 1980s, however, these trends had reversed, and Atbara had lost the prominence it had enjoyed for more than half a century. Arguably, this drastic change was a product of the policies of the military regime of Ja`far Nimeiri, which ruled the Sudan from May 1969 to April 1985. This period witnessed an unprecedented level of repression against the labor movement in general and the railway workers in particular. By the time of Nimeiri's downfall in 1985, the railway workers movement had been crushed, the railway department itself had been ruined, and Atbara had sunk into decay. The primary goal of this chapter, therefore, is to examine the conditions that led to Atbara's political and economic decline, and to chronicle the struggle of its railway workers against the powerful forces unleashed by the May regime.

This chapter contends that beyond the repressive policies of the May regime, the decline of Atbara must be examined in the context of the profound socioeconomic changes that took place during the 1970s and 1980s. The open-door policy of the May regime, the intensification of capitalist investment—particularly in agriculture—and the growing emphasis on road transport had a huge impact on the Sudan Railways. Moreover, the collapse of the railway workers' movement was a direct result of the coercive policies of the May regime, the dramatic changes in the political landscape in the country, and the internal problems of the movement itself.

THE MAY REGIME AND ITS LEGACY[1]

The year 1969 marked the beginning of a new era in postcolonial Sudanese history. In addition to major socioeconomic transformation, Nimeiri's policies changed the political map of the Sudan in a lasting way. Within two years of his coming to power, Nimeiri had dealt serious blows to both the sectarian establishment and the Sudanese left. In 1972 he concluded the Addis Ababa Agreement, which ended the seventeen-year civil war and brought relative peace and stability to the South. However, Nimeiri's policies in the early 1980s led to resumption of the civil war, which has continued until today. The resumption of civil war, Nimeiri's authoritarian rule, and acute economic hardships became the main catalyst for the popular uprising of April 1985, which brought down the May regime.

The policy of the May regime toward the labor movement can be divided into two distinctive phases: May 1969 to July 1971, and July 1971 to April 1985. During the first phase, the regime raised radical, socialist slogans, and exhibited great hostility toward the sectarian parties. Although the Sudanese Communist Party (SCP) had long opposed military coups, the junta's antisectarian and radical pronouncements appealed to certain elements within the SCP, who believed that they could transform the coup into a revolutionary regime. Hence, the SCP mobilized a large number of trade unions and gave the new regime strong popular support, without which it could not have survived.

Following the coup, the junta dissolved parliament, banned all political parties, restricted freedom of the press, and ruled through decrees. The supreme authority in the country was vested in a Revolutionary Command Council (RCC). Three of the RCC members had close ties to the SCP: Babikir al-Nur, Hashim al-`Atta, and Farouq Hamdalla. The civilian cabinet also included a number of prominent Communists, such as Farouq `Abu `Isa, Mahjoub `Uthman, and Joseph Garang. The influence of the SCP on policy during the first two years was manifested in the nationalization of foreign-owned businesses and banks and in the introduction of several educational and social reforms.

Nonetheless, from the beginning, relations between the SCP and the May regime were marred by serious tension. A military coup that raised socialist slogans created a major dilemma for the SCP; while some factions within it put great hopes in the junta and were willing to cooperate with it, most were not. Prominent among those in the former group were `Umar Mustafa al-Makki, Ahmad Sulayman, and Mu`awiyya Ibrahim, who became convinced that the new regime could bring about radical changes. `Abd al-Khaliq Mahjoub—the secretary general of the SCP—and the bulk of the party considered what happened in May 1969 as nothing more than a military coup, led by petty bourgeois elements.[2] Mahjoub was not prepared to compromise the party's autonomy and risk losing the strong social base it had built over the years among workers, tenants, students, and women. In the end, the party split into two factions: Mu`awiyya Ibrahim and his group joined the regime, while `Abd al-Khaliq Mahjoub and the bulk of the party remained cautious and continued to criticize the regime's policies.[3]

Differences between the SCP and the May regime centered on a number of key issues, the most important of which was the future of the party itself. The centerpiece of the regime's philosophy was to establish a single party, representing workers, peasants, soldiers, the national bourgeoisie, the progressive intelligentsia, and the armed forces. This line of thought was advocated by the Pan-Arabist elements within the RCC, including Nimeiri himself, who hoped to model the new party after Egypt's Arab Socialist Union. Consequently, this group demanded that the SCP dissolve itself and become part of a popular front, embracing progressive elements in the country. Another source of conflict was the junta's effort to form a union with Egypt and Libya. The SCP was apprehensive about the Sudan's union with what it considered petty bourgeoisie regimes.

Tensions between the SCP and the May regime rose steadily toward the end of 1970 and the first half of 1971. In November 1970, for instance, Nimeiri's faction ejected Babikir al-Nur, Hashim al-`Atta, and Farouq Hamdalla from the RCC for their support of the SCP position. `Abd al-Khaliq Mahjoub was briefly banished to Egypt. After his return, he continued to criticize the regime, which led to his detention in a military camp in the southern part of Khartoum in the summer of 1971. However, with the help of some Communist officers, `Abd al-Khaliq Mahjoub escaped and remained in hiding until the coup of July 1971.

To the bulk of the SCP, the expulsion of the three RCC members was nothing less than a right-wing coup. Following their expulsion, the three officers and their leftist comrades in the army began to make plans to overthrow Nimeiri. On July 19, 1971, Hashim al-`Atta staged a coup and arrested Nimeiri and leading members of the RCC as well as many senior army officers. The aim of the July coup, according to al-`Atta, was to return to the "revolutionary path" from which the May regime had strayed. The extent to which the SCP was involved in the coup is still a subject of great debate. The official view of the SCP was that the military wing of the party had acted unilaterally despite the strong opposition of the civilian leadership.

Al-`Atta's coup lasted only three days. He and his comrades overlooked the fact that the public was not ready for a Communist takeover. They also failed to gain the support of the bulk of the army. Another critical factor was the hostility of neighboring countries, particularly Egypt and Libya, which were not willing to tolerate a Communist regime in the Sudan and were prepared to go to any length to topple it. For instance, Anwar Sadat of Egypt had begun to make plans to dispatch Sudanese troops stationed at the Suez Canal to restore Nimeiri to power. On July 22, a Khartoum-bound British Airways flight carrying Babikir al-Nur and Farouq Hamdalla was forced by Libyan jet fighters to land in Tripoli, where the two officers were arrested and later handed over to Nimeiri.

On the afternoon of July 22, troops loyal to Nimeiri staged a counter-coup and restored him to power. A period of bloodshed followed: Hashim al-`Atta, Babikir al-Nur, Farouq Hamdalla, and several leftist officers were executed by firing squad. `Abd al-Khaliq Mahjoub; al-Shafi` Ahmad al-Shaykh, president of the Sudanese Workers' Trade Union Federation (SWTUF); and Joseph Garang were hanged. A general witch-hunt of Communists ensued. Hundreds of SCP members, trade-union leaders, and other leftists were rounded up and detained.

Although Nimeiri emerged victorious, he realized that he could not rely on the support of the army alone. Hence, he began to search for a new ally. It was in this context that he made peace with the South. Although the Addis Ababa Agreement increased his popularity in the South, it remained unpopular in the North and continued to be criticized by the sectarian parties.

Following the destruction of the SCP and the peaceful settlement of the civil war, the May regime proceeded to build its political institutions. One of the most important steps in this direction was the launching of the Sudanese Socialist Union (SSU). Although the idea of establishing a single-party system was conceived during the early days of the regime, the SSU did not take shape until 1974. Former Communists and pan-Arabists, who dominated the SSU, envisaged a radical, mass-based organization that could shift the balance of power away from the sectarian forces in the country. However, following the failed Communist coup, Nimeiri turned away from these groups and began to rely on technocrats—namely university lecturers, lawyers, engineers, doctors, and civil servants—who dominated his cabinet and became his close advisors. They included J`afar Muhammad `Ali Bakheit, Mansour Khalid, Ibrahim Mun`im Mansur, Bashir `Abbadi, Ahmad `Abd al-Halim, and Muhammad `Uthman Abu Saq. Most of these technocrats had received graduate degrees from Western European and American universities. They were highly westernized in outlook and lifestyle. Although they had no particular ideological orientation, they all shared anti-Communist and antisectarian sentiments. They stressed economic development as the only means to "modernize" the country and weaken sectarian domination. In fact, throughout its existence, the SSU was plagued by lack of clear ideological vision, elitist tendencies, and rampant bureaucracy. Moreover, Nimeiri's increasing authoritarianism and the rampant corruption and inefficiency prompted some of the technocrats—such as Mansour Khalid and Ibrahim Mun`im Mansur—to defect.

In the meantime, sectarian parties continued to mount opposition to Nimeiri's rule from their bases in Libya and Ethiopia. They made several coup attempts, but failed to topple the regime. In the end, both sides were exhausted and decided to come to terms with one another. As a result of the so-called "national reconciliation," which was launched in the late 1970s, leaders of the sectarian parties and the Muslim Brothers returned to the country and joined the May regime.

Nimeiri's incorporation of sectarian and Islamicist forces had serious repercussions. Of particular importance was his alliance with the Muslim Brothers, who seized the opportunity and built a strong political and economic base. The most vivid example of their growing influence on Nimeiri was the introduction in September 1983 of the so-called *shari`a* laws, and the execution in January 1985 of Mahmoud Muhammad Taha, leader of the Republican Brothers movement and a fierce critic of the Muslim Brothers. As mentioned earlier, these policies as well as the resumption of civil war and the acute economic hardships became the catalyst for Nimeiri's downfall.

One of the most important legacies of Nimeiri's rule was the profound transformation of the Sudanese economy and society. The post–July 1971 period witnessed a remarkable shift to the right as the regime abandoned its socialist slogans and reversed the economic policies of the first two years. It encouraged foreign investment, particularly from Western Europe, the United States, Japan, and the oil-producing Arab countries. In the context of the Cold War environment, Nimeiri's anti-Communist policies appealed to Western countries. A spate of loans from the

United States, Britain, the International Monetary Fund, and the World Bank poured into the Sudan. The greater part of foreign capital was directed toward agriculture.

The promotion of capitalist agriculture was part of the so-called "breadbasket" policy, which was premised on the notion that given its abundant land and water resources, the Sudan could supply food to the entire Middle East. To achieve this goal, a number of agricultural schemes, financed by Arab capital, were launched. Saudi Arabia and Kuwait provided the lion's share of this investment.[4]

Among the most important projects developed during this period were the Rahad Scheme and the Jongeli Canal. The latter involved the construction of a 175-mile canal bypassing the White Nile sudd as a means of improving the river flow to meet Egypt's growing demand for water. However, the crown jewel of the breadbasket strategy was the 350-million-dollar Kenana Sugar Scheme in which Lonrho, a British conglomerate, was a major investor. Another important project was the one-million-acre cattle farm, developed by AZL International, a subsidiary of Arizona, Colorado Land and Cattle Company.[5] Arab and Western European capital was also involved in the development of such industries as textiles, matches, soap, and glass. Some of these industries were later taken over by the Kuwaiti-owned Gulf International.

The breadbasket strategy was hampered by a number of factors. Most projects failed as a result of poor planning, high cost, mismanagement, and corruption. Eventually these projects drained the country's economy and increased its foreign debt. Following the usual prescriptions of the IMF and the World Bank, the government devalued the Sudanese currency and removed subsidies from consumer goods, which impoverished the overwhelming majority of the working population.

Nonetheless, the breadbasket strategy had its beneficiaries; these included a small group of foreign and local Sudanese entrepreneurs. The most notable foreigners were Roland Rowland of Lonrho and `Adnan Kashogi, the Saudi businessman whose dubious deals in the Sudan and close links with Nimeiri generated a major controversy.[6] Local beneficiaries included Khalil `Uthman, who—with the help of Kuwaiti financing—established Gulf International Corporation, and Muhammad `Abdu Rabbou, a Sudanese of Yemeni origin with strong connections to South Korean businesses. Members of Nimeiri's family established the Wad Nimeiri Cooperative Society, which engaged in various commercial activities and amassed considerable wealth.

By the early 1980s a new class of Sudanese bourgeoisie had emerged. It included merchants, agricultural entrepreneurs, civil servants, army officers, and a large number of parasites.[7] Members of this class flaunted their wealth in ways that were alien to Sudanese society. They engaged in conspicuous consumption of luxury goods, lived in opulent houses, owned expensive cars, held lavish wedding ceremonies, and spent most of their time in Europe and North America.

On the other hand, the open door and the breadbasket policies created tremendous economic hardships for urban workers who could not cope with the rising cost of living. At the same time, rural folk who had been displaced by famine and civil wars flocked in large numbers to the urban centers, particularly the towns of Khartoum, Khartoum North, and Omdurman. Thousands of refugees and unemployed people swelled the streets of the capital in the late 1970s and early 1980s and posed a serious threat to the regime's stability. After a series of riots in the mid-1970s, the government launched a crude campaign known as *kasha* (rounding up) to expel unemployed and displaced people from the capital. But the kasha did not stop the flow of rural immigrants, famine victims, and displaced persons. It was these groups who spearheaded the popular uprising of April 1985.

THE MAY REGIME AND THE LABOR MOVEMENT

The dramatic shift in the orientation of the May regime was clearly reflected in its policy toward the labor movement. During the "leftist" phase, between 1969 and July 1971, the regime made persistent efforts to elicit the support of the labor movement, particularly the Sudan Workers' Trade Union Federation (SWTUF). The SWTUF was responsible for organization of the famous June march, in which thousands of workers participated to show their support for the new regime. Four months after the May coup, the government issued a decree ordering a 25 percent reduction in housing rent for low-income workers.[8] The Labor Department was elevated to a Ministry of Labor, headed by Taha Ba`shar, a psychiatrist and prominent member of the SCP. A committee, chaired by al-Shafi` Ahmad al-Shaykh and made up of representatives of several trade unions and employee associations, was named to reform existing labor legislation. The minister of labor told the committee to develop labor legislation that reflected "socialist concepts and ideals." Based on the committee's recommendations, a Consolidated Labor Code was enacted in November 1970. The code stipulated new guidelines for establishment of trade unions and gave apprentices and workers in small establishments the right to form unions. The legislation led to a dramatic increase in the number of unions and their memberships. The code also emphasized the need for labor "unity" and prohibited formation of trade-union federations that could compete with the SWTUF. Moreover, the legislation protected union leaders from dismissal and retaliation by employers. To ensure workers' participation in decision making, the code created three councils in which workers, employers, and the government were represented. These were the Supreme Labor Council, headed by the minister of labor and charged with the task of making policies on all aspects of work organization and industrial relations; the Manpower and Training Council; and the Work Relations Council. The last two were advisory bodies to the Supreme Labor Council. The code stated that in each council, workers' representatives should constitute at least half of the membership.

In return for these concessions, workers were asked to forgo wage demands, increase production, and support the May regime. Moreover, workers lost the right to strike, which was prohibited and considered a criminal offense.[9] In other words, the new legislation actually increased government control of trade unions. Even these limited reforms were soon removed. Two months after its promulgation, the Consolidated Labor Code was repealed and pre-1969 labor legislation was reinstated. The Trade Union Act of 1971 revoked the right of apprentices to form trade unions and made a sharp distinction between white- and blue-collar workers in terms of rights and pay. The new legislation clearly stated that the role of trade unions was to increase production and defend the rights of their members within the framework of the existing laws. It also gave the minister of labor unlimited authority to deal with unions and empowered the registrar of trade unions to suspend the activity of any union that engaged in "illegal" activity. Finally, the legislation made strikes a criminal offense punishable under the State Security Act.[10]

The hostility of the May regime toward the labor movement increased dramatically after the July 1971 coup. As far as Nimeiri was concerned, the SWTUF was nothing more than a shadow of the SCP, and he accused its members of being implicated in the failed coup. This was Nimeiri's justification for the execution of al-Shafi` Ahmad al-Shaykh. But many of al-Shafi`'s close associates asserted that he was not involved in planning the coup, nor did he support it. One of those intimately familiar with the events of July 1971 was al-Hajj `Abd al-Rahman, who was secretary of the SWTUF at the time. According to al-Hajj, the July coup came as a big surprise to leaders of the federation, including al-Shafi` himself. He recalled that a day after the coup, Hashim al-`Atta held a meeting with the federation's leaders in an attempt to enlist their support. During the meeting, both al-Hajj and al-Shafi` made it clear that they must first consult with the rank and file before they declared a position toward the coup. According to al-Hajj, Hashim al-`Atta was not pleased with this response and left the meeting highly disappointed. After the meeting, the SWTUF leaders agreed that the federation should adopt a neutral position toward the coup. Al-Hajj and al-Shafi` were stunned when a few hours later they heard a statement broadcast on Omdurman radio declaring that the SWTUF supports the coup. Al-Hajj related that al-Shafi` was enraged and vowed to distribute a leaflet stating the neutrality of the SWTUF.[11] The leaflet was distributed on July 22, during a march the SCP had organized to support the new regime. However, a few hours later, al-`Atta was ousted and Nimeiri returned to power.

As mentioned earlier, the period after July 22 witnessed a wave of executions and detentions involving hundreds of Communists and leftist labor activists. Al-Hajj himself was detained for two years despite the fact that he was a member of the SCP faction that had broken away from the party and supported the May regime. He later recalled that during his detention he was questioned several times by both Nimeiri and Abu al-Qasim Muhammad Ibrahim about al-Shafi`'s involvement in the July coup. During one of these visits al-Hajj recalled that Abu al-Qasim Mohammad Ibrahim asked him about the link between the July coup and the SWTUF. According to al-Hajj, "I told him that there was no link between them; the SWTUF is a democratic institution that represents the workers, while the July coup was a political movement. I told him that I am not saying this because I am afraid. At that moment, I didn't care if I lived or died. My sole purpose was to prove that al-Shafi` was innocent."[12] Al-Hajj's story is consistent with the general image of al-Shafi`—that of a trade-union leader who, despite his political affiliation, was a fierce defender of the autonomy of the labor movement.

Following the purge of Communist and leftist elements from trade unions, the government established in 1973 a preparatory committee to hold elections for the SWTUF. For the next several years the federation was dominated by pro-May elements such as `Abdalla Nasr Ginawi of the Survey Department, Muhammad `Uthman Jumm`a, Mahjoub al-Zubair, and Taj al-Sir `Abdoun. Moreover, in its effort to co-opt the labor movement, all trade unions became a tributary of the SSU.

The ideology underpinning the attitude of the May regime toward the labor movement was best expressed by Ja`far Muhammad `Ali Bakheit, the political philosopher of the regime. In a series of articles published in *al-Sahafa* newspaper in May 1975, Bakheit outlined what he considered the proper role of the labor movement in Sudanese society.[13] He began by asserting that the SSU was not a labor party but a vehicle through which workers could become part of the ruling institutions. He argued that trade unions should strive to transform the labor movement into a viable economic force. Unions, according to Bakheit, should promote literacy among the rank and file and educate their leaders by sending them to universities and training centers. With the approach of the twenty-first century, he continued, the labor movement should abandon such old-fashioned concepts as class struggle, which stemmed from the experience of the industrial revolution in Europe. Bakheit contended that Marxist concepts of class oppression and the dictatorship of the proletariat were not only outdated but irrelevant to the Sudan, where family ties superseded class loyalties.

THE RAILWAY WORKERS AND THE MAY REGIME

The railway workers of Atbara received the lion's share of Nimeiri's reprisals in the aftermath of the July 1971 coup. In the ensuing wave of detentions and dismissals, 245 railway workers were discharged. The majority of these were from the workshops and the traffic division, which were known for many years as Communist strongholds.[14] Although some of them were reinstated, the purge of leftist elements from the railways continued throughout Nimeiri's rule.

In order to weaken the railway workers' movement, Nimeiri decided to undermine the institution from which they drew their power, namely the railway department. His strategy involved increasing government control of the department and changing its administrative and organizational structure, with the ultimate goal of breaking up the concentration of workers in Atbara.

Until the late 1960s the Sudan Railways was an independent government agency, directed by a board, with a separate budget and considerable administrative autonomy. Following the May coup, the board was dissolved and the SR was brought under direct government control. After the failed Communist coup in July 1971, the government converted the SR into the Sudan Railways Corporation (SRC). The corporation was run by a board of directors, which included the general manager and representatives from the ministries of transport and communications, finance and economic planning, and civil service; two trade-union officers; and four experts in economics and transport.[15] Under the general manager were the directors of the various divisions. During the same year, the catering and the steamers divisions became separate units.

In February 1974, the minister of transport and communications formed two subcommittees to study the organizational structure and the conditions of service in the SR. A month later, the harbor division was separated, which deprived the SRC of a major source of income.[16] New social services, research, and training divisions were established and attached to the general manager's office. Although there was a strong need to reform the railways, Nimeiri's primary goal was to disperse the railway workers of Atbara and decrease their political influence.

WAGE STRUCTURE AND WORKING CONDITIONS

One of the central issues in the struggle between the labor movement and the May regime was the wage structure inherited from the colonial period. In 1974 the government introduced a new job classification scheme, with the intention of narrowing the wage gap between workers in the public and private sectors, and providing clear job descriptions for various categories of employees.[17] According to the new scheme, the minimum monthly wage for the lowest paid worker rose from LS 16.170 to LS 18.150. However, given its complex job hierarchy, the implementation of the scheme in the SRC faced serious difficulties. In 1975 the SRC formed a committee to reform its own wage structure, but it took the corporation three years to implement the recommendations of the committee. It was only after workers protested that the first phase of the scheme was introduced in 1978. The new wage structure adopted by the SRC is shown in Table 6.1.

Table 6.1   Sudan Railways Job Evaluation Scheme, 1978

Grade	Minimum wage	Maximum Wage
I	23.075	31.825
II	25.642	40.642
III	36.532	41.542
IV	42.700	48.100
V	57.192	62.967
VI	68.000	76.325
VII	85.775	97.075

The new scheme drew sharp criticism from the railway workers who resented the fact that they had not been consulted during its preparation. Their strongest objection, however, was that the new scheme did not reflect the varying skill levels among railway employees. According to the new wage structure, a fitter who completed technical school was placed in the same grade as the engine cleaner, who had elementary education. Similarly, the foreman and charge man would remain in the same grade for more than thirty years without promotion.

In response to workers' opposition, the wage scheme was revised and reintroduced in 1980, and is shown in Table 6.2.[18]

However, the rapid rate of inflation rendered these wage increases meaningless. Between 1970 and 1980, for instance, the cost of living in the country rose by about 102.6 percent. Moreover, following World Bank and IMF recommendations, the government withdrew its subsidies from such basic commodities as sugar, flour, and petrol, which sparked off a wave of labor unrest by various groups of workers. In the early 1980s, railway workers engaged in fierce battles with the May regime over the issues of wages and living conditions. At the heart of this struggle was the Sudan Railways Workers' Union (SRWU), whose position during the May regime deserves special attention.

The SRWU during the May Regime

Under the May regime, the SRWU vacillated between collaboration and confrontation. As mentioned previously, the period after the abortive communist coup witnessed increased repression of leftist elements. As a result, the leadership of the

Table 6.2   Sudan Railways Revised Job Evaluation Scheme, 1980

Grade	Wage
I	40.67
II	49.25
III	58.75
IV	73.00
V	93.81
VI	118.40
VII	124.66

SRWU was captured by anti-Communist and sectarian leaders such as Musa Mitay, who became the union president from 1972 to 1974. Musa joined the SSU and became a member of its central committee. Early in 1973 he was honored by the government, and during the ceremony, Nimeiri embraced him and invited him to his house.[19]

However, Musa's relation with the May regime was short lived. The SRWU leadership came under growing pressure from the rank and file to press for wage increases and improvements in working conditions. For example, in response to a 1973 increase in the price of sugar, cooking oil, and other consumer goods, railway workers marched to union headquarters and forced the executive committee to declare a general strike.[20] Other unions in various government departments followed suit. Strikes and demonstrations spread to other Sudanese towns such as Khartoum, Wad Medani, and Kosti, forcing the government to reverse its price increase.

The anti-Nimeiri forces took advantage of the deteriorating economic conditions and established links with the SRWU. After the May coup, the sectarian parties and the Muslim Brothers formed a National Front, whose main goal was to overthrow Nimeiri and restore parliamentary rule. Although the front operated from exile, it managed to establish a strong base inside the country, particularly among the students of Khartoum University, where its sympathizers controlled the student union. In an attempt to organize a popular uprising similar to that of October 1964, the front encouraged various student organizations and labor unions to declare a general strike. In September 1973 Khartoum University and secondary school students organized large-scale demonstrations in Khartoum. The unrest spread to other towns, prompting the government to declare a state of emergency. What came to be known as the *Sha`ban intifada* (September uprising) was perhaps the most serious threat to the May regime since 1971. In sympathy with the students, the SRWU declared a general strike, demanding a wage increase and other improvements. The government response to the unrest was swift and severe. In addition to deploying the police and the army to suppress demonstrations, it closed down Khartoum University for several months and arrested many student and trade-union leaders. Musa himself was detained for eight months.[21]

The defeat of the September uprising was followed by a campaign against labor activists and union leaders, many of whom were either dismissed or detained. The government tried to create an atmosphere of terror among the railway workers by recruiting informants and placing spies in the workplace and in residential neighborhoods. This campaign paved the way for the emergence of pro-government leaders who dominated the SRWU. They were best exemplified by the late Muhammad al-Hasan `Abdalla, who held the post of SRWU president from 1974 to 1978. The executive committee included `Uthman Ali Fadl—general secretary—and Kambal Bashir—treasurer.

The new SRWU leadership not only supported the May regime but also helped in its campaign to weaken the railway workers' movement. In addition to their open collaboration with the government, `Abdalla and his group engaged in several controversial activities. For instance, in the mid-1970s, the SRWU leaders became involved in buying and selling consumer goods such as sugar, sorghum, charcoal, flour, cooking oil, and meat. In justifying these activities, union leaders contended that their objective was to combat the rampant black market and provide workers with consumer goods at low prices. However, there was widespread suspicion among the rank and file that union leaders, particularly `Abdalla, had amassed considerable wealth from these commercial dealings. Despite his vast experience as a trade-union leader and his remarkable organizational skills, `Abdalla's reputation was seriously damaged, and he came to be viewed by many workers as corrupt and opportunist.

Faced with deteriorating living conditions and a pro-government union, the railway workers decided to take matters into their own hands. On April 2, 1978, thousands of workers in Atbara marched to the union's headquarters and demanded the resignation of the executive committee and election of a new one. When `Abdalla tried to address the angry crowd, he was physically attacked but managed to escape with police help. It was only after the railway management promised to take action within forty-eight hours that workers agreed to disperse. As the deadline passed and no decision was made, workers staged another demonstration and occupied the union headquarters. In an attempt to resolve the dispute, a delegation from the Peoples' National Assembly arrived at Atbara. The delegation appealed to workers to return to work and chose representatives to negotiate with the government.

During the negotiation with the government, workers' representatives remained adamant about their demands of holding new elections and reducing the prices of consumer goods. On April 6 the minister of transport and communications visited Atbara to contain the situation. But his reiteration of the government position that the executive committee would not be dissolved without the approval of the general assembly convinced workers of the futility of negotiations and prompted them to declare a work slowdown until their demands were met.

On April 11 Abu al-Qasim Muhammad Ibrahim, the vice president, went to Atbara, where he was scheduled to address the railway workers at the football stadium. The workers refused to meet him there and insisted that he address them at the SRWU headquarters. Abu al-Qasim gave a provocative speech in which he reiterated the government refusal to dissolve the executive committee, and went on to say that the "May Revolution" would not tolerate strikes.[22] The vice president's remarks did nothing but toughen the workers' position. In the end, however, the government conceded by agreeing to dissolve the executive committee and hold new elections. This episode was dubbed the April *intifada* and was regarded by the railway workers as another landmark in a long history of struggle.

An episode that took place during the meeting between the vice president and the railway workers had a profound impact on the railway workers' movement. It was reported that at the beginning of the meeting, the vice president asked the workers to explain the reasons for their opposition to `Abdalla's leadership. However, the presence of a large number of security agents and the fear of reprisals forced many workers to remain silent. The only person who dared to stand up and attack `Abdalla and his group was a worker named `Abbas al-Khidir al-Hussain. `Abbas's speech prompted huge applause and cheers by workers, and encouraged others to stand up and assail `Abdalla. The episode instantly elevated `Abbas from an obscure figure to a hero. Prior to this, `Abbas was known only as a very pious person who had no involvement in the labor movement. However, he was known to be a sympathizer with the Muslim Brotherhood movement. His speech in front of the vice president gained him great popularity among the workers and changed his career forever. During subsequent union elections, `Abbas became the president of the SRWU.

Despite their precarious position, the leftists won five seats on the executive committee. This meant that the committee was sharply divided along ideological lines, with the Muslim Brothers and sectarian elements on one side, and the leftists on the other. Given their deep hostility toward the Communists, it is not surprising that the Muslim Brothers and their sectarian allies expelled the five leftist members on the grounds that they were "obstructionists."[23]

Under `Abbas al-Khidir al-Hussain's leadership, the SRWU witnessed major changes not only in its ideological orientation but also in its organizational structure. A new constitution was officially adopted on June 15, 1979. The general assembly, which consisted of 265 members representing the various railway divisions, remained the highest authority.[24] The executive committee consisted of eighty-five members of whom eighteen came from the workshops, twelve from the headquarters, twelve from the engineering division, seven from the stores, six from the steamers, six from the catering division, and six from each of the four regional centers. The committee elected the president, the vice president, the secretary and his assistant, and the treasurer and his deputy. According to the constitution, these officers had to reside in Atbara.[25]

The Islamicist orientation of the new leadership was clearly reflected in the content and language of the new constitution. The preamble stated that the main objective of the SRWU was to "preserve the unity and the basic rights of the railway workers and the country," and to safeguard the trade-union movement against "ideological deviance and dogmatism." It went on to emphasize that the union should endeavor to unite the railway workers and inculcate them with the "noble Sudanese ethos" that reflected the country's Muslim tradition.[26] It was stated that the main goal of the SRWU was to defend workers' rights, improve their working conditions and educational standards, and help them acquire technical skills both locally and abroad. Moreover, the union should encourage workers to establish cooperative societies and help each other in case of illness and need. In other words, from the perspective of the new leaders, the SRWU should refrain from politics and focus on occupational and social issues. But given the harsh economic realities facing workers, it was difficult to maintain this line. Under pressure coming from below, the SRWU staged a major confrontation three years later with the May regime.

THE 1981 STRIKE AND ITS AFTERMATH

On April 2, 1981, the SRWU submitted a petition to the government, demanding a reduction in the prices of consumer goods, the supply of Atbara hospital with medicine and equipment, the provision of school supplies, the eradication of the black market, and the enforcement of price control measures. However, the government dismissed these demands as nothing more than a conspiracy orchestrated by the Communists and the "enemies of the revolution." In response, the SRWU announced a general strike, scheduled for April 20, 1981. Two days before the strike, the government dismissed thirty union leaders.[27] At this point, the executive committee split on how to respond; while one faction called for an immediate general strike, the majority advocated the delay of the strike until other avenues were exhausted. Consequently, a delegation was sent to Khartoum to negotiate with the authorities.

At the beginning of the negotiations, workers' representatives made it clear that they would not proceed unless the dismissed thirty union leaders were reinstated. Government officials insisted that the dismissed workers must submit written appeals, and then each case would be dealt with separately. Workers' representatives rejected this proposition and insisted that their colleagues must be returned. As the deadlock continued for three weeks, workers' frustration grew. On May 30 the SRWU announced that unless workers demands were met, it would stage a five-day strike. On the following day, the government dissolved the SRWU, alleging that it was organizing an illegal strike that was part of a larger conspiracy. In response, the SRWU announced another five-day strike.[28] Nimeiri was infuriated and decided to take drastic action against the railway workers.

On June 16, Nimeiri issued a republican decree, in which he authorized his security agents to arrest the SRWU leaders and announced the formation of a committee to plan the decentralization of the SRC. The committee was asked to submit its report within three weeks. Finally, the decree stipulated the establishment of a "strategic railway battalion" composed of retired and active soldiers to operate and maintain the railway system during the strike.[29]

The following day Nimeiri delivered a speech in al-Ubayyid, capital of Kordofan Province, during which he assailed the railway workers, describing them as parasites who were draining the country's resources.[30] Nimeiri defended his dismissal of the thirty union leaders by stating that he had strong evidence that they were members of the Communist Party, and went on to point out that it was the union's president who recommended their dismissal.[31] Nimeiri took this opportunity to attack the railway corporation, describing it as a failed institution that had become a financial liability. Perhaps the most critical point in the president's speech was his announcement that after the completion of the Khartoum–Port Sudan road, the country would no longer depend on the railways.[32] The proclamation that the country would no longer depend on the railways encapsulated the president's real agenda, which was the dismantling of the SRC. At the heart of this process was decentralization of the corporation, with the ultimate goal of abolishing the headquarters at Atbara. Most important, railway workers were given a twenty-four-hour ultimatum to either return to work or be evicted from their railway houses.

Another republican decree was issued on September 5 in which Nimeiri ordered the decentralization of the Sudan Railway Corporation and appointed a committee to supervise the process. The committee included al-Rashid al-Tahir Bakr; Badr al-Din Sulayman, minister of finance; Mustafa `Uthman Hasan, minister of transport; and Hayder Kabsun, minister of public administration. According to the decentralization plan, the headquarters of the SRC would be transferred to Khartoum, the store division to Port Sudan, while the workshops would be distributed to various regions.[33]

Faced with the prospect of losing their houses and a prolonged, exhausting strike, the railway workers resumed work on September 18, 1981. By then the strike had cost the corporation LS 2,681,000.[34]

Following the strike, a deep sense of defeat and uncertainty prevailed among the railway workers. Their greatest concern was the looming decentralization, which would entail the dismantling of Atbara workshops and the transfer of thousands of workers to various regional railway centers. The prospect of transfer caused a great deal of anxiety, despair, and even sarcasm among workers, who taunted each other by saying "in a few weeks you are going to be in Babanusa, Haya, or Nyala." As a result of low morale, productivity declined to the extent that the railway management instructed supervisors to refrain from giving the workers the impression that they were defeated. Instead, the strike and the subsequent measures were portrayed as "unfortunate developments."[35]

After the dissolution of the SRWU and detention of its leadership, the government decided to form a preparatory committee to draft a new constitution for the union. The government appointed Musa Mitay as president of the preparatory committee. Musa recalled that he was summoned by `Umar Muhammad al-Tayyib, the vice president and head of the notorious Public Security, who informed him about the appointment. As a veteran trade-union leader who understood the temperament of the railway workers, Musa knew the repercussions of this action. He recalled the conversation between him and the vice president:

> the vice president told me, Musa: we want to appoint you as president of the SWRU. I was shocked. I paused and then said, your Excellency, I have never been appointed to this position; I only held it through elections; the railway workers would not accept this decision. Therefore, I cannot accept this appointment. When the vice president insisted, I told him that I would accept the appointment with the condition that the government release the detained SRWU leaders and allow them to return to Atbara with me. `Umar paused and then said, you got your wish.[36]

The following morning, `Abbas al-Khidir al-Hussain and his colleagues were released, and they returned with Musa to Atbara, where they were received by a large crowd of workers.

The strike of 1981 was a turning point in the history of the SRWU. The railway workers paid a heavy price and never recovered. Many veteran union leaders such as al-Hajj `Abd al-Rahman and Hasan Ahmad al-Shaykh maintained that both the timing of the strike and the manner in which it was conducted reflected a great deal of immaturity and lack of experience on the part of union leaders. They argued that `Abbas al-Khidir al-Hussain and his colleagues dragged the workers into an unnecessary confrontation with a ruthless regime that had powerful and sophisticated security apparatus. According to al-Hajj `Abd al-Rahman, long strikes usually require a great deal of mobilization and are difficult to sustain. He recalled that in the past, strikes were usually carried out gradually, by a limited group of workers in strategic railway divisions. For instance, a strike by workers in the running shed workshop alone could halt train movement and shut down the entire system. After they returned to work, workers in the electric or signaling divisions would go on strike, which would have the same effect on railway operations. In other words, a succession of strikes by a small group of workers could affect the whole system without wasting workers' energy. Finally, the strike of 1981 gave Nimeiri a golden opportunity to settle his score with the railway workers and implement his grand scheme of dismantling the SRC.

THE CAMPAIGN AGAINST THE SRC

As mentioned earlier, the centerpiece of Nimeiri's scheme of dismantling the railways was decentralization. The idea of reforming the administrative structure of the railways certainly preceded Nimeiri. With the expansion of the railway network in the 1950s and 1960s, a number of regional divisions were established. These were the Northern, Southern, Eastern, Western, and Central divisions. The railway management felt that it was necessary for Atbara to delegate some authority to regional centers.[37] But Nimeiri's objective was purely political and went far beyond simple administrative reforms. His primary goal was to disperse the railway workers of Atbara and end once and for all their political clout.

In October 1982 Khalid Hasan `Abbas, minister of transport and communications, issued a decree stipulating the reorganization of the administrative structure of the SRC. The decree appointed five regional directors and seven advisors to the general manager, whose office had been transferred from Atbara to Khartoum. A host of senior railway personnel were removed because of their objection to decentralization. They included Muhammad Ahmad al-Tayyib, the general manager at the time; Isma`il Ahmad Muhammad, chief mechanical engineer; `Abd al-Salam Salih, chief civil engineer; Ahmad `Abd al-Rahman, deputy chief mechanical engineer; and several officials.

Decentralization created a great deal of confusion in railway operations. The transfer of the general manager's office to Khartoum, while his deputy remained in Atbara, impeded decision making and coordination. Moreover, heads of railway divisions lost a great deal of their authority to regional managers. Decentralization also ran into practical difficulties. For instance, it was impossible to transfer the heavy machinery and equipment from the Atbara workshops because most of these machines had been installed during the colonial period. Railway engineers and technicians warned that if these machines were dismantled, there was no guarantee that they would be reassembled.[38]

Another long-term strategy in Nimeiri's campaign against the railways was the building of paved roads, linking the central parts of the country with Port Sudan harbor. With the notable exception of the Khartoum–Wad Medani road, which was built in the 1960s, the Sudan had very few paved roads. However, in line with the breadbasket policy of the 1970s, the May regime began to promote road transport. For example, the 1977–1983 six-year plan allocated LS 242 million for road construction, while the rail system was allocated LS 78 million. Moreover, imported trucks and lorries were given favorable treatment by the customs department, and their number increased dramatically. For example, between 1970 and 1974, the number of imported lorries rose from 11,000 to 24,000, and reached 182,821 in 1982.[39] In addition, the total volume of road transport rose from an estimated 9 million-ton kilometers in 1970 to about 2.6 billion-ton kilometers in 1976—exceeding that of the railway, which stood at 2.1 billion-ton kilometers.[40]

The leading advocates of road transport were members of the new commercial bourgeoisie, the main beneficiaries of the breadbasket strategy. They included large firms such as the Sudan-Kuwaiti Company, Wad Nimeiri Cooperative Society, and several individuals.

Government emphasis on road transport and its deliberate neglect of the railways generated major controversy. Naturally, the leading critics of road transport were the staff of the ministry of transport and communications, railway employees, and some economists. They argued that the railways served low-income passengers, and its revenue went to the public treasury, while road transport benefited mainly large firms and private individuals. Therefore, they reasoned, the government should increase its funding of the railways.[41] These critics also pointed out that road transport would undoubtedly increase the public bill for petroleum, which consumed 60 percent of the country's foreign exchange. Moreover, the manner in which paved roads were used would rapidly destroy them. For instance, while the Khartoum–Port Sudan road was originally designed for trucks with a maximum capacity of 33 tons, it was actually being used by trucks carrying 70 tons. If this continued, these critics argued, the roads would be unusable in three years.

On the other hand, proponents of road transport insisted that despite the high cost, the time saved was so great that shippers were willing to pay the greater cost. They pointed out that while transport time on the Khartoum–Port Sudan road was between two and three days, priority freight on the railways often took seven to eight days and regular freight about ten to fifteen days. But railway officials argued that they were not against building paved roads per se; rather, these roads should be built as "feeder roads"[42]—a proposition made two decades earlier by K.D.D. Henderson, a former British colonial administrator, who wrote,

> Road construction and maintenance in Sudan conditions are very much more costly than the railway, and the road allocation could more profitably be spent on building feeder services from production areas to railhead.[43]

Political repression, administrative reorganization, and the decline of public funding had a catastrophic effect on the SRC. By early 1980 the corporation was in shambles. The decline was manifested not only in loss of revenue but also in operation, shortage of equipment, track maintenance, train delays, increased accidents, and growing apathy among the workforce. The following section will shed light on these crises and their impact on workers.

THE COLLAPSE OF A NATIONAL INSTITUTION

While the SRC had been hailed in the 1960s as a revenue-generating government agency, it became a financial liability in the 1970s. This could be attributed to a host of factors. According to railway officials, the leading cause of the corporation's decline was the loss of its autonomy and increased government control, particularly under the May regime. The SRC was not allowed to manage its finances or operate on a commercial basis. For instance, the corporation was forced by the ministry of finance to transport consumer goods such as sugar, petrol, cotton, and wheat at unreasonably low rates. It was the under pricing, railway officials claimed, that led to the chronic deficits in the 1970s and 1980s. Table 6.3 shows the SRC deficits during the 1974–1984 period.[44]

Continuing deficits forced the SRC to borrow from the central bank and international donors. But given the general economic conditions of the country, the cen-

Table 6.3   Sudan Railways Corporation Deficits, 1974–1984

Year	LS
1974/75	7,574,304
1975/76	3,521,116
1976/77	6,219,988
1977/78	8,836,082
1978/79	14,766,486
1979/80	11,386,816
1980/81	23,528,436
1981/82	3,225,101
1982/83	21,512,718
1983/84	47,730,000

tral bank was in no position to help the corporation. For instance, in 1981 the SRC needed $8 million to purchase spare parts. The council of ministers requested the Sudan Bank to provide the corporation with a monthly subvention of $250,000. Of that amount only $4,203 was provided.[45] Another factor behind the SRC financial crisis was the separation of the Port Sudan harbor, which deprived the corporation from a major source of foreign exchange.

The financial difficulties of the SRC were exacerbated by the fact that many government departments that depended on it for transporting their materials and equipment failed to pay their bills. For instance, in 1982 government departments owed the railways an estimated LS 11 million.[46] During the same year, a committee representing various government agencies recommended that the ministry of finance and the petroleum corporation pay the SRC LS 17 million annually to keep it afloat. Deliberate government neglect was another factor behind the SRC crisis. For example, the budget allocated to the SRC for the fiscal year 1983–1984 was $29 million, while its outstanding debts and interest charges stood at $22 million.[47]

Since the late 1970s, international donors had become involved in financing major railway projects. The European Economic Community (EEC) financed renovation of the Abu Zabad–Babanusa line to increase freight carried between Kordofan and the Bahr al-Ghazal. The United States Agency for International Development (USAID) provided $4 million for the purchase of spare parts for American-made locomotives. The Federal Republic of Germany provided 18.9 million marks, of which nine million were earmarked for the purchase of spare parts for German diesel engines, three million for tools and equipment, and the rest for constructing a brick factory at al-`Akad, south of Atbara. In 1983 the SRC approached the French government for a loan in the amount of 40 million francs for the purchase of oil tankers, and also asked the Japanese government to provide a $2 million loan to purchase spare parts for shunting locomotives. The government of Romania agreed to build new workshops at Atbara and help upgrade the workshops at Sinnar and Khartoum. According to a World Bank study in 1984, in order to make the SRC a profitable institution, it would need a capital investment of about $55.6 million.[48]

The financial crisis of the SRC affected every aspect of its activities. By 1983 the SRC operated a single track of 4,786 kilometers. The system used a wide variety of steam locomotives and diesel engines, most of which were imported from Britain and America. However, as a result of poor maintenance and lack of spare parts, fewer than half of the diesel and steam engines were functioning in the early 1980s. Exacerbating the problem was the shortage of shunting locomotives, which forced railway employees to use main-line locomotives for shunting purposes. The use of main-line locomotives (which were designed for high-speed trains) for shunting purposes seriously damaged these engines. In 1979–1980, for instance, the SRC bought forty-six British locomotives; two years later, twenty needed spare parts, and four years later, they were all immobile.

The introduction of diesel engines required changing track gauge, from 50 lb to 75 lb and 90 lb. About 500 kilometers of track had been relaid in 1977–1981. Light diesel locomotives were used on heavy tracks, while the steam locomotives were confined to the light lines of Babanusa–Wau and Damazin–Sinnar. However, the task of upgrading the whole system was far beyond the SRC's abilities.

Compounding the problem of track maintenance were frequent sandstorms and rains that caused great damage. Financial loss caused by track breakdown in 1981 alone was estimated at $3.3 million. Unable to maintain the track, the SRC was forced, for safety considerations, to reduce train speed, often to no more than 10 kilometers per hour. In 1983 the Sudan government invited a team of specialists from Kampsax—a Dutch consulting firm of engineers and economists—to make plans for upgrading the track between Port Sudan and Haiya. The project was expected to cost $31 million, of which $21 million was promised by the EEC.[49]

With regard to wagons, only half of the total 495 passenger wagons were functioning in 1982. Two hundred wagons were more than twenty years old. The shortage of wagons led to further deterioration because it was no longer possible to reshuffle wagons in and out of service for maintenance purposes. Of the 5,268 freight wagons, 1,716 were out of service and the figure was expected to rise to 3,850 in 1983. The only innovation during this period was the replacement of the old vacuum system by a pressurized air system, which improved safety. This project began in 1980 and by 1982, one-third of the vacuum system had been changed.[50]

One of the most vital aspects of railway operations was the communication system. In the early 1980s most of the control equipment was forty years old. The telephone system had been operated by imported dry-cell batteries that often died and shut down the whole communication system. The signaling system on several lines had also become dysfunctional. For instance, between Sinnar and Kosti, the system had totally broken down, rendering it impossible for station staff to know the exact location of approaching trains until they actually arrived.

In 1976 the SRC took some steps to modernize its record and information system by establishing a computer center. The center had been rented, which cost the SRC $2,290 per month. In 1980 the United Nation Development Programme (UNDP) provided funds to upgrade the system, and an Indian expert was hired to manage it.[51]

The brunt of the crisis was felt in the Atbara workshops, on which the entire railway system depended. The workshops had the capacity to overhaul eight mainline engines and two shunting locomotives, two hundred freight wagons, and twenty-five passenger wagons per month. But lack of spare parts and outdated machinery led to the collapse of the maintenance system. Of the 277 machines, 119 were more than thirty years old. The cranes, for instance, were installed in 1929. To maintain machines, workers had to take parts from one locomotive to repair another. Complicating the problem was the severe shortage of fuel, oxygen, and acetylene, as well as frequent power failures.

Low pay and deteriorating working conditions precipitated a sharp decline in productivity and workers' morale. The SRC came under heavy criticism from government officials and international donors, who blamed it for maintaining a large, redundant, and unproductive labor force. Those critics argued that wages alone constituted 70 percent of the corporation's expenditure. However, railway workers countered by saying that the labor force considered lazy and unproductive in the 1980s was the same one that had made the SRC successful in the 1960s. They blamed government policies and mismanagement for deterioration of working conditions and low productivity. In an interview with a group of reporters from *Sudanow* in November 1982, workers described their struggle in maintaining an aging fleet of locomotives and rolling stock. They bitterly complained about the lack of such basic materials as iron, copper, zinc, and nails, and how they were reduced to using scrap to repair machines.[52] In some remote areas, railway employees lived in squalid conditions, with severe shortages of basic consumer commodities. As one worker put it, "in some remote stations there is nothing but God in heaven and the station master on earth."[53] Moreover, workers at the Atbara workshops resented the presence of the strategic battalion, whose members lacked adequate skills for railway operations.[54]

As a result of deteriorating working conditions, the SRC lost a large number of its technical employees, who were attracted by better pay in other government departments and private firms. A railway engineer was paid 46 percent less than his counterpart in the National Electricity Corporation. It is not surprising that between 1980 and 1982, sixty-five out of seventy-five engineers left the SRC for better paying jobs.[55]

In its final months in office, the May regime made a half-hearted attempt to address the problems of the SRC. In November 1984 the ministry of transport and communications organized a five-day conference on "the Role of the Sudan Railway Corporation in the Sudanese Economy." The conference was attended by senior officials from the ministries of transport and communications, finance, and energy and mining; the Bank of Sudan, the People's National Assembly, the Business Association, the University of Khartoum, and the railway workers' union. There were also representatives from the World Bank and the EEC. The deliberations were dominated by the subject of privatizing the SRC, which generated heated debate between the ministry of finance and the ministry of transport and communications. Representatives from the latter blasted the ministry of finance for forcing the railways to transport basic consumer goods at an artificially low rate, thereby depriving the SRC of the revenue it needed to maintain and improve its services.[56] In his opening remarks, Khalid Hasan `Abbas, minister of transport and communications, defended his ministry's record in managing the SRC, and launched an offensive against the pricing policy of the ministry of finance, which in his view had crippled the corporation. The minister also blamed the deterioration of the SRC on inflation, shortage of foreign exchange, and low freight rates. To prove the low cost of rail transport, the minister pointed out that the transportation of a sack of sorghum by rail from Gedarif to Nyala would cost about LS 5, compared to LS 30 by lorry.

Transport officials were supported by some members of the People's National Assembly. For instance, Yassin `Umar al-Imam—the assembly's president—and Mahmoud Hasan Jiha—a member of the assembly's budget committee—argued that given the central role of the SRC in the country's development, it must be compensated by those government departments benefiting from its services.[57] Six months earlier the People's National Assembly had adopted a resolution calling on the ministry of finance and the central bank to give priority to SRC projects and help it obtain foreign currency. The resolution also emphasized that the SRC should remain the primary carrier of all public sector requirements.

Advocates of privatization of the SRC maintained that it should follow the example of other public sector institutions that were privatized. In their view, privatization would improve efficiency and productivity and increase revenue. Opponents, however, countered by stressing that privatization of the SRC would lead to loss of government control over such a vital national institution. It would also raise the transportation cost of basic consumer goods, thereby increasing their prices. Naturally, the leading opponent of privatization were the railway workers themselves, who were concerned with the prospects of massive layoffs. They cited the example of the Sudan Airways, which got rid of 60 percent of its workforce following its privatization. Despite these objections, the conference recommended the transformation of the SRC into a private company and the provision of about $134 million to help it achieve that goal. The minister of transport formed a committee, chaired by Ibrahim ʿAbaidalla, vice president of the People's National Assembly, to plan for the establishment of the new company. Indeed, these plans did not see light, for a few months later the May regime was overthrown.

The combined effects of political repression and reorganization under the May regime had dealt a serious blow to the railway workers' movement. By the end of the regime, the movement had been crippled. The restoration of parliamentary rule in 1986 provided an opportunity for the revival of the SRC and the trade-union movement. But the "Third Democracy" came to an end on June 30, 1989, when a group of army officers, backed by the Islamic National Front, took over power and inaugurated one of the most authoritarian regimes in Sudanese history. Hundreds of trade unionists, political activists, students, and leaders of civic associations were detained, tortured, and killed. In its effort to establish a theocratic state in the Sudan, the Islamicist regime launched a large-scale campaign against what it considered secular forces. Consequently, thousands of civil servants, army and police officers, doctors, engineers, teachers, and workers lost their jobs.

As far as the railway workers were concerned, the Islamicist regime continued the job Nimeiri had begun several years earlier, but with greater ferocity. Following the June coup, the SRWU was dissolved, and hundreds of railway employees were dismissed. The biggest blow, however, was the dismissal of approximately two thousand railway workers between 1990 and 1992, many of whom were trade-union activists. Moreover, the idea of privatizing the SRC was revived and pursued with great vigor. In a newspaper interview in 2000, ʿUmar Muhammad Nur, general manager of the SRC, announced that certain sections of the Atbara workshops would be sold to the private sector, and asserted that this would definitely entail laying off thousands of workers.[58] Meanwhile, the government continued to give preference to road transport. In the 1990s a number of paved roads linking al-

Ubayyid, Kosti, Atbara, and Dongola to Khartoum were built. The country became more and more dependent on road transport. The SRC became totally dysfunctional, limiting its activities to a few passenger and freight trains.

TRAGEDY AND DECLINE

The first casualty of the decline of the SRC was the town of Atbara and the workers. As we have seen, throughout the 1970s and early 1980s, the railway workers had become the primary target of Nimeiri's regime. Moreover, the escalating inflation took a heavy toll on the city's working population. Economic hardships forced people to either seek additional sources of income or leave the city altogether. They also had a profound impact on family life. Coupled with this was the collapse of infrastructure and social services in the city, which were reflected in chronic power failure and severe shortage of drinking water, medicine, and public transport.

One of the most important manifestations of Atbara's decline was the sharp increase in outward migration. The city that was hailed in the 1950s and 1960s for its low cost of living and strong communal bonds had become an inhospitable place in the 1980s. Although there are no official demographic figures, it is evident that a large number of Atbara's residents moved to other Sudanese towns such as Khartoum, Port Sudan, and Kassala, where they found alternative means of livelihood. Moreover, like other Sudanese, many young Atbarawis migrated to the Arab oil-producing countries such as Saudi Arabia and the Gulf states, as evidenced by the existence of several Atbarawi associations in these countries. The elderly and those without technical skills either remained in the city or returned to their villages in the rural areas.

The demographic composition of Atbara had begun to change in the early 1980s. The widespread famine, which struck many parts of the Sudan, led to the dispersal of thousands of refugees who flocked to northern Sudanese towns. Atbara, for instance, received a large influx of refugees and displaced persons from the Nuba Mountains. These immigrants settled in a large shantytown along the bank of Atbara River, south of Umbakol and al-Mawrada. The camp continued to attract a growing number of refugees and became a den of prostitution, beer brewing, and criminal activity. As a result, the municipal authorities decided to move the camp to a new quarter on the outskirts of the city. The new quarter, which was called *Hay al-Wuhda* (Unity quarter), consisted of huts and hovels and lacked any services.[59]

The impact of economic hardships was clearly felt in family life. As mentioned in chapter 2, household structure among the railway workers was based on the principal of the male worker as the breadwinner. This structure rapidly changed in the 1980s and 1990s. With the meager incomes of their husbands, wives began to play a leading role in providing income to their families. They sold vegetables, food, and handcrafts in neighborhood markets and developed other survival strategies.[60] One of those was the *sanduq* (rotating credit), which had been an integral part of urban life in the Sudan for many decades. In the past, people resorted to the san-duq to meet expenses of weddings, death, illness, and other emergencies. How-ever, the function of the sanduq changed in 1980s and 1990s, as it became a regular supplement to family income.[61]

Economic hardships also forced families to make major adjustments in their consumption habits. For instance, in the past, leftovers were either thrown away or given to animals. This was no longer the case: remaining pieces of bread were dried and used as *maraqa* (soup cubes with onions).[62] Many families had to aban-don the old Sudanese habit of males and females eating separately because, as one woman put it, "there isn't enough *mullah* [stew] to be divided into two plates."[63] Although these economic crises gave women the opportunity to work outside the home and increased their role in decision making within the household, they also placed a heavy burden on them. In the case of retired workers, for instance, women became the primary breadwinners.[64]

To cope with these difficulties, the people of Atbara resorted to their old tradi-tions of communal solidarity and social networks. This was best exemplified by the Atbara Town Development Committee, which was officially launched in 1984. The purpose of the committee was to raise funds to rebuild the city's infrastruc-ture and improve its social services. The committee collected donations from char-ity organizations such as al-Shaykh al-Ja`ali Charity Society, private individuals, and, most important, the Atbarawi emigrants in the Gulf states and Saudi Arabia.

The committee divided its work among a number of subcommittees, each fo-cusing on a certain arena such as social affairs, health, education, agriculture, en-ergy and roads, and publicity. Between 1984 and 1991 the Atbara Town Development Committee completed a number of projects, financed by individual entrepreneurs and donations. These projects included the supply of Atbara hospi-tal with equipment and the building of maternity and diabetes units. In addition, the committee built three clinics, a secondary school for girls, and a vocational in-stitute for women. Other projects included the completion of four asphalt roads and three wells for drinking water.[65]

After coming to power in 1989, the present Sudanese government restricted the committee's activity on the grounds that it was a leftist organization engaging in subversive activities. This suspicion stemmed from the fact that several members of the committee were former trade-union activists dismissed by the government. However, after a great deal of struggle, the committee was allowed to resume its activities in the late 1990s.[66] Among the most important projects completed dur-ing this second phase were the provision of Atbara hospital with dialysis equip-ment, the establishment of a cloth factory, and the renovation of five major roads in the city. One of the most ambitious campaigns the committee launched was to establish a medical college in Atbara.

More recently, members of the Atbarawi Diaspora in Europe and North Amer-ica launched an Internet discussion group to disseminate information about their town and to maintain links with one another. Their efforts and that of the Atbara

Town Development Committee show that despite the city's economic decline, its spirit is still alive.

CONCLUSION

By the early 1980s, the world the railway workers of Atbara made had begun to crumble. Their social and political institutions collapsed, and their community and family life were ravaged by acute economic hardships. Paradoxically, destruction of the railway workers' movement was carried out by a regime that claimed to represent the working people. In its effort to co-opt the railway workers, the May regime eliminated the dedicated and experienced labor activists and paved the way for the emergence of inexperienced and opportunist leaders whose actions have contributed to the demise of the movement.

NOTES

1. For Nimeiri's period, see Peter Woodward, *Sudan, 1898–1989: The Unstable State* (Boulder: Lynne Rienner, 1990), 137–200; Tim Niblock, *Class and Power in Sudan: The Dynamics of Sudanese Politics, 1898–1985* (Albany: State University of New York, 1987); Mansour Khalid, *Nimeiri and the Revolution of Dis-May* (London: KPI, 1985).

2. It was reported that only twelve out of thirty-three members of the party's central committee supported the regime; see `Abd al-Qadir Yasin, *Al-idrab al-siyasi fil Sudan* (Political strikes in the Sudan) (Cairo: Dar al-Ahali, 1995).

3. Gabriel Warburg, *Islam, Nationalism, and Communism in a Traditional Society: The Case of Sudan* (London: Frank Cass, 1978).

4. Carole Collins, "Colonialism and Class Struggle in Sudan," *Middle East Research and Information Project* 46 (1976): 3–20; Peter O. Khoff and Karl Wohlmuth, eds., *The Development Perspectives of the Democratic Republic of Sudan: The Limits of the Breadbasket Strategy* (Munich, Cologne, and London: Weltforum Verlag, 1983); Norman O'Neill and Jay O'Brien, eds., *Economy and Class in Sudan* (Aldershot: Gower, 1988).

5. Norman O'Neill, "Imperialism and Class Struggle in Sudan," *Race and Class* 20, no. 1, (1978): 17.

6. For the best account of Khashogi's dealing, see Mansour Khalid, 92–161.

7. Fatima Babiker, *The Sudanese Bourgeoisie: Vanguard of Development?* (London and Khartoum: Khartoum University Press and Zed Press, 1984).

8. Niblock, *Class and Power in Sudan*, 245.

9. Abdel Rahman El-Tayib Ali Taha and Ahmad El-Jack, eds., *The Regulations of Termination of Employment in the Sudanese Private Sector: A Study of the Law and Its Application* (Khartoum: Khartoum University Press, 1973), 13, and Abdel Rahman El-Tayib Ali Taha, "The Industrial Relations System in the Sudan," in *An Introduction to the Sudanese Economy*, ed. Ali Muhammad El-Hasan, (Khartoum: Khartoum University Press, 1977).

10. Taha, "The Industrial Relations System," 183–200.

11. Al-Hajj `Abd al-Rahman, interview by author, Khartoum, 23 August 1995.

12. Ibid.

13. NRO Miscellaneous, 1/888/2500–2501, and *al-Sahafa*, 3 May 1975.

14. Nabawia Mohammad Mahgoub, "The Conditions of Railway Workers during the May Regime, 1969–1983" (B.Sc. diss. University of Khartoum, May 1993), 57.

15. *Sudan Railways Corporation* (Khartoum, 1983), 10.

16. Ibid., 11–12.

17. Mahgoub, "The Conditions of Railway Workers," 31.

18. Ibid., 43.

19. *Al-`Ummal*, 1973, 7.

20. Ibid., 58

21. Musa Mitay, interview by author, 12 October 1999.

22. SRWU, *Amal wa inqaz* (Hope and salvation) (Khartoum: SRWU, 1982), 2–5.

23. Mahgoub, "The Conditions of Railway Workers," 68.

24. SRWU, *Al-Nizam al-Asasi lil Nagaba al-`Aama li `Ummal al-Sika Hadid* (Constitution and bylaws of the Sudan Railways Workers Union) (Atbara: SRWU, n.d.), 6–7.

25. Ibid., 8.

26. Ibid.

27. Mahgoub, "The Conditions of Railway Workers," 69.

28. This long strike was carried out in a series of five-day strikes. Because of security watch, the announcements of these strikes were made during Muslim prayers. According to eyewitness accounts, `Abbas al-Khidir al-Hussain led the prayers and waved the fingers of his right hand to indicate the number of days for the strike; Hasan Ahmad al-Shaykh, interview by author, Atbara, 13, October 1999.

29. *Al-Ayyam*, 17 June 1981, 3.

30. Ibid.

31. Mahgoub, "The Conditions of Railway Workers," 71.

32. Ibid.

33. *Al-Ayyam*, 6 September 1981.

34. Ibid.

35. *Sudanow*, October 1981, 35.

36. Musa Mitay, interview.

37. Hashim Muhammad Ahmad, interview by author, Oxford, England, 17 July 1997.

38. Ibid.

39. *Waraqa hawl mashakil al-sika hadid al-tamwiliyya wa al-maliyya, wa al-taswiqiyya, wa al-tijariyya, wa al-ta`rifiyya* (Memorandum on financial, marketing, commercial, and pricing problems of the railways) (Khartoum 1995).

40. C. Wilkins, "Road Transport in the Sudan," in *An Introduction to the Sudan Economy*, ed. Ali Mohamed El-Hasan (Khartoum, Khartoum University Press, 1977), 102–22.

41. Ibid.

42. Ahmad, interview.

43. K.D.D. Henderson, *Sudan Republic* (New York and Washington: Frederick A. Praeger, 1965), 148.

44. *Sudanow*, December 1984, 11.

45. Ibid., 10.

46. Ibid., November 1982, 17.

47. Ibid., August 1983, 27.

48. Ibid., December 1984, 10.

49. Ibid., August 1983, 27.

50. Ibid., November 1982, 17.

51. Ibid., August 1983, 26.

52. Ibid., November 1982, 18.

53. Ibid.

54. Ibid., October 1981, 29.

55. Ibid., November 1982, 18.

56. Ibid., December 1984, 9.

57. Ibid.

58. *Al-Ray al-`Am*, 18 March 2000.

59. Khidir Mahmoud Babikir, "Ahamm al-Taghiyrat al-Ijtima`iyya wa al-Iqtisadiyya li Hijrat Sukkan Jibal al-Nuba ila Hawadir al-Mudiriyya al-Shamaliyya–Atbara and al-Damer" (Master's thesis, University of Khartoum, 1994), 100.

60. On the development of these survival strategies in the 1990s, see Nada Mustafa Mohammed Ali, "Coping amidst Crisis: The Narratives of Five Sudanese Women" (Master's thesis, American University in Cairo, 1993).

61. Ibid., 121.

62. Ibid., 67.

63. Ibid., 64.

64. Ibid.

65. Handbook of Atbara Town Development Committee (Atbara, n.d.).

66. Hasan Ahmad al-Shaykh, interview by author, Atbara, 13 October 1999. At the time of the interview, al-Shaykh was the president of the committee.

CONCLUSION

The experience of the railway workers of Atbara illuminates important themes that are at the heart of the current debate on labor and working-class history and the transformation of colonial and postcolonial societies. Of particular significance is the political and social role of labor in African and Middle Eastern societies, the success and failure of the socialist movements in these societies, the struggle between religion and secular ideologies, workers' relationship with the state, and the place of labor in today's world.

Within the Sudanese context, the railway workers of Atbara can be considered pioneers who played a pivotal role in the transformation of their society. These workers formed the core of a permanent, stable workforce, employed in a modern industrial enterprise with a particular structure of authority, discipline, and work ethos. Atbara workers, most of whom were rural immigrants, embraced the values of the railway industry and used it as a basis for their collective identity. In a country where the overwhelming majority of the population were farmers and nomads, the railway workers developed a strong sense of distinctiveness and regarded themselves as harbingers of modernity and progressive social change. Their affiliation with the railway industry and its pivotal role in the country's economy allowed them to make legitimate claims for entitlements and citizenship.

The railway workers of Atbara also pioneered the establishment of civil society institutions in the Sudan. In their efforts to face the challenges of city life and wage employment, these workers created extensive social networks that ranged from regional and mutual aid societies to social clubs and unions. Atbara workers drew upon elements of their rural culture and constructed a new identity that reflected their rural background, railway employment, and urban life. They created a working-class culture that incorporated modern notions of class solidarity, wage labor, and Sudanese cultural values, and demonstrated that solidarity was not limited to collective actions during labor protests but was exhibited through daily interactions and companionship. The Atbarawis took great pride in their simple way of life and their strong communal bonds, and have become known as people who cherished such values as modesty, thrift, and hard work.

The experience of the railway workers of Atbara also illustrates the ability of African workers to mold such institutions as trade unions to suit their own needs and aspirations. They established an effective and dynamic trade union that fostered the emergence of leadership from the grassroots and produced many of the country's most eminent labor leaders. As we have seen, the activities of the SRWU transcended the struggle for wages and occupational concerns and became deeply embedded in Atbara's social and political life.

Arguably, one of the most significant aspects of the experience of the railway workers movement was its close alliance with the Sudanese left. On one level, this alliance defies the essentialist notion, which perceives religion as the only force that shapes and transforms Muslim society. This issue is of particular importance in view of the global decline of the left and the recent resurgence of the Islamicist movements in Africa and the Middle East, and their relentless effort to establish "Islamic" states in these societies. This in turn begs the question, What is the role and the place of labor in the Islamicists' project? In this regard, Sudan's recent experience may provide important insights. Since 1989 the military regime of the National Islamic Front has embarked on a vigorous program of Islamization of the state and society, and exhibited an unprecedented hostility toward trade unions and civic organizations. Hundreds of trade-union leaders and political activists were persecuted. In addition to purging the civil service, the police, and the army from what the regime perceived as "secular" and anti-Islamicist elements, the government has actively pursued a policy of privatization and the dismantling of public sector institutions. In the end, the policies of the Islamicist regime have benefited a small group of party loyalists who amassed considerable wealth, while the overwhelming majority of working people have suffered an unparalleled level of economic deprivation.

On the other hand, the inability of the SCP to mobilize the railway workers beyond the issues of occupational demands illustrates the complex interplay between the cultural and the structural factors that shape workers' consciousness and behavior. As an orthodox Marxist-Leninist party, the SCP adopted the proletarianization paradigm, which perceived the working class as a homogeneous entity by virtue of its location within the socioeconomic structure. This essentialist approach overlooked the floating and shifting nature of working-class identity and the fact that workers have their own motives and strategies and their own ways of conceptualizing their needs and goals.

The collapse of the railway workers' movement and the decline of Atbara as a center of labor activism reveal a great deal about the nature of the postcolonial African states, their attitude toward social movements and civic organizations, and the impact of the neocolonial order on the labor movement. As we have seen, successive postcolonial Sudanese governments, both civilian and military, exhibited great hostility toward the labor movement. Paradoxically, the destruction of the railway workers' movement in particular was carried out by a regime that raised progressive slogans and claimed that it represented the interests of the working people. In addition to its large-scale repression, the alliance of the May regime and foreign capital unleashed powerful social and political forces that led to the demise of the Sudan Railways as an institution and as a powerful force for change.

However, it is important to point out that the railway workers themselves did contribute to the demise of their movement. In view of their previous successes, their numerical strength, and their strategic position in the country's economy, the railway workers developed a strong sense of invincibility. Quite often, they evinced little interest in linking their struggle with that of other workers. As we have seen, on several occasions in the 1960s, the SRWU broke rank with the Sudanese Workers' Trade Union Federation (SWTUF) and refused to participate in a number of strikes. It was this parochialism and the feeling of invincibility that contributed to the demise of the railway workers' movement. Moreover, the emergence of inexperienced union leadership had serious consequences. This became vivid in the early 1980s when the SRWU single-handedly engaged in futile battles against Nimeiri's regime and provided him with a golden opportunity to destroy the railway workers' movement.

Despite the decline of their movement, the railway workers of Atbara have created an enduring legacy and can be considered one of the principal makers of contemporary Sudan. These workers inaugurated a powerful social movement and developed many innovative ways and sophisticated strategies that became a model for resisting the repressive regimes that ruled the Sudan. The railway workers of Atbara established a tradition of militancy and a culture of protest that was drawn upon by successive generations of Sudanese labor organizers, civic leaders, and political activists. General strikes and civil disobedience have become an integral part of Sudanese political culture and have proven themselves effective tools for bringing about political change. This was manifested in the October 1964 and April 1985 uprisings that led to the downfall of the military regimes of General 'Abboud and Ja' far Nimeiri, respectively. Despite Sudan's current predicament, the City of Steel and Fire has remained a symbol of defiance, modernity, and hope.

Appendix 1: Petition to Establish a Cooperative Society by the Natives of Umbakol and Ghourayba, Residing in Atbara

بسم الله الرحمن الرحيم

وصلى الله على سيدنا محمد وعلى آله وصحبه وسلم

(قول تعالى)

تعاونوا على البر والتقوى ولا تعاونوا على الإثم والعدوان

سم - (الصندوق التعاوني لأبناء أميكول - العربية · بعطبرة)

رئيس   الحاج محمد حسين أبو سام

القانون

(١) تنعقد بجنة مسؤولة لنذلك وعدد بعطبرة بأن يندفع كل منهم شهريا مبلغ معين قدره بيما للازلاج أعذارهم الشرعية وهذا المبلغ يودع بالبريدة كأمانة غير قابل للبيع - ولا تشتراك يحمل يوم واحد سهل شهر

(٢) اذا نافر أحد فرد عند الدفع لهذه شهريه تنعقد اللجنة لإدارته وتبحث في سبب التأخير وينتهى لأمر محبه بإجراءات بتوقيعاه

(٢) لا تقضى الصندوق اى عضو لإدارته بعد مضى سنة كامل مشتراية ناشيم او لا يعدم تسليسة اى فرد مسل المشتركه لا يعدم مضى سنة كامل مسر تاريخ اشتراك وبستنى من ذلك الإعضاء الشرعيه التى تبتدى اللجنة لإدارته بعد ذلك

(٤) يعد مضى سنه كامله مداماع الاشتراك يقدم للمشترك العضو ما يستحق مبلغ الضروري بعد ان تقدم في ذلك طلبا لنائب الرئيس ولا شترك اسه يعطى كلما يطلبه عند التفقد على يعطى المبلغ الذى تواعد عليه اللجنة لإدارة وينظر في ميعاد سراه وتوفيد منه يعطى عمل استئلام وتسجيل المبلغ

(٥) في حاله ترك المشترك العدم او نفع عليه انه يقدم طلبا الى نائب الرئيس بما لوقته اما بالانفصال او الاستمرار - واذا توفى احد المشتركين فيعطى جميع مبلغ لو توفى به الته الشرعيه

(٦) اذا اراد المشترك لانفصاله اختياريا يلزم نائب الرئيس قبل شهر من التاريخ الذى يرغب فيه لانفصاله وحينئذ يدفع له جميع مبلغ ولا يقبل استئذار مره اخرى

(٧) اللجنة لإدارية تتكون من نائب الرئيس والسكرتير والأمين ولها عضاء وكيلها ان تجتمع يوم ٨ من كل شهر لمراجعة الحسابات

(٨) لا تشرع اللجنة الإدارية في عمل شيء حتى اذا اكان لها مدير يسم سلطاتها هم ما بوازى الثلاثه او اكثر

(٩) نائب الرئيس - عليه ان يرأس جمعات اللجنة ولا احد اعضاء طلب ذلك اكثر المعتا واجمعيه حتى ان تكون وله تقديم اقتراحات بارتفاعه اما الانفصال

(١٠) السكرتير - عليه تدوين قرار الجمعية في دفتر والعلام المشتركين مسرا باللجنة يراد انعقادها المباحث في إحلال كتابيه بعث

TRANSLATION OF APPENDIX 1

Petition to establish a cooperative society by the natives of Umbakol and al-Ghourayba, living in Atbara.

Atbara, 13/11/1933

District Commissioner, Atbara:

With respect, we submit the following petition:

We, the natives of Umbakol and al-Ghourayba, al-Debba District, Dongola Province, wish to establish a cooperative society, which will be governed by the attached rules and regulations. We are confident that you will approve this valuable project, which will bring many benefits and help us meet our needs, safeguard our community, maintain our dignity, and protect ourselves against indigence. In-

deed, this is what our righteous government endeavors to achieve in empathy with venerable and poorly paid subjects like us. May God protect your just rule.
Signatures

President of the society	Vice President	Secretary
Muhammad Hasan Abu Sham	`Ubaid Hamid	Sa`id Muhammad Rahama

Treasurer: `Abdalla Medani
Members: `Abdalla al-Hasan, Bashir Ahmad Kindi, al-Shaykh Muhammad Malik,
        al-Tahir Muhammad Hamid, and al-Khidir al-Hajj Muhammad
Constitution of the Cooperative Society of the Natives of Umbakol and al-Ghourayba, Living in Atbara.
Name: The Cooperative Society of the Natives of Umbakol and al-Ghourayba, living in Atbara.

1. Some natives of the above mentioned villages, residing in Atbara, agreed that each will subscribe 100 millimes monthly to meet their emergency needs. Subscriptions are due on the first day of each month and would be deposited in an interest-free post office account.

2. If any member fails to pay his dues for two consecutive months, the administrative committee will examine his reasons and make a decision by voting.

3. Loans will be available for members after one year after the establishment of the society. The member can apply for a loan only after one year from the date he joined the society. However, under unusual circumstances, the committee has the discretion to approve a loan to a person who has been a member for less than a year.

4. After one year, the member can apply for a loan by submitting a written application to the society's vice president, with the understanding that he may not be approved for the total amount requested. The executive committee would decide the amount and the terms of the loan and would obtain a receipt from the borrower stating these conditions.

5. In case of retirement or job transfer, the member must inform the vice president in writing of whether he wants to resign or retain his membership. If a member dies, all his assets would be given to his legal heirs.

6. If a member decides to terminate his membership, he must give the vice president a one month notice, in which case all his assets would be refunded, but he would not be eligible to rejoin the society.

7. The executive committee consists of the vice president, the secretary, the treasurer, and members. It meets on the eighth day of each month to review the accounts.

8. The administrative committee cannot hold a meeting unless two-thirds of its members are present.

9. The vice president presides over the meetings of the administrative committee and has the discretion to call meetings at any time deemed necessary. He has the authority to decide membership applications and dismissals.

10. The secretary's duty is to record the minutes of the meetings and to inform members of the general assembly about the committee's decisions and call upon them to help with paper work.

11. The treasurer's duty is to collect the monthly subscriptions and keep records of all financial transactions. He is personally responsible for any shortfalls in the society's funds.

12. No withdrawal from the society's account can be made without a receipt bearing the signatures of the vice president, the secretary, and the treasurer.

13. Each member has the right to review his own account as well as the society's financial transactions.

14. The cost of stationeries and supplies will be collected from members with their monthly subscriptions.

15. The executive committee shall serve for a one-year term, to be followed by general elections.

16. This cooperative society was formed on the first of November 1933.

Appendix 2: Petition to Establish a Cooperative Society for the Natives of `Omudiyyat Kuri, Residing in Atbara

جناب المحترم مفتش مدينة عطبرة

بمزيد الإحترام نرفع هذا لحنا لكم نحن ابناء كوري بمديرية دنقلا
والمقيمين بعطبرة الآن فضلوك

أقندم بما اتنا فكرنا نعمل مستودعه نتجارده جبري لنقصد منه
ازالة الوطناء الشرئيه التي نطرأ على أي فرد وتتم الاهاليه
على يد يدفع كل شخص مائة مليم شهريا والمبلغ يودع بالخزينه
ضمانة موجبة كما نؤده ومنع لهذا النقصد وسري نقفله
اعتبارا امه اول نيا به ١٩٤٤ فارها نتقدم بالرطمع عليه والتصديه
لنا بذلك وتتم هزين الشمر افندم

١ / ١ / ١٩٤٤

الرئيس   الاعضاء
الحاج الشومه   الطيب الملك   نائب الرئيس
                        حمد توفك   سكرتير
            عثمان عبد الرحيم   امه انصروه
هناك بشاه - محمد محمود - مكاوي عبد الجباح - حسن عبد الله سيد احمد
حمد النياس - الرشيد محمد جلدي - حسين دبالك - علي بوسف

بسم الله الرحمن الرحيم وبه نستعين

وصلى الله على سيدنا محمد وعلى آله وصحبه وسلم

(قال تعالى)

تعاونوا على البر والتقوى ولا تعاونوا على الاثم والعدوان

الاسم — صندوق التعاون الخيري للابناء جنينة عمودية كوري المقيمه بعيلك مدمرية هيبنا ملك — كوري — السدر — التلر — موره — الكاسبه النعاء

الرئيس — ابراهيم الشوسه

نائب الرئيس — انقف الملك

الصندوق — عثمان حميد عبد الرحيم

— حمد سوكه

الاعضاء — خالد عثمان — محمد محجوب — مكاوي الملك — مسد عبد الله سيد احمد — محمد البلح — حسن الزبن الرشيد محمد حلمداء — جميعلي دباوك — على دويسا

اولا — تنعقد بعضه مد وطني النظام اعضاء المقيمه بعطه باله يتبرع كل منهم شهريا مبلغ معينه قدره ١٠٠ مليم لازاله المضار هم السريعه وهذا المبلغ يودع بالكوميته كاملا ته غير قابل للتزييع — والاشتراك محمل يوم واحد مكل شهر

٢ — اذا تأخر اي فرد مد الدفع لمده شهرية تنعقد اللجنه الادارية وتعيثه نسبه المتأخير وتبنى الامر حسما الاصوات بالنظام

٣ — لا يقبل الصندوق اي سحبه الا بعد مضى سنة كامله مد تاريخ تأسيسه ولا يجوز تسليف اي فرد من المشتركه الا بعد مضى سنه كامل مد تاريخ الشترك ويستثنى من ذلك اللضرا الشرعيه التي تشترط اللجنه الادارية لغرفه منه مد مله ان لا يعطى لا اكثر من نصف ما استحقا فيها الصندوق

٤ — ويمضى سنه كامله مد تاريخ الاشتراك يكون للمشترك الحق بان يستلف مبلغا قدرما يعاد لتقديم في ذلك طلبا لنا تجا الرئيس ولا يشترط انه لا يعطى لكل ما يطلبه مد الننقود بل يعطى المبلغ الذي توافقه عليه اللجنه الادارية

وتنظر في سداد رده وتوجد منه ايصالا عند استلام تسديدالمبلغ

(٥) في حالة ترك المشترك الخدمة او نقل عليه أن يقدم طلبا الى نائب
الرئيس بما يوافقه اما بالانفصال او الاستمرار ـ واذا توفى
أحدالمشتركين فتعطى جميع مبلغه لورثته بواسطه بينة شرعيه

(٦) اذا اراد المشترك الانفصال اجتنابا عليه ان يعلم نائب الرئيس
قبل شهر من التاريخ الذي يريد فيه الانفصال وحينئذ يدفع
جميع مبلغه ولا يقبل اشتراكه مرة اخرى

(٧) اللجنة الادارية تتكون من نائب الرئيس والسكرتير والامين والاعضاء
وعليها انه يجتمع يوم ٨ من كل شهر لمراجعة الحسابات

(٨) لا يشرع اللجنة الادارية في عمل اي شئ الا اذا كان الموجود ديهست
اعضائها لهوما يوازي الثلثيه او اكثر

(٩) نائب الرئيس عليه أنه يرأس جمعيات اللجنة ولا جمع ان طالب
من السكرتير انعقادا لجمعيه تحت اي ظرف وله تقديم طلبات
الانضمام والانفصال

(١٠) السكرتير ـ عليه تدوية قرار الجمعيه في دفتر واعلام المشتركين
على اي لجنة يراد انعقادها والمساعدة في الاعمال التابعه

(١١) امين الصندوق ـ عليه تحصيل الاشتراكات وحفظ حسابات في دفتر
وحفظ صور الايصالات ويكون مسؤولا عن اي عجز حدث في مالة الصندوق

(١٢) لا يصح اي مبلغ من الصندوق سالم نكد بيد الامين ايصال موقعا عليه
من نائب الرئيس والسكرتير او رئيسه نقم

(١٣) لاي مشترك الحق بانه يسأل عن قيمه حسابه وماليته بالصندوق

(١٤) اذا طلع الامر لمشترى اوراقه اوردفاتر او طبع ردوده فعليه قيمة
ذلك من المشتركين مع الاشتراك الشهري

(١٥) تعمل اللجنة الادارية لمدة سنه من تاريخ انتخابي وبعد ذلك
تنعقد لجنة تضم جميع المشتركين لانتخاب لجنة اخرى بالاصوات

(١٦) يأسس هذا الصندوق من أول مينا يناير ١٩٢٤ بمصلحة المديريه

TRANSLATION OF APPENDIX 2

Petition to establish a cooperative society for the natives of `Omudiyyat Kuri, residing in Atbara (from Hussainarti to Kuri, al-Sadar, al-Takar, Moura, al-Rikabiyya, and al-Naf`ab).

The Honorable District Commissioner, Atbara:

With utmost respect, we, the natives of `Omudiyyat Kuri, Dongola Province, residing in Atbara, wish to submit the following petition:

We have agreed to establish a cooperative society to help us meet our emergency needs. We have agreed that each member shall pay a monthly subscription of 100 millimes, to be deposited in an interest-free post office account. The following rules and regulations were adopted effective January 1, 1934. We would be grateful if you kindly approve them.

1/1/1934

President

Ibrahim al-Shush

Members:

Al-Tayyib al-Malik	Vice President
Hasan Sorkati	Secretary
`Uthman Ahmad `Abd al-Rahim	Treasurer

Khalid `Uthman, Muhammad Mahjoub, Makkawi Muhammad al-Hajj, Hasan `Abdalla Sidahmad, Hasan al-Tuhami, al-Rashid Muhammad Jallab, Ahmad Hasan `Ali Dabalok, `Ali Yusuf

Constitution

President: Ibrahim al-Shush

Vice president: al-Tayyib al-Malik

Treasurer: `Uthman Ahmad `Abd al-Rahim

Secretary: Hasan Sorkati

Members: Khalid `Uthman, Muhammad Mahjoub, Makkawi Muhammad al-Hajj, Hasan `Abdalla Sidahmad, Hasan al-Tuhami, al-Rashid Muhammad Jallab, Ahmad Hasan `Ali Dabalok, and `Ali Yusuf.

1. Some natives of the above mentioned villages, residing in Atbara, have agreed that each shall pay a monthly subscription of 100 millimes, to meet their emergency needs. Subscriptions are due on the first day of each month and would be deposited in an interest-free post office account.

2. If any member fails to pay his dues for two consecutive months, the administrative committee will examine his reasons and reach a decision through voting.

3. Loans will be available for members after one year after the establishment of the society. The member can apply for a loan only after one year from the date he joined the society. However, under unusual circumstances, the committee has the discretion to approve a loan to a person who has been a member for less than a year.

4. After one year, the member can apply for a loan by submitting a written application to the society's vice president, with the understanding that he may not be approved for the total amount requested. The executive committee would decide the amount and the terms of the loan and would obtain a receipt from the borrower stating these conditions.

5. In case of retirement or job transfer, the member must inform the vice president in writing of whether he wants to resign or retain his membership. If a member dies, all his assets would be given to his legal heirs.

6. If a member decides to terminate his membership, he must give the vice president a one month advance notice, in which case all his assets will be refunded, but he will not be eligible to rejoin the society.

7. The executive committee consists of the vice president, the secretary, the treasurer, and members. It meets on the eighth day of each month to review the accounts.

8. The administrative committee cannot hold a meeting unless two-thirds of its members are present.

9. The vice president shall preside over the meetings of the administrative committee and has the discretion to call meetings at any time deemed necessary. He has the authority to decide membership applications and dismissals.

10. The secretary's duty is to record the minutes of the meetings and to inform members of the general assembly about the committee's decisions and call upon them to help with paper work.

11. The treasurer's duty is to collect the monthly subscriptions and keep records of all financial transactions. He is personally responsible for any shortfalls in the society's funds.

12. No withdrawal from the society's account can be made without a receipt bearing the signatures of the vice president, the secretary, and the treasurer.

13. Each member has the right to review his own account as well as the society's financial transactions.

14. The cost of stationeries and supplies will be collected from members with their monthly subscriptions.

15. The executive committee shall serve for a one-year term, to be followed by general elections.

16. This cooperative society was formed on the first of January 1934.

Appendix 3:
Executive Officers of the Workers' Affairs Association and the Sudan Railways Workers' Union, 1948–1984

Executive Committee of WAA, 1948

Muhammad `Ali Mahdi	President
Dahab `Abd al-`Aziz	Secretary
Hussain al-Sayyid	Treasurer
Qasim Amin	Assistant Secretary
`Abd al-Rahim `Awad al-Karim	Members
Hafiz al-Amin	
Ahmad Muhammad Shagarabi	
Bashir Jad al-Sayyid	
Ahmad Siddiq	
Bashir Hussain	
Hussain Muhammad Farraj	
`Abdalla Muhammad Nur al-Din	
Al-Nur al-Zain Haiba	
Ibrahim Sir al-Khatim	
Mahjoub `Ali	

Executive Committee of WAA, 1949

Muhammad `Mahmoud Daoud	President
`Abdalla Bashir	Secretary
`Abdalla al-Hajj	Members
`Atta al-Mannan Hussain	
Hafiz al-Amin	
`Awad Hamada	
Hussain Muhammad Farraj	
Al-Shafi` Ahmad al-Shaykh	
Muhammad Ahmad `Abdalla	
Ahmad Muhammad Da'oud	
Mahjoub `Ali	
`Abdalla Muhammad Nur al-Din	

Executive Committee of the Sudan Railways Workers' Union (SRWU), 1950

`Abd al-Qadir `Ali Hamid	President
Al-Shafi` Ahmad al-Shaykh	Secretary
`Ali Muhammad Bashir	Assistant Secretary
Musa Ahmad Mitay	Members
`Abdalla Muhammad Nur al-Din	
Isma`il Matran	
`Uthman al-Ruffa`I	
Khidir Muhammad Hussain	
Ahmad Muhammad `Ali al-Tom	
Mahjoub Sulayman Shora	
Ahmad Muhammad Da'oud	
`Uthman `Umar al-Masri	

1951–1952

`Abd al-Qadir `Ali Hamid	President
`Abdalla Bashir	Secretary
Al-Hajj Muhammad `Abd al-Qadir	Assistant Secretary
Musa Ahmad Mitay	Members
`Awad al-Seid Muhammad Mustafa	
Hasan Mahjoub	
Muhammad Sulayman Hussain	
Muhammad `Abdalla	

Ahmad Muhammad `Ali al-Tom
Hussain al-Sayyid
`Ali Muhammad Bashir
Mahjoub `Ali
Muhammad `Abd al-Majid
`Uthman `Umar al-Masri
`Umar al-Hasan Sanad
`Abdalla Sidahmad
Mahjoub Sulayman Shora
Hasan Sa`id
Muhammad al-Bashir Hammad
1952–1953

Khabir Sulayman	President
`Ali Muhammad Bashir	Secretary
Bashir Ahmad Hussain	Treasurer
Al-Hajj `Abd al-Rahman	Assistant Secretary

1953–1954

Musa Ahmad Mitay	President
Ahmad Muhammad al-Faki	Secretary
Hashim al-Sanusi	Assistant Secretary

1955–1956

Hussain al-Sayyid	President
Mahjoub `Uthman	Secretary
Rabi` `Abd al-Fadil	Treasurer
Muhammad `Uthman al-Mudir	Assistant Secretary

1964

Musa Ahmad Mitay	President
Muhammad `Uthman al-Mudir	Secretary
`Abd al-Rahman Mustafa	Vice President
Mirghani `Abd al-Rahman	Treasurer
Al-Sir Mirghani al-Bob	Assistant Secretary

1965

Muhammad al-Hasan `Abdalla	President
Hashim al-Sa`id	Secretary
Muhammad al-Hasan `Abdalla	Assistant Secretary

1966

Muhammad al-Hasan `Abdalla	President
Hashim al-Sa`id	Secretary
Sayyid Hussain Tahir	Assistant Secretary

1967

Muhammad al-Hasan `Abdalla	President
Hashim al-Sa`id	Secretary
Ja`far `Ali Gamar	Assistant Secretary

1968

Muhammad al-Hasan `Abdalla	President
Muhammad `Uthman al-Mudir	Secretary
Musa Ahmad Mitay	Treasurer

1972-1973

Musa Ahmad Mitay	President
Al-Sir Mirghani al-Bob	Secretary
Khalifa al-Makki	Treasurer

1974–1977

Muhammad al-Hasan `Abdalla	President
`Uthman `Ali Fadl	Secretary
Kambal Bashir	Treasurer

1978–1979

`Abbas al-Khidir al-Hussain	President
Hussain Muhammad al-Hussain	Secretary
Hasan Ahmad Mitary	Treasurer

1980–1983

`Abbas al-Khidir al-Hussain	President
Sir al-Khatim Ahmad Muhammad	Secretary
Hasan Ahmad Mitary	Treasurer

1984–1985

Ibrahim `Abaidalla	President
Khidir Ibrahim al-Bashir	Secretary
Hasan Muhammad Ahmad Idris	Treasurer

Appendix 4:
Executive Officers
of the Sudan
Railways Staff Union

1965–1966

Al-Tayyib Yusuf	President
Hasan Mahmoud Hasanain	Secretary
Wadi` Kamil	Treasurer

1967–1969

`Abd al-Salam Ahmad Mahjoub	President
Al-Tayyib al-Asaid	Secretary
Sayyid `Ali Hussain	Treasurer

1971–1973

Bashir Muhammad Bashir	President
Hasan Hajj al-Tom	Secretary
Hasan Hajj Musa	Treasurer

1974–1975

Muhammad `Arafa al-Sayyid	President
Muhammad al-Hasan Sir al-Khatim	Secretary
`Uthman Jubara	Treasurer

1975–1977

Mustafa Ahmad Nuri	President
Muhammad al-Hasan Sir al-Khatim	Secretary
Muhammad Ahmad Khayri	Treasurer

1978–1981

Hasan Hajj Musa	President

Muhammad al-Hasan Sir al-Khatim	Secretary
Muhammad Ahmad Khayri	Treasurer

1982–1986

Hasan Khidir al-Hussain	President
Hasan Ahmad al-Shaykh	Secretary
Al-Zakki Hamid Nugud	Treasurer

APPENDIX 5:
BIOGRAPHICAL
INFORMATION OF SOME
SRWU OFFICERS

`Abbas al-Khidir al-Hussain
Born in 1947 at Daim al-Garrai in Shendi District, he joined the SR workshop division in 1962. He held the post of SRWU president from 1978 to 1981 and led the famous 1981 strike.

Al-Hajj `Abd al-Rahman
He was born in 1921 at Korti, Meroe District, Northern Province. After completing his primary education at Atbara East Elementary School, he attended Atbara Technical School and joined the SR in 1931 as a fitter apprentice in the workshops division. Al-Hajj was one of the founders of the WAA and was an executive member of the SRWU for several years. In 1966, al-Hajj was elected to represent his constituency in the National Assembly. In the late 1960s, he became the secretary general of the Sudanese Workers' Trade Union Federation.

`Ali Muhammad Bashir
Born in 1926 at Umbakol, he joined the SR workshop division in the early 1940s. He was a member of the Society of the Old Boys of Technical School and one of the founders of the WAA. As a result of his activities against the `Abboud regime, he was dismissed in 1961. In 1965 `Ali Bashir was elected to represent his constituency in the national parliament. He later joined the department of labor in Khartoum until his retirement.

Al-Shafi` Ahmad al-Shaykh
He was born in 1922 at Shendi, where he completed his intermediate education and then joined the Atbara Technical School. He was one of the founders of the WAA. Al-Shafi` was instrumental in the establishment of the Sudanese Workers' Trade Union Federation and became its first president in the 1950s and 1960s. He became minister of labor in the transitional government that followed the October

uprising in 1964. He resumed his trade union activity and his position as the president of the SWTUF from 1965 until his execution by Nimeiri in 1971.

Dahab `Abd al-`Aziz

Born in 1912 at Wadi Halfa, Northern Province, Dahab joined the workshops division of the SR in 1934. Dahab played a leading role in the establishment of the WAA and was a member of its executive committee in 1948. In the 1950s he represented the SRWU in the Sudanese Workers' Trade Union Federation.

Hashim al-Sa`id

He was born at al-Barkal, Northern Province. After finishing Meroe Elementary School, he went to Port Sudan, where he joined the Sudan Railways as an apprentice. He moved to Atbara in 1947 just before the famous July strike. Hashim was an active member of the Communist Party and was elected general secretary of the SRWU several times in the 1960s.

Hussain Ahmad al-Hajj

He was born in 1923 at Umbakol, Meroe District, Northern Province, and joined the SR as a switchman in 1939. He was one of the founders of the WAA and a member of its executive committee in 1947. Hussain was a member of the executive committee of the SRWU from 1950 to 1953.

Mahjoub `Ali

Born in 1910 at al-Sayyala village near Atbara, he joined the SR in the 1920s. He was one of the founders of the WAA and the SRWU.

Mahjoub `Uthman

Born in 1923 at al-Kunaysa village, Meroe District, he began his railway career in 1941 as a carpenter in the workshop division. He was the secretary of the Ahli Club, which was a major center of political activity during the nationalist struggle in the late 1940s. He was dismissed in 1961 as a result of his activities against the military regime of Ibrahim `Abboud. In 1962 he was appointed an administrator in the labor department.

Muhammad Ahmad Shajarabi

Born in 1913 at Korti, Meroe District, Northern Province, he joined the SR as a permanent-way worker in 1935. He was a member of the executive committee of the WAA in 1947.

Muhammad al-Hasan `Abdalla

Born in 1929 at Umbakol, Meroe District, Northern Province, he joined the SR in 1948 in the management division. `Abdalla was one of the most prominent leaders of the railway workers' movement and became the president of the SRWU from 1974 to 1978.

Musa Ahmad Mitay

Born at al-Takar village in Meroe District, he joined the SR in 1942 as a permanent-way worker in the engineering division. He was one of the founders of the WAA. He was a member of the SRWU executive committee and was the union's president for four sessions.

NOTES

1. NRO, NP 2/34/393–410.
2. A unit of native administration, headed by an `*umda* (chief).

GLOSSARY

anadi	drinking houses
ardeb	a measure of capacity; 1 ardeb = 198 litres
baraka	blessing, grace
dar	land, homeland
dhura	sorghum
dura	millet
feddan	unit of land measurement; 1 feddan = 1.038 acres or 0.420 hectares
foul	fava bean
hosh	enclosure
`ishash	straw
jalous	mud, denoting mud-built houses
kala	work team
khalifa	successor
khalwas	Quranic schools (sing. Khalwa).
muwaladin	offsprings of Sudanese and Egyptians
piastres	a unit of Sudanese currency
qadi	Muslim judge
sanduq	rotating credit
saqiya	waterwheel operated by animals or irrigated field
sayyid	formerly a religious title of respect, now roughly equivalent to "Mr."

shari'a	Islamic law
shaykh	tribal or religious leader
sirdar	title of the commander-in-chief of the Egyptian Army
soul	Turkish for sergeant major
Sufism	Muslim mysticism
tarbush	hat
tariqa	a Sufi order or brotherhood
tulbas	daily laborers
`umda	headman of a village or groups of villages

BIBLIOGRAPHY

ORAL SOURCES

`Abd al-Qayum `Abd al-Wahid: he was a carpenter in the railway workshops in the early 1950s. He was transferred to the steamers division at Kosti. He represented his division in the SRWU until the early 1990s. He now lives in Columbus, Ohio, where he had numerous informal conversations with the author in January and February 2001.

`Abd al-Rahman al-Bashir: the son of a permanent-way worker, `Abd al-Rahman joined the SR in the early 1960s and became a trade-union activist until his dismissal in 1992 by the current Sudanese government. Interviewed in Atbara, 12 October 1999.

`Abdalla `Abd al-Wahid: a native of al-`Akad village near `Atbara and former employee of the Public Works Department. Interviewed in Atbara, 11 October 1999.

Ahmad Fath al-Rahman: served in the Sudan Railways Police Force from 1949 until his retirement in 1978. Interviewed in al-Magal, Meroe District, September 15, 1999.

Ahmad Muhammad Salih: served in the Sudan Railways Police from 1949 until his retirement in 1977. Interviewed in al-Magal, 29 September 1999.

Ahmad Muhammad Shami: a prominent member of the Sudanese Communist Party, who was the leader of the SCP branch in Atbara from 1954 to 1964. Interviewed in Khartoum, 1 September 1996.

Al-Hajj `Abd al-Rahman: a well-known trade-union activist (see appendix 5). Interviewed in Khartoum 23 August 1995.

Al-Tayyib Muhammad al-Tayyib: a leading expert on Sudanese oral tradition and folklore, who grew up in the vicinity of Atbara. Interviewed in Khartoum, 23 October 1999.

`Awadalla Dabora: the owner of the famous Dabora Bookshop, the oldest bookshop in Atbara. Interviewed in Atbara, 11 October 1999.

Bushra Bahna `Abd al-Malik: a Copt whose father had joined the Sudan Railways in 1907. Bushra was born in 1933 in Atbara, and worked for the Sudan Railways from 1950 to 1961. After his retirement, he owned a bar in Atbara, which was burnt down by a mob in 1982, following the announcement of September Laws. In the early 1990s, he migrated to England where he currently lives. Interviewed in London, 26 February 2000.

Hasan Ahmad al-Shaykh: former employee in the accounting division of the SR. He was the general secretary of the Sudan Railways Staff Union until his dismissal in 1992. At the time of the interview, he was the president of the Atbara Town Development Committee. Interviewed in Atbara, 13 October 1999.

Hasan Khalifa (al-`Atbarawi): a well-known Sudanese singer and political activist, who was known for his patriotic songs. Interviewed in Atbara, 12 October 1999.

Hashim al-Sa`id: a prominent leftist and trade-union leader who was the secretary general of the SRWU in the late 1960s. Interviewed in Khartoum, 23 August 2001.

Hashim Muhammad Ahmad: an engineer who joined the Sudan Railways in April 1964. He became chief engineer from 1978 to 1980, then the general manager of the SRC from 1984 to July 1987. Hashim is also a political activist and trade unionist. He is currently a leading figure in the National Democratic Alliance, a coalition of various groups opposing the present Sudanese government. Interviewed in Oxford, England, 17 July 1996.

Hussain Babikir: a schoolteacher in Atbara and a political activist. Hussain was the chair of a committee responsible for the distribution of consumer goods in Atbara during the popular uprising of April 1985. Interviewed in Atbara, 12 October 1999.

Ibrahim al-Hasan: a prominent merchant and religious figure in Atbara. His ancestors had migrated from Morocco to the Sudan. Ibrahim is the leader of the Tijaniyya Sufi Brotherhood. Interviewed in Atbara, 16 October 1999.

Louis Nashid: a Copt who served in the management division of the Sudan Railways for many years. He died in December 1999. Interviewed in Atbara, 13 October 1999.

Mahjoub Jadalla: A World War II veteran who joined the Sudan Railways Police Force in 1945 after his discharge from the army. He retired in 1978 and is currently a taxi driver in Atbara. Interviewed in Atbara, 11 October 1999.

Muhammad `Ali Mustafa: a native of al-Dakhla village and former railway employee and trade-union activist. Interviewed in Atbara, 13 October 1999.

Musa Mitay: a prominent trade-union leader (see appendix 5). Interviewed in Atbara, 12 October 1999.

ARCHIVAL MATERIALS

National Records Office (NRO), Khartoum, Sudan

The archives of the Sudan government are kept in the National Record Office (previously the Central Records Office), Khartoum. Documents in the NRO are listed by class number, box number, and file number. The following materials have been used:

CAIRINT: This classification deals mainly with intelligence and general administration in the early years of Anglo-Egyptian rule. The following files were used: 1/50/290; 1/51/293; 1/55/311; 3/161/61; 3/168/69

CIVSEC: Designates files of the civil secretary department. The following materials deal with the railway department and labor in general—Civsec 1: 1/8/29; 1/58, 20/1–20/5, 37/3, 65/12

Civsec 2: 30/9–16.

Dakhlia: Contains the archives of the ministry of the interior: 1/4/15; 1/5/13; 10/1/1; 15/3/9; 50/25/182; and 99/3/5.

Departmental Reports: Contains the files of various government departments. Sudan Railways annual reports are listed in Class 4 and 30.

Miscellaneous: 1/176/2283–2285; 1/27/1694; 1/188/2500; 1/235/3051–3052.

Northern Province

This is the most important archival material for this study. Files here cover all aspects of the administration of the province in general and Atbara in particular. NP 1: All files in Class 1, 2, and 3; all files in NP 2: Atbara List, Class 1.

Security: Contains the papers of the public security intelligence branch, 12/2/10

University of Durham Library, Palace Green (Sudan Archives)

Below is a list of officials whose papers were used. For specific reference and full citation, see notes.

W. J.R. Andrews

A.J.V. Arthur

E.G. Baker

E.A. Balfour

E. Barrow

I.M. Beasley

J.A. Bright

J. Cameron

S.J. Claydon

H.C. Franklin

C.R. Harvey

F.L. Harwood

A.C. Parker

G.W. Power

H. Quinlan

G.R. Storrar

F.R. Wingate

G.K. Woods

Public Record Office (PRO), London

FO 371: The following files deal with the history of the Sudan railways and labor: 22003–23363, 24632, 27494, 4137–80, 53252, 63088, 63252, 69170, 69209, 69235–6, 1022930, 113779, and 11378.

OFFICIAL PUBLICATIONS

British Government

General Staff, Handbook of the Egyptian Army, 1912.
Reports by His Majesty's Agent and Consul-General on the Finances, Administration, and
      Conditions of Egypt and the Sudan, 1899–1919.
Reports by His Majesty's High Commissioner on the Finances, Administration, and Con-
      ditions of Egypt and the Sudan, 1920.
Reports on the Finances, Administration, and Conditions of the Sudan, 1921–1945.

Sudan Government

Department of Statistics, First Population Census of the Sudan, 1955/56.
Population and Housing Survey, Atbara, 1964/65.
Transport Statistics Bulletin.

Sudan Railways

Waraqua hawl mashakil al-sika hadid al-tamwiliyya wa al-maliyya, wa al-taswiqiyya, wa
      al-tijariya, wa al-ta`rifiyya (Memorandum on financial, marketing, commercial, and
      pricing problems of the railways), Khartoum 1995.
Sudan Railways Corporation, *History of the Sudan Railways*, Khartoum, 1983.
General Rules Book, 1909, 1925, 1930, 1939, 1959, and 1958 editions.
Archives of the Sudan Railways Corporation.
The Sudan Railways Bulletin, 1945–1955.
Sudanese Communist Party, Thawrate sha`b, Khartoum, n.d.
Sudan Railways Workers' Union
Silver Jubilee of the SRWU, Atbara, July 1997.
Amal wa inqaz, Khartoum: 1982.
Al-Nizam al-Asasi li nagabat `ummal al-Sikah Hadid, 12 April 1978.
Dirasah ihsaiyyah tahliliyyah shamila li maslahat al-sikah al-hadid al-Sudaniyya, Khar-
      toum, Nubar, 1968.
Mudhakirat nagabat `ummal al-sikah hadid (Memorandum by the Sudan Railways Work-
      ers Union), Atbara, 1968.

NEWSPAPERS AND MAGAZINES

Al-Iza `a wa al-Talvizion
Al-`Arabi
Atbarabian
Al-Ayam
Al-Ray al-`Am
Al-Sahafa
Sudanow

UNPUBLISHED THESES AND DISSERTATIONS

Ahmad, Muhammad Idris. "Madinat Atbara: dirasah fi gughrafiyat al-mudun." Master's thesis, Cairo University, 1978.

Ali, Nada Mustafa Mohammed. "Coping amidst Crisis: The Narratives of Five Sudanese Women." Master's thesis, American University in Cairo, 1993.

Babikir, Khidr Mahmoud "Ahamm al-Taghiyrat al-Ijtima `iyya wa al-Iqtisadiyya li Hijrat sukkan Jibal al-Nuba ila Hawadir al-Mudiriyya al-Shamaliyya-Atbara and al-Damer." Master's thesis, University of Khartoum, 1994.

Due, John F. "Rail and Road Transport in the Sudan." Faculty Working Papers, University of Illinois at Urbana-Champaign, July 1977.

El-Rayh, Abdel Rahim. "Political Process in Atbara Town." B.A. diss., University of Khartoum, 1970.

Lindsay, Lisa A. "Putting the Family on Track: Gender and Domestic Life on the Colonial Nigerian Railway." Ph.D. diss., University of Michigan, 1996.

Mahgoub, Nabawia Mohammed. "The Conditions of Railway Workers during the May Regime, 1969–1983." B.Sc. diss., University of Khartoum, May 1983.

Taha, Abdel-Rahman El Tayib Ali. "The Sudanese Labor Movement: A Study of Labor Unionism in a Developing Society." Ph.D. diss., University of California, Los Angeles, 1970.

PUBLISHED MATERIALS: BOOKS AND ARTICLES

Abdin, Hasan. *Early Sudanese Nationalism, 1919–1924.* Khartoum: Khartoum University Press, 1986.

Atkins, Keletso. *The Moon Is Dead! Give Us Our Money! Cultural Origins of an African Work Ethics, Natal, South Africa, 1843–1900.* Portsmouth, NH: Heinemann, 1993.

Babikir, Fatima. *The Sudanese Borgeoisie: Vanguard of Development?* London and Khartoum: Khartoum University Press and Zed Press, 1984.

Baker, William, et al. *Sports in Africa: Essays in Social History.* New York and London: Africana Publishing Company, 1987.

Bakheit, Jaafar Muhammad Ali. *Communist Activities in the Middle East, 1919–1927, with Special Reference to Egypt and the Sudan.* Khartoum: Khartoum University Press, 1969.

Bashari, Mahjoub `Umar. *Ruwwad al-Fikr al-Sudani.* Khartoum: Dar al-Fikr, 1981.

Beinin, Joel, et al. *Workers on the Nile: Nationalism, Communism, Islam, and the Egyptian Working Class, 1882–1954.* Princeton: Princeton University Press, 1987.

Berlanstein, Lenard, ed. *Rethinking Labor History: Essays on Discourse and Class Analysis.* Urbana: University of Illinois Press, 1993.

Beshir, Mohammed Omer. *Revolution and Nationalism in the Sudan.* London: Rex Collings, 1974.

Bozzoli, Belinda. *Class, Community and Conflict: South African Perspective.* Johannesburg, 1987.

Castells, Manuel. *The Power of Identity.* Malden: Blackwell Publishers, 1997.

Chotterjee, Pantha. *The Nation and Its Fragments: Colonial and Post-Colonial Histories.* Princeton: Princeton University Press, 1993.

Clignet, Remi, and Maureen Stark "Modernization and Football in Cameroon." *Journal of Modern African Studies* 12, no. 3 (1974): 409–21.

Collins, Carole. "Colonialism and Class Struggle in Sudan." *Middle East Research and Information Project* 46 (1976): 3–20.

Cooper, Frederick. *Decolonization and African Society: The Labor Question in French and British Africa*. Cambridge: Cambridge University Press, 1996.

———. "From Free Labor to Family Allowances: Labor and African Society in Colonial Discourse." *American Ethnologist* 16 (November 1989): 745–65.

———. On the African Waterfront: Urban Disorder and the Transformation of Work in Colonial Mombassa. New Haven: Yale University Press, 1987.

———. "Our Strike: Equality, Emancipation, Anti-colonial Politics and the 1947–48 Strike in French West Africa." *Journal of African History* 37 (1996): 81–118.

———. "Work, Class and Empire: An African Historian's Retrospective on E.P. Thompson." *Social History* 20 (May 1995): 235–41.

Cooper, Frederick, ed. *Struggle for the City: Migrant Labor, Capital, and the State in Urban Africa*. Beverly Hills: Sage, 1983.

Coplan, David. "Fictions That Save: Migrants' Performance and Bathoso National Culture." In *Reading Cultural Anthropology*, edited by George E. Marcus. Duke: Duke University Press, 1992.

Coquery-Vidrovitch, Catherine. "The Process of Urbanization in Africa (from the origins to the Beginning of Independence." *African Studies Review* 34 (April 1991): 1–98.

Crisp, Jeff. *The Story of an African Working Class: Ghanaian Miners' Struggles, 1870–1980*. London: Zed Books, 1984.

Daly, M.W. *Imperial Sudan: The Anglo-Egyptian Condominium, 1934–1956*. Cambridge: Cambridge University Press, 1991.

———. *Empire on the Nile: The Anglo-Egyptian Sudan, 1898–1934*. Cambridge: Cambridge University Press, 1986.

Duffield, Mark. *Maiurno: Capitalism and Rural Life in Sudan*. London: Ithaca, 1981.

El-Amin, Mohammed Nuri. *The Emergence and Development of the Leftist Movement in the Sudan during the 1930s and 1940s*. Khartoum: Khartoum University Press, 1984.

———. "The Sudanese Communist Movement: The First Five Years, Part 1." *Middle East Studies* 32 (July 1996): 22–40; Part 2, 32 (October 1996): 251–263; Part 3, 33 (July 1997): 128–51.

El-Hasan, Ali Muhammad, ed. *An Introduction to the Sudanese Economy*. Khartoum: Khartoum University Press, 1975.

Epstein, A.L. *Politics in an Urban African Community*. Manchester: Manchester University Press, 1958.

Fair, Laura. *Pastimes and Politics: Culture, Community, and Identity in Post-Abolition Urban Zanzibar, 1890–1945*. Athens: Ohio University Press, 2001.

Fawzi, Saad El Din. *The Labor Movement in the Sudan, 1946–1955*. London: Oxford University Press, 1957.

———. "The Wage Structure and Wage Policy in the Sudan." *Sudan Notes and Records* 36 (1955): 158–80.

Freund, Bill. *The African Worker*. Cambridge: Cambridge University Press, 1988.

Grillo, R. D. *African Railwaymen: Solidarity and Opposition in an East African Labour Force*. Cambridge: Cambridge University Press, 1973.

Gutkind, P.R. Cohen, et al. *African Labor History*. Beverly Hills and London: Sage Publications, 1978.

Hamza, Kamal. *Murshid Baladiyat Atbara* (Guide to Atbara municipality). Khartoum: Tamadun Press, 1958.

Harries, Patrick. *Work, Culture, and Identity: Migrant Laborers in Mozambique and South Africa, C. 1860–1910.* Portsmouth, NH: Heinemann, 1994.

Henderson, K.D.D. *Sudan Republic.* New York and Washington: F. A. Praeger, 1965.

———. *A Survey of the Anglo-Egyptian Sudan, 1898–1944.* London and New York: Abbey Press, 1946.

Hill, Richard. *Sudan Transport.* London: Oxford University Press, 1965.

Hoffman, David L. *Peasant Metropolis: Social Identity in Moscow, 1929–1941.* Ithaca and London: Cornell University Press, 1994.

Holt, P.M., and M.W. Daly. *A History of the Sudan: From the Coming of Islam to the Present Day.* London and New York: Longman, 1988.

Hunt, Nancy Rose. *A Colonial Lexicon: Of Birth Ritual, Medicalization, and Mobility in the Congo.* Durham and London: Duke University Press, 1999.

Jeffries, Richard. *Class, Power and Ideology in Ghana: The Railwaymen of Sekondi.* Cambridge: Cambridge University Press, 1978.

Khalid, Mansour. *Nimeiri and the Revolution of Dis-May.* London: KPI, 1985.

Khoff, Peter O., and Karl Wohlmuth, eds. *The Development Perspectives of the Democratic Republic of Sudan: The Limits of the Breadbasket Strategy.* Munich, Cologne, and London: Weltforum Verlag, 1983.

Kirk-Greene, Anthony. "Imperial Administration and the Athletic Imperative: The Case of the District Officer in Africa." In *Sports in Africa: Essays in Social History*, edited by William Baker and James A. Mangan. New York and London: Africana Publishing Company, 1987, 81–113.

Klubock, Thomas Miller. *Contested Communities: Class, Gender, and Politics in Chile's El Teniente Copper Mine, 1904–1951.* Durham: Duke University Press, 1998.

Lindsay, Lisa. "Domesticity and Difference: Male Breadwinners, Working Class Women, and Colonial Citizenship in the 1945 Nigerian General Strike." *American Historical Review*, 1, no. 13 (June 1999):783–812.

Little, Kenneth. "The Role of Voluntary Associations in West African Urbanization." *American Anthropologist* 59 (1957): 579–96.

Lockman, Zachary, ed. "Railway Workers and Relational History: Arabs and Jews in British-Ruled Palestine." In *Comparing Jewish Societies*, edited by Todd M. Endelman. Ann Arbor: University of Michigan Press, 1997, 235–66.

———. *Workers and Working Classes in the Middle East: Struggles, Histories, Historiographies.* Albany: State University of New York, 1994.

Lubeck, Paul. *Islam and Urban Labor in Northern Nigeria: The Making of a Muslim Working Class.* Cambridge: Cambridge University Press, 1986.

Malik, `Abd al-Raham `Abbas. *Adwa `ala al-ujur wa mustawa al-ma `isha.* (Khartoum: Sudan Workers Trade Union Federation, 1968).

Mandala, Elias. *Work and Control in a Peasant Economy: A History of the Lower Tchiri Valley in Malawi, 1859–1960.* Madison: University of Wisconsin Press, 1990.

Martin, Phyllis M. *Leisure and Society in Colonial Brazzaville.* Cambridge: Cambridge University Press, 1995.

Maylam, Paul, and Lain Edwards, eds. *The People's City: African Life in Twentieth Century Durban.* Portsmouth, NH: University of Natal Press and Heinemann, 1996.

Mohammed, Sayed El-Bushra. "The Evolution of the Three Towns." *African Urban Notes* 6, no. 2 (1971): 8–23.

Niblock, Tim. *Class and Power in Sudan: The Dynamics of Sudanese Politics, 1898–1985.* Albany: State University of New York, 1987.

Oberst, Timothy. "Transport Workers, Strikes and the Imperial Response: Africa and the Post World War II Conjuncture." *African Studies Review* 31, no 1 (1988):117–134.

O'Brien, Jay. "Formation of the Agricultural Labor Force in the Sudan." *Review of African Political Economy* 26 (1983): 15–34.

———. "The Political Economy of Semi-proletarianization under Colonialism: Sudan, 1925–50." In *Proletarianization in the Third World*, edited by B. Munslow, and H. Finch. London and Dover: Croom Helm, 1984, 12–147.

O'Neill, Norman. "Imperialism and Class Struggle in Sudan." *Race and Class* 20, no. 1 (1978): 1–19.

O'Neill, Norman, and Jay O'Brien, eds. *Economy and Class in Sudan.* Aldershot: Gower, 1988.

Pinckney, Frederick George Agustus. *Sudan Government Railways and Steamers.* London: Institution of Royal Engineers, 1926.

Ranger, Terence. "Pugilism and Pathology: African Boxing and the Black Urban Experience." In *Sports in Africa: Essays in Social History*, edited by William Baker and James A Mangan. New York and London: Africana Publishing Company, 1987, 196–213.

Robertson, Claire. *Sharing the Same Bowl? A Socioeconomic History of Women and Class in Accra, Ghana.* Bloomington: University of Indiana Press, 1984.

Al-Sahzali, Salah al-Din. "The Structure and Operation of Urban Wage-Labour Markets and the Trade unions." In *Economy and Class in Sudan*, edited by Norman O'Neill and Jay O'Brien. Aldershot & Brokfield: Avebury, 1988, 239–76.

Sandbrook, Richard, and Robin Cohen, eds. *The Development of an African Working Class.* London: Longman, 1975.

Sandes, E.W.C. *The Royal Engineers in Egypt and the Sudan.* Chatham: Institution of Royal Engineers, 1937.

Sikainga, Ahmad Alawad. *Slaves into Workers: Emancipation and Labor in Colonial Sudan.* Austin: University of Texas Press, 1996.

Stromquist, Shelton. *A Generation of Boomers: The Pattern of Railroad Labor Conflict in Nineteenth-Century America.* Urbana and Chicago: University of Illinois Press, 1993.

Suliman, Ali A. *Wages and Labor Problems in the Sudan.* Khartoum: Khartoum University Press, 1974.

Taha, Abdel Rahman El-Tayib Ali. "The Industrial Relations System in the Sudan." In *An Introduction to the Sudanese Economy*, edited by Ali Mohammad El-Hasan. Khartoum: Khartoum University Press, 1975, 183–200.

———. "Reflections on the Structure and Government of the Sudan Railways Workers' Union." *Sudan Notes and Records* 15 (1974): 61–69.

Taha, Abdel Rahman E. Ali, and Ahmad El-Jack eds. *The Regulations of Termination of Employment in the Sudanese Private Sector: A Study of the Law and Its Application.* Khartoum: Khartoum University Press, 1973.

Al-Tayyib, al-Tayyib Hasan. *Mudhakirat `an al-Haraka al-`Ummaliyya.* Khartoum: Khartoum University Press, 1989.

Thompson, E.P. *The Making of the English Working Class.* New York, 1966.

Van Onselen, Charles. *New Babylon: Studies in the Social and Economic History of the Witwatersrand, 1886–1914.* London: Longman, 1982.

Warburg, Gabriel. *Islam, Nationalism, and Communism in a Traditional Society: The Case of Sudan.* London: Frank Cass, 1978.

———. *Sudan under Wingate: Administration in the Anglo-Egyptian Sudan, 1899–1916.* London: Frank Cass, 1971.

White, Louise. *The Comforts of Home: Prostitution in Colonial Nairobi.* Chicago: University of Chicago Press, 1990.

Wilkins, C. "Road Transport in the Sudan." In *An Introduction to the Sudan Economy*, edited by Ali Mohamed El-Hasan. Khartoum: Khartoum University Press, 1977, 102–22.

Williams, C.R. *Wheels and Paddles in the Sudan, 1923–1946.* Edinburgh: Pentland Press, 1986.

Wood, Gerard K. "Training Native Engine Drivers on the Sudan Railways." *Crown Colonist* 5 (1935): 552–54.

Woodward, Peter. *Sudan, 1898–1989: The Unstable State.* Boulder: Lynne Rienner, 1990.

Yasin, `Abd al-Qadir. *Al-idrab al-siyasi fil Sudan* (Political strikes in the Sudan). Cairo: Dar al-Ahali, 1995.

INDEX

`Abbadi, Bashir, 152

`Abbas, Khalid Hasan, 164, 169

`Abbas, Khalifa, 91

`Abboud, Ibrahim: military coup of, 2, 118, 123, 127, overthrow of, 134

`Abd al-`Aziz, Dahab, 105–106, 115, 137

`Abd al-Jalil, Shatir al-Busayli, 91

`Abdalla, Muhammd al-Hasan: and the May regime, 159–160; as a leader of the SRWU, 133, 136, 141

`Abd al-Latif, `Ali, 37

`Abd al-Qadir, Salih, 37

`Abd al-Rahim, Muhammad, 90

`Abd al-Rahman, Al-Hajj: early career as a railway worker, 8, 50, 92, 105–106, 116, 137–39, 141, 163; persecution 128–32, 155, 163; poetry 1, 143–45; role in the labor movement, 105–106, 116, 137–39, 141

`Abd al-Raziq, `Awad, 101–102

`Abdoun, Taj al-Sir, 156

Abu Hamad, 26, 28, 57

Abu `Isa, Farouq, 150

Abu Saq, Muhammad `Uthman, 152

Abu Sham, Muhammad Hasan, 54, 69–70, 79, 88

Abu Shush, Bashir, 70

Abu Shush, Ibrahim, 54

Abyssinian Quarter, 66–67

Adam, Daoud, 50–51

Adam, Taj al-Sir Hasan, 115, 128

Al-Ahli Club, 89. *See also* Social and Sport Clubs

Al-Amal Club, 85, 109. *See also* Social and Sport Clubs

Al-`Atta, Hashim, 150–51

Al-Azhari, Isma`il, 141

Al-Bawga, 52, 57

Al-Bawga Men's Society, 79. *See also* Mutual aid associations

Al-Dakhla: early settlement, 31–32, 34–35; land appropriation in, 66–67; planning of, 66–69, 126; social and political activities in 84, 133

Al-Damer, 32, 107

Al-Dar Club, 86. *See also* Social and Sport Clubs

Al-Fadl, Muhammad, 124

Al-Fadli, Yahya, 117

Al-Faki, al-Rayyah, 69–70, 88

Al-Faki Medani, 66–68, 72, 126, 131

Al-Hasaya, 68, 126

Al-Hayyia al-Raqta Team, 83. *See also* Social and Sport Clubs

Al-Hilal Club, 84. *See also* Social and Sport Clubs

Al-Hussain, `Abbas Al-Khidir: leadership of the SRWU and confrontation with the May regime, 160–164
Al-Liwa al-Ahmar magazine, 115
Al-Liwa Club, 83. *See also* Social and Sport Clubs
Al-Mahdi, Sayyid `Abd al-Rahman, 9–11, 102
Al-Mahi, al-Sadiq, 135
Al-Marrikh Club, 85. *See also* Social and Sport Clubs
Al-Mawrada, 67, 70, 85, 126, 133
Al-Mirghani, Sayyid `Ali, 9–11, 88, 103. *See also* Khatmiyya
Al-Mugran, 32, 69
Al-Murba`at, 66, 126
Al-Najm al-Ahmar Club. *See* Social and Sport Clubs
Al-Nikhaila, 32
Al-Nil Club, 84–85. *See also* Social and Sport Clubs
Al-Nisr Team, 84. *See also* Social and Sport Clubs
Al-Nur, Babikir, 150–51
Al-Qala`, 66
Al-Qayqar, 32, 85
Al-Rashid Studio, 92–93
Al-Saflawi, Sirour Muhammad, 69–70, 88, 133
Al-Sa`id, Hashim: poetry, 143; as trade union leader, 8, 76, 92, 106, 116, 128, 137, 141
Al-Sarraj, al-Tayyib, 90
Al-Sayyala, 126
Al-Shabiba Club, 84. *See also* Social and Sport Clubs
Al-Shaykh, al-Shafi` Ahmad: early career in the Sudan Railways 50; execution, 151, 155; trade union leader, 8, 108, 114–17, 127, 138
Al-Shaykh, Hasan Ahmad, 163, 172
Al-Tayyib, Hasan al-Tayyib: literary activities 50, 92–93, 100; as trade union leader, 8, 105–107, 115
Al-Umara` Club, 85. *See also* Social and Sport Clubs
Al-Watan Club, 83. *See also* Social and Sport Clubs

Amal wa Ahlam film, 92
American Mission School, 72–73
Amin, Qasim, 8, 50, 105, 115–16
Anglican School, 126
Anglo-Egyptian Condominium, 9–10
`Aqud, Mirghani, 109
Ashiqqa Party, 11, 70, 89, 100–101, 107, 114–15
Atbara Club, 35–36, 38, 81. *See also* Social and Sport Clubs
Atbara Golf Club, 36. *See also* Social and Sport Clubs
Atbara Municipal Council, 70–71, 86
Atbara Secondary School, 126, 131
Atbara Technical School, 48, 50, 103, 131
Atbara Town Development Committee, 172–73. *See also* Mutual aid associations
Atbarabian magazine, 55–56

Babanusa, 47, 167
Badr, Muhammad Mutwali, 70
Bakheit, J`afar Muhammad Ali, 152, 156
Bardaweil, Muhammad `Abeidi, 105
Ba`shar, Taha, 154
Bashir, `Ali Muhammad, 130, 132, 141
Bayram, Ahmad Hasan, 70
Berber Boys' Society, 79. *See also* Mutual aid associations
Berber Province, 52, 57
Breadbasket policy, 153–54
British Quarter, 67, 71. *See also* Hay al-Sawdana
Burhaniyya, 79

Catholic Mission Club, 82. *See also* Social and Sport Clubs
Church Missionary Society School, 72
Committee of Inquiry, 108–109
Consolidated Labor Code, 154
Cooper, B., 55
Coptic Orthodox Benevolent Society, 36
Coptic school, 126
Copts, 36, 70, 72, 79–80. *See also* Egyptian community in Atbara
Corps of Royal Engineers, 25, 29–30
Crawley, H. D., 55
Creed, T. P., 52

Dabora, `Awadalla, 76–77, 92, 109
Dabora Bookstore, 92
Dangagla, 53. *See also* Nubians
Democratic Unionist Party (DUP), 134, 137
Deng, `Abdalla, 93
Dibble, Harry, 50, 83
Dibble Team, 83. *See also* Social and Sport Clubs
Diggle, P. G., 52, 83
Dongola Men's Society, 79. *See also* Mutual aid associations
Dongola Province, 33, 53, 57
Dunbar, J. H., 55

Eastern European artisans, 25
Egyptian Army Railway Battalion, establishment of, 12, 25; mutiny and evacuation of, 11, 36–39; organization of, 29–30
Egyptian Club, 36, 82. *See also* Social and Sport Clubs
Egyptian community in Atbara, 33, 70, 79–80; Sudan Railways workforce, 49. *See also* Copts
Egyptian Movement for National Liberation (EMNL), 101
Engine Drivers, 47
English Union Golf Club, 36
Ethiopian community in Atbara, 33
European Economic Community (EEC), 167, 169

Family life among railway workers, 74–77, 171–72
Funj Kingdom, 9, 32
Fur Kingdom, 9

Garang, Joseph, 150
Gedarif, 27
General Gordon, 26
Gezira Scheme, 37
Ghanaian railway workers, 5, 57
Ginawi, `Abdalla Nasr, 156
Girouard, Lieutenant E. Percey, 29
Gordon Memorial College, 47, 50, 59, 72, 101
Graduates' General Congress, 10, 88, 100

Greeks: artisans in the Sudan Railways, 29, 36; community in Atbara, 25, 33, 70, 80
Gulf International Corporation, 153

Halfawiyyin, 53. *See also* Nubians
Hamdalla, Farouq, 150–51
Hammer and Sickle Society, 47, 82. *See also* Social and Sport Clubs
Hay al-Darawish, 34
Hay al-Sawdana, 126–27. *See also* British Quarter
Hay al-Tamargiyya, 34
Hay al-`Ummal, 126
Hellenic Society, 36. *See also* Greeks

`Ibaid, `Abdalla, 131
Ibrahim, Abu Al-Qasim, 155, 160
Idris, Muhammad `Umar, 90
Indian artisans in the Sudan Railways, 33
International Federation of Free Trade Unions (ICFTU), 117
International Labor Organization (ILO), 128
International Monetary Fund (IMF), 153, 158, 167
`Ishash quarter, 34, 66–68
Italians: air raids on Atbara, 99; artisans in the Sudan Railways, 25, 33, 58; occupation of Kassala, 99

Ja`aliyyin, 9, 32, 33, 67–68
Jadalla, Yusuf, 131
Jami`yat al-Shabiba al-Wataniyya bi Atbara, 39
Jelessi, 32

Kannur, 52, 54, 69
Kareima, 26, 33, 53
Kashogi, `Adnan, 153
Kassala, 27, 99
Kerma, 26
Khalid, Mansour, 152
Khalifa, Hasan Ahmad, 49–50, 78
Khalil, `Abdalla, 118
Khatmiyya, 9–10, 70, 79, 88, 101
Kenana Sugar Scheme, 153
Kordofan and Dar Fur Society, 79. *See also* Mutual aid associations

Kordofan Province, 26, 34, 70
Kosti, 27–28
Kosti Youth Association, 79. *See also* Mutual aid associations
Kuri People Society, 79. *See also* Mutual aid associations
Kuwaiti investment, 152–53. *See also* Breadbasket policy

Labor aristocracy, 7–8
Labor Board, 105–106
Longfield, W. E., 29. *See also* Corps of Royal Engineers
Lonrho Company, 153
Lord, P. C, 29. *See also* Corps of Royal Engineers
Lubodi, 85. *See also* Social and Sport Clubs

Macauley, G. B., 29. *See also* Corps of Royal Engineers
Mahas, 53. *See also* Nubians
Mahas People's Society, 79. *See also* Mutual aid associations
Mahdists, movement, 9, 101; prisoners, 33
Mahdiyya, 9
Mahjoub, Muhammad Ahmad, 107
Mahjoub, `Abd al-Khaliq: attitude toward the May regime, 150; execution by Nimeiri, 151; leadership of the Sudanese Communist Party, 102. *See also* Sudanese Communist Party (SCP)
Mahlawi, Ibrahim Hasan, 90–91, 109
Malja al-Qirish, 78, 92. *See also* Mutual aid associations
Maltese artisans, 33, 58
Manasir, 9, 53
Manpower and Training Council, 154
Mansour, Ibrahim Mun`im, 152
Masonic Society, 80–81
Meroe, kingdom of, 32
Meroe district, 33, 57
Midwinter, Sir Edward, 29. *See also* Corps of Royal Engineers
Mitay, Musa Ahmad, early career in the Sudan Railways, 57; relation with the May regime, 159; as trade union leader, 117, 129, 132, 141

Mograt Cooperative Society, 79. *See also* Mutual aid associations
Muddathir, Hasan, 90
Mursal, Shakir, 127
Musa, Sulayman, 88, 105–107, 115
Muslim Brothers, 82, 161
Mutual aid associations, 77–81, 172–73
Muwaladin, 49

National Unionist Party (NUP), 117
Nile–Red Sea Line, 26, 28
Nimeiri, Ja`far: military coup of, 123, 149; overthrow of, 154; policy toward the Sudanese Communist Party, 150–53; policy toward Sudan Railway Workers' Union, 161–64; reorganization of the Sudan Railway Corporation, 13, 149, 164–66
Nimir, Babo, 47
Northern Peoples' Club, 85. *See also* Social and Sport Clubs
Nuba, 70
Nuba Mountains, 101
Nubian Cooperative Society, 79. *See also* Mutual aid associations
Nubian Union Club, 85. *See also* Social and Sport Clubs
Nubians, 33, 58
Nur al-Din, Muhammad, 115

October uprising (1964), 134
Old Boys of Technical School Club: during strikes of 1947–48, 108; during World War II, 100; establishment and activities, 85–86, 89. *See also* Social and Sport Clubs
Omdurman School for Stone Masons, 47
Omer, al-Jinaid Ai, 115

Parker's Cup, 82, 86
Parker's Stadium, 82–83, 86
People's National Assembly, 169–70
Pole, Sir Felix, 39
Poles: artisans in the Sudan Railways, 33, 47, 80
Port Sudan, 28, 32
Port Sudan Club, 35

Qadiriyya, 79
Quinland, Hugh, 50

Railway strikes: in 1961, 130; in 1981,
    161–164; background, 98–104; post
    World War II, 104–109. *See also* Sudan
    Railways Workers' Union
Red Sea Club, 35
Republican Brothers, 89, 152
Revolutionary Command Council (RCC), 150
Rida, Abu Bakr Ali, 124
Robertson, J. W., 98
Rubatab, 9, 53, 57, 68
Russell, R. E., 32. *See also* Corps of Royal
    Engineers

Sabah al-Khair, Qasmalla, 105
Sabbagh, Joseph Latif, 91
Sa`idi laborers, 29, 30, 33
Saqiyya system, 53–54
Shaiqiyya, 9, 53–54, 67–68
Shami, Ahmad, 115, 131, 139
Sinnar railway line, 27
Social and Sport Clubs, 82–89
State Security Act, 155
Storrar, G. R., 35
Sudan Government Military Railways, 27
Sudan Government Railways, 33; labor
    force in early years, 28–31; organi-
    zation, 33–34
Sudan-Kuwait Company, 165
Sudan Railways (SR):expansion, 26–27,
    43–44, 124; *General Rules Book* , 45,
    55; labor force, 27–28, 47–51; organi-
    zation 27–28, 44- 47, 156–57; revenue
    and expenditure, 28, 44, 124–25; role in
    the administration of Atbara, 66; wage
    structure, 58–60, 113; during World
    War II, 99–100
Sudan Railways Bulletin, 56, 91
Sudan Railways Cooperative Society, 8.
    See also Mutual aid associations
Sudan Railways Corporation, 156; finan-
    cial conditions, 157–58, 163–68,
    170–71; reorganization by Nimeiri, 157,
    164–66; wage structure, 157–58
Sudan Railways Police Force, 50–51

Sudan Railways Workers' Union (SRWU):
    and the `Abboud regime, 130–134;
    foundation and development of, 114,
    117–118; executive officers, 140; and
    the May regime, 156–163; organization
    of, 136–137
Sudan Workers Trade Union Federation
    (SWTUF), 114–117, 127, 135–36, 151,
    154–55
Sudanese Communist Party (SCP): failed
    coup, 151; and the labor movement, 2,
    11, 101, 115, 131, 134, 139; and
    Nimeiri's coup, 150; split of, 150
Sudanese Movement for National Libera-
    tion (SMNL), 11, 101. *See also*
    Sudanese Communist Party (SCP)
Sudanese Socialist Union (SSU), 152, 156
Sudanese Women's Union, 139–40
Sudanese Youth Union, 139
Supreme Labor Council, 154
Syrians, 25, 70

Taha, Mahmoud Muhammad, 152. *See
    also* Republican Brothers
Thomas Team, 83. *See also* Social and
    Sport Clubs
Tijaniyya, 79
Town Building Regulations, 34
Trade Union Act of 1971, 155
Trade Union Congress (TUC), 117
Trade Union Ordinance, 114, 127, 129

Ugandan railway workers, 5, 57
Umbakol Cooperative Society, 79. *See
    also* Mutual aid associations
Umbakol quarter, 66–67, 126, 133
Umma Party, 70, 100, 103, 115, 134
`Ummal al-Darisa, 45
United Front for the Liberation of the
    Sudan, 116
United States Agency for International
    Development (USAID), 167
`Uthman, Khalil, 153

Wad Ahmad, Mahmoud, 32
Wad Nimeiri Cooperative Society, 153,
    165

Wadi Halfa, 26–28, 29, 32, 57
Wadi Sayyidina School, 101
Wakefield Commission, 113
West African immigrants, 33, 70
White Flag League, 11, 37–38
Work Relations Council, 154
Workers Affairs Association (WAA), 89,
    106–114
Workers' Club, 128
Workers' Congress, 114
World Bank, 153, 158, 167, 169

World Federation of Trade Unions
    (WFTU), 116, 127
World War II: impact on Atbara, 98–101,
    104; Sudan's involvement in, 98–100

Zagalona, 66
Zakariyya, Ibrahim, 115
Zarruq, Mubarak, 92, 107
Zayn al-`Abdein, `Abd al-Wahab, 101–102
Zayn al-`Abdein, Ahmad, 101–102
Zulu mine workers, 3

About the Author

AHMAD ALAWAD SIKAINGA is Associate Professor of History and African-American and African Studies as well as Director of the African Studies Center at the Ohio State University.